The Bank of America Guide to

MAKING THE MOST OF YOUR MONEY

H. Darden Chambliss, Jr.

Dow Jones–Irwin
Homewood, Illinois 60430

Library of Congress Cataloging-in-Publication Data

Chambliss, H. Darden.
    Bank of America guide to making the most of your money / H. Darden Chambliss, Jr.
        p.   cm.
    ISBN 1-55623-283-7 (pbk.)
    1. Finance, Personal.   I. Title.
HG179.C49   1990
332.024—dc20   89–34677
                                                                    CIP

Printed in the United States of America

1 2 3 4 5 6 7 8 9 0   BP 6 5 4 3 2 1 0 9

Contents

Preface   v

Introduction: Finding Yourself in This Book   ix

Chapter 1: Budgeting Your Money to Match
              Your Needs   1

Chapter 2: Banks and Banking   23

Chapter 3: Accounts: Checking, Savings, and
              Variations   37

Chapter 4: Getting and Using Credit   59

Chapter 5: Planning Your Future   89

Chapter 6: Saving for Security and Satisfaction   107

Chapter 7: Investing for the Future   119

Chapter 8: Providing for a College Education   137

Chapter 9: Planning for Retirement   149

Chapter 10: Buying and Selling a Home   161

Chapter 11: Planning Home Improvements   185

Chapter 12: How to Get Information and Advice   195

Chapter 13: Matching Your Money Plan to Your
              Psychological Needs   213

Index   231

Preface

I have admired for a long time the way that Bank of America provides guidance to its customers on personal finance. Their materials are authoritative, helpful, and noncommercial.

So I was enthusiastic when I was approached by an old friend from the days when I was a business writer for the Associated Press, Ron Rhody, now Senior Vice President for Corporate Communications at the bank. He asked me to take the bank's materials, expand on them, and produce a book for the public.

This is it. It is a book designed for anyone who would like to do a better job of managing their personal finances. It's addressed to those who never took the time to master this part of their lives, those just starting out and those suddenly forced by death or divorce to manage money for the first time.

It's based principally on the bank's highly regarded Consumer Information Report series. I also interviewed subject experts at the bank and went to a number of other organizations for information and an additional perspective.

The people at the bank—being bankers, and conservative by nature—were sometimes a little unsure about the casual tone of some of this book. But they held steadfastly to the view that it had to be written in the way that was most helpful to the reader, not bankers.

I also added a psychological dimension, wholly separate from the bank's materials. My source was a clinical psychologist who has done special work on dual-income couples and their problems, including financial management. She is my daughter, Catherine Chambliss, Ph.D, chair of the psychology department at Ursinus College, Collegeville, Pennsylvania. She is the author of *Group Involvement Training* (New Harbinger Publications) and is currently writing a book on dual-earner families. She and her husband, Alan Hartl, also a clinical psychologist, have a private practice, Psychotherapy Associates. They developed the self-tests employed in Chapters 12 and 13 and are responsible for most of Chapter 13.

The discussions on goal-setting techniques that appear in several places, particularly in Chapter 5, "Planning Your Future," are adapted from my experience as a strategic planner. They make use of training I received from an innovative organization in San Francisco, Interaction Associates.

I am greatly indebted to many people for information and advice. I can't mention them all, but there are several I would be remiss not to thank publicly: June Stevens of Reston, Virginia, for hours spent collecting and organizing information from organizations around the country (some of which are listed below); two patient and lucid stockbrokers from Smith Barney, Sheila Kowal of Denver and Greg Venit of Washington, D.C.; realtor Robin Butler of ReMax in Vienna, Virginia (who sold me a condominium in the process); the many people who helped refine and calibrate the psychological quizzes used in the book, including Don and Kay Chambliss of Fresno, California, and evening-class students at Ursinus College; Walter Bussewitz of Rockville, Maryland, a colleague from my days at the Associated Press who is now a chartered financial consultant; two long-time, dear friends who provided advice and encouragement, Ray B. King of Abilene, Texas (district agent of Northwestern Mutual Life) and Barbara Shelton of Norris, Tennessee; and some agreeable critics and guinea pigs, David and Valerie Chambliss, Elisabeth Chambliss, John Hensley, and Blake Chambliss.

In addition, many organizations were helpful with literature and answers to specific questions. Readers will be encouraged to know that there is a plethora of information on personal finance available free or at little cost. Most communities have some form of consumer information service. Help was lavished on us by one, the Office of Citizen Assistance, Consumer Affairs Division, Alexandria, Virginia. Other organizations that were particularly helpful included Investment Company Institute (ICI), 1600 M Street NW, Washington, DC 20036; the American Association of Retired Persons, 1909 K Street, NW, Washington, DC 20006, an excellent source of information on a variety of personal finance subjects; the Credit Bureau, Inc., P.O. Box 4091, Atlanta, GA 30302; the National Association of Realtors, Economics and Research Division, 777 14th Street NW, Washington, DC 20005; International Association for Financial Planning, Two Concourse Parkway, Suite 800, Atlanta, GA 30328; American Council of Life Insurance, 1850 K Street NW, Washington, DC 20006-2284; and the National Foundation for Consumer Credit, 8701 Georgia Ave., Suite 507, Silver Spring, MD 20910.

There is a great deal of information available from the federal government. A series of concise bulletins on specific subjects is available from the Federal Trade Commission, Bureau of Consumer Protection, Washington, DC 20580.

The Consumer Information Center of the General Services Administration, P.O. Box 100, Pueblo, Colorado 81009, publishes a flier listing almost 200 booklets from 43 government organizations. Included are:

- The U.S. Department of Agriculture's comprehensive "Managing Your Personal Finances" (82 pages, about $6)

- An excellent directory of public and private, national, state and local sources of consumer information and help, "Consumer's Resource Catalogue," U.S. Office of Consumer Affairs (91 pages, free)

To all these individuals and organizations, and to the many others I have not mentioned by name, I am truly grateful.

As a final note, I would caution the reader to seek out specific professional advice before making important money decisions. A book like this can help stimulate your thinking and get you asking questions, but it can't replace expert counsel by someone who understands your circumstances.

Darden Chambliss

Introduction:
Finding Yourself
in This Book

You bought this book looking for help in money matters and we intend to be helpful in a different and special way.

We'll help you find yourself in this book so you can fit the information to your own needs and personality. Our goal is to help you find the answers that work best for you as a unique individual. As we'll emphasize again and again, effective money management consists of making the choices that will give *you* the most satisfaction, with the least stress.

Some people berate themselves because they feel that they aren't putting away as much money as they've been taught they should. Or that their investments aren't growing as fast as they're supposed to. Or that they spend too much money on the wrong things. Or that they ought to be willing to take more risks.

Says who?

The point is that you don't have to let other people's biases—not even those of "experts"—make you question your own desires. Most people who write money-management advice really want you to be conservative, numbers oriented, and basically a saver. They're distressed that most of us are not like that, and much of their advice is designed to protect us from ourselves. In addition, a lot of budget and spending advice operates on the bias that practicality should be the sole criterion, that emotional rewards are suspect.

All of which is one reason why money management is, for some people, a very frustrating pursuit. They don't do it the way people say they should—and even if they did, it wouldn't feel good. Thumbing the pages of a passbook just doesn't cut it for the person who aches for the feel of Corinthian leather.

So the first point to realize is that you can and should match your money management plans to your own characteristics. That reduces the stress of trying to do what doesn't come naturally and frees you from the tension of attempting to divine other people's expectations. When you set out to "get more for your money," you can ask "more what?"—and answer that question in terms of the factors that make *you* happy.

Moreover, as you go about the task of implementing a money plan, you'll find that it's easier to follow if it's one you've designed yourself, with an appreciation for where you'll hit rough spots and what kinds of rewards will strengthen your resolve. And what's true for individuals is even more true for couples: it's a lot easier, and more satisfying, to follow a plan if it explicitly accommodates your differences and builds upon the interests and desires you have in common. One partner may require a larger cash cushion than the other to feel comfortable and it's good to resolve this up front. Also, if you both really enjoy an expensive activity, such as dining out and entertaining, you can agree where to sacrifice in other categories to provide money for this.

To help you sharpen your awareness of your own attitudes toward money matters, we have asked the help of the psychologists at Psychotherapy Associates in Collegeville, Pennsylvania. They have developed a test that you can take and score yourself (Chapter 13). You may learn some things about yourself that you didn't know before, or you may merely confirm some assumptions. The test is nonjudgmental, and it may give you a warm feeling to have your own weirdness formally recognized.

For couples, this test can be both entertaining and useful beyond the purposes of this book. Our psychologist consultants encourage partners to take the test independently, then compare answers and discuss the results, especially the differences.

In addition to tailoring this book to reflect your own personality, we take other steps to help you customize it to your particular situation. We offer techniques to help you plan, to think of things that could happen—good and bad—for which you might want to set aside reserves or at least make explicit allowances in your thinking. We devote an entire chapter to sources of advice and information available from experts (Chapter 12). Besides telling you where to go for information, we make some suggestions about ways to deal with experts to make the experience as comfortable as possible. We offer some intimidation insurance and assertiveness psyching.

Throughout the book, we strive to be user-friendly. We avoid jargon, and we try to explain everything fully. We'd rather run the risk of overexplaining than the opposite. If sometimes we seem to state the obvious, don't take offense. There isn't an explanation in the book that at some point or other the author didn't need.

Chapter One

Budgeting Your Money to Match Your Needs

Budgets are the place to start with money planning. At a minimum, budgets should at least give you a way to organize your money activity and understand it better. But they can do a lot more.

Budgets can help you direct your money to the places that will give you the greatest satisfaction.

They can boost your self-discipline, giving you clear targets, a way of keeping score, and rewards for success.

They can help ensure that money is there when you need it.

They can be research tools, helping you gather information to make better spending decisions. (How much money would you really free up for other purposes if you got rid of that other car?)

They can be powerful aids to your investment strategies, helping to make sure you have the maximum amount of money available for extra return through investments. For instance, good budget control can ensure that you have just enough money in your checking account to keep service charges to a minimum, and just enough to meet big bills as they come due, so that every cent beyond that can be at work earning a maximum return.

Budgets can be strong planning tools, forcing you to think ahead. And for couples, they can be aids to communication, helping you to be clear with each other about your feelings concerning money and the things money buys.

Although budgets can be all of these, too often the budget is a source of frustration and, for couples, arguments. A budget that's out of whack can be the symbol of everything that seems to be going wrong in a life — a job not going well enough, money not coming in fast enough, expenses running away with themselves, bad habits and personal excess. The best thing some people can say about budgets is that they're a boring, time-consuming paperwork exercise that doesn't really help them with their goals.

In this chapter, we'll try to do more than prevent your budget from being a nagging pain. We'll try to make it a positive force that helps you get more satisfaction from your hard-earned dollars.

WHAT DO YOU WANT YOUR BUDGET TO DO?

The first thing to decide is how you intend to use your budget, what you want it to do, and how much effort you're prepared to spend managing it. Make that decision before you try to create your budget, because it will influence the categories you select and the detail with which you will track your spending.

If your budget isn't designed to fit you specifically, it won't work. Budget keeping is tough enough to do well under the best of circumstances. Trying to do it with rules written for other people makes it just about impossible.

Let's take a look at several kinds of budgets, each of which serves its own special purpose.

A Casual Budget

Maybe you're fairly well fixed, and money isn't that important to you right now. You don't think it's worth the effort to fine-tune your spending or saving practices. So you want a simple system, one that won't take much of your time, that will organize your spending and make sure money is there when you need it.

In that case, you'll prefer a short, casual budget, with broad categories, and you probably won't review it very often or closely. Some people, in fact, write a new budget only when their income changes, and never look at it again until they write a new one. That's better than not writing one at all. For certain people, this style of budgeting may be all they really need: a periodic evaluation and sensitizing process that guides them in making their purchasing decisions.

A Tight Budget

Maybe your income and expenses are so tight that there is little room to maneuver. You want a budget that's clear and simple, one that will make it easy to spot problems quickly. For you, budget *writing* isn't the problem: money is.

In that case you'll want a short budget with a few, clear categories. You'll want to check how you're doing frequently, perhaps every month when you balance your checkbook.

A Diagnostic Budget

You may want to use your budget as an instrument to gather information for making better purchasing decisions. If so, you'll want to create descriptive subcategories you can use and then discard. A diagnostic budget is the one to use if, for example, you want to track the costs of your second car to see whether you can really afford it — or how much money would be freed for other purposes if you didn't have it.

A Problem-Solver Budget

You may want your budget to help you deal with some specific discipline needs: controlling your credit card charges, helping you deal with runaway clothing and cosmetics costs, getting a handle on bills that are persistently overdue. If so, you'll want to select categories and possibly subcategories to help you track spending in detail and identify problem areas.

A Long-Range Planning Budget

You may want to use your budget as the blueprint for personal planning and saving. In that case you'll use your budget to set a two-, three-, or even five-year plan that projects what your needs will be and how much money that will take. You'll think of the things you want and need most, and then plan ways to provide for them over the years as your income grows.

A Goal-Directed Budget

You may want to design a budget to help you reach some specific goals, such as establishing an emergency account, saving for specific large purchases (perhaps the down payment on a car or home), or setting up an investment program for more income now or retirement income later. If so, you'll want enough categories to help you exert strong control on spending. You may also want to devise some diagnostic subcategories to help you find candidates for reduction. Be prepared to commit a chunk of time to this activity.

STEPS IN WRITING A BUDGET

Assuming you have an idea of what kind of budget you want and need, let's walk quickly through the basic steps involved in writing a budget.

Determine Net Income

First, you need to determine what amount of money you're working with. Use the Money Planner Worksheet for income (Figure 1-1). It's easiest to do this on an annual basis, but later you'll want monthly figures for writing your actual budget. So, at the bottom, just divide the final total by 12.

As you fill out the worksheet, you'll need to decide whether to take the high side or the low side in making projections about future income. Once you put a figure down and start planning on the basis of it, it gets embedded in your mind. It can be discouraging later if you find you're sticking to your new budget on the *spending* side, but the *income* isn't doing its part.

To allow for contingencies, you can borrow a technique from corporate strategic planners: for variable items such as raises, bonuses, commissions, tips, gains from investments, and gifts, use a spread: worst case (lowest), best case (highest), and median (midway point between the two), or select a "best guess." For this purpose you'll need to devise a slightly more complicated worksheet, or complete more than one. The technique is illustrated in Figure 1-2.

Like some people, you may find it easiest to assume that income in the coming year will be the same as in the past year. If so, place contingency income—possible raises, bonuses, overtime pay, and the like—outside your mainstream figuring. Later, you can increase the budget when hoped-for money actually comes in.

Some people, however, find that Spartan approach too depressing: to stick to their tiny budget next month, they need to be able to look forward to the bump in pay they're expecting in a few months. But they should be realistic: is that raise really in the bag, or is it just a hope?

Couples should make sure that they are honest with each other and in agreement on income estimates from the start of their budget writing. Getting a raise should be a happy event, not a burdensome obligation that one partner imposes on the other. And it can be very destructive to a budget plan if one partner goes along with a modest projection just to be agreeable but is mentally fudging up the money available for spending.

Let's go back to the worksheet (Figure 1.1) on page 5 now. Start with your salary or wages. Don't subtract from this figure any voluntary deductions from your paycheck, such as charity donations. Even though they aren't part of your take-home pay, you still control this spending and you should list it as an expenditure later on.

Now add any additional income from tips, commissions, and bonuses, less taxes. Then enter income from any other sources in the right column on the worksheet.

Figure 1-1   Money Planner Worksheet: Income

Income

A. SALARY, WAGES, ETC.

1. Gross salary, wages
   (principal wagearner) $_____

2. Minus deductions

   a. Federal and state
      income tax $_____

   b. FICA, Social
      Security $_____

   c. Health insurance $_____

   d. Other $_____

   e. Total deductions
      (add a through d)   ($_____)

3. Take-home pay (subtract 2e from line 1
   and enter result in Income column) $_____

4. Other gross salary, wages
   in household $_____

5. Minus deductions   ($_____)

6. Other take-home pay (subtract line 5
   from line 4 and enter in Income column) $_____

7. Commissions, tips, bonuses $_____

8. Minus taxes   ($_____)

9. Take-home pay (subtract line 8
   from line 7 and enter in Income column) $_____

B. OTHER INCOME

10. Net profit from business, farm, trade,
    profession* $_____

11. Interest, dividents from savings, stocks,
    bonds, other securities, notes* $_____

12. Net profit from sales of assets* $_____

13. Net profit from rental property* $_____

14. Payments from others
    (e.g., alimony, child support) $_____

15. Tax refunds, rebates $_____

16. Cash gifts	$_____
17. Social Security benefits*	$_____
18. Income from IRAs, SEPs, Keoghs*	$_____
19. Pensions, annuities*	$_____
20. Veterans' benefits	$_____
21. Unemployment benefits	$_____
22. Disability benefits	$_____
23. Life insurance benefits	$_____
24. Income from trusts*	$_____
25. Royalties, residuals*	$_____
26. Less taxes on 'other Income' ($_____)	
27. Other income	$_____

TOTAL INCOME
   (add all lines in Income column) $_____

                                Divide by 12 $_____
                                                        /mo.

*Allow for tax effects. Either use the after-tax
amount or collect these amounts at line 26.

I know, you might look at that long list of "other" income sources and say "Don't I wish!" It's true that almost everyone gets almost all of their income from the first couple of items. Still, it doesn't hurt to remind yourself that there are ways to get money that are more fun than working, such as being paid dividend income.

Now add up all your income. The bottom line is what you'll carve up into a budget.

Describe Your Past Spending

The flip side of Income is Expenses. If you have already been keeping track of spending, chart last year's figures on the Money Planner Worksheet for expenses (Figure 1-3).

It will make it easier to develop the year-to-year comparisons you'll need later if you convert all your past spending to monthly totals. You may have trouble doing this with your lump sum expenditures—property taxes, the new tires for the car, the new clothes dryer, that expensive spring vacation. List such expenditures by name under the appropriate category. Divide the amount you paid by 12 to get monthly totals and put those in the Last Year (Monthly) column. If you financed a purchase through a credit card or charge account, and are still paying on it, enter the monthly payment for that purchase.

If you don't have a good, consolidated record of past spending, you'll want to do some research. It's a chore, but do it with your eye fixed sharply on the applied use of the information: you're doing it to help you make better decisions to give you more pleasure for your money. It's worth the effort.

Gather your existing records from as far back as you can manage. A full 12 months will help give you a feel for costs that are seasonal. Checkbook stubs, especially if they are not too terse or cryptic, can give you much of what you need. If you keep old bills, they can also help. So can past credit card bills, especially those that break out specific expenditures.

Figure 1-2   Example of Estimating Projected Income

	Last Year	Worst Case	Best Case	Guess
1. Gross salary, wages	$45,000	$45,000		
(George gets $2,500 raise)			$47,500	$45,000
2. Commissions, tips, bonuses	750			
(Jan's bonus increases)			1,500	1,500
3. Minus deductions	(6,800)	(6,590)	(7,920)	(7,000)
4. Take-home pay	38,200	39,160	41,080	39,500
5. Interest, dividends from savings, stocks, bonds, other securities, notes	1,600	1,600		
(Mutual fund up)			2,000	2,000
6. Net profit from sales of assets	0			
(Sell boat)		950	1,500	1,500
7. Tax refunds, rebates *(Income tax rebates)*	400	400	400	400
8. Cash gifts	500	500	750	750
TOTAL INCOME	$40,700	$42,610	$45,730	$44,150
Divide by 12:	$3,392/mo.	$3,551/mo.	$3,811/mo	$3,679/mo.

Figure 1-3   Money Planner Worksheet: Expenses

	Last Year (Monthly)	Budget Year (Monthly)
A. HOUSING		
1. Rent, home loan payment	$_____	$_____
2. Property taxes, assessments*	_____	_____
3. Property insurance (homeowner, tenant)*	_____	_____
4. Maintenance, repairs	_____	_____
5. Utilities a. Oil,* gas, electricity	_____	_____
b. Other fuel	_____	_____
c. Telephone	_____	_____
d. Water, sewer	_____	_____
e. Cable TV	_____	_____
f. Garbage collection	_____	_____
6. Home furnishings*	_____	_____
7. Other (homeowners' association fees, household help)	_____	_____
B. PERSONAL MAINTENANCE		
8. Food	_____	_____
9. Clothing a. Purchases	_____	_____
b. Laundry, dry cleaning, repairs	_____	_____
10. Transportation a. Gas, oil	_____	_____
b. Repair, maintenance*	_____	_____
c. Parking, tolls	_____	_____
d. Auto insurance	_____	_____
e. License registration	_____	_____
f. Public transportation	_____	_____
g. Cab fare	_____	_____

11. Health care

    a. Health insurance $_____ $_____

    b. Doctor's visits   _____   _____

    c. Prescriptions, medicine _____   _____

12. Child/dependent care
(including babysitters,
nursery school fees)   _____   _____

13. Personal care
(including barber,
hairdresser, cosmetics)   _____   _____

14. Self-improvement

    a. Education   _____   _____

    b. Books, magazines,
       newspapers   _____   _____

15. Entertainment, recreation

    a. Vacations*   _____   _____

    b. Other (including movies,
       sports, restaurants,
       hobbies)   _____   _____

16. Gifts, holiday expenses   _____   _____

17. Union dues, memberships _____   _____

C. OBLIGATIONS

18. Regular payments to
others (including alimony,
child support, other
court-ordered
payments)   _____   _____

19. Contributions, dues
(voluntary, including
those deducted from
your paycheck)   _____   _____

20. Debt payments

    a. Installment loan
       payments (for
       vehicles, furniture,
       etc.)   _____   _____

    b. Credit card, charge
       accounts   _____   _____

D. CASH RESERVE: SAVINGS AND INVESTMENTS

21. Short-term savings $_____ $_____

22. Long-term savings
    (including pension)   _____   _____

23. Life insurance   _____   _____

24. Investments (including
    stocks, bonds,
    real estate)   _____   _____

TOTAL EXPENSES   _____   _____

*Set-Aside Accounts for which you'll accumulate funds, as explained in text.

You'll probably have a lot of trouble reconstructing what you did with your cash, but do the best you can. Later, we'll discuss ways to keep track of cash in the future.

As you go through this exercise, think ahead to your objectives. Keep your eye out for interesting patterns and surprises. If some expense seems to show up more often or in larger amounts than you expected, make note of it. That could be a candidate for budget correction or a change in spending practices. Note seasonal fluctuations, in utility bills, for instance. Watch out for anything that can be helpful to you in writing a better budget and making better spending decisions.

As already noted, you'll want to convert all your past spending to monthly totals. Record this information as your Last Year budget on the Money Planner for expenses.

Write Yourself a New Budget

Before you write your new budget, you may have to fiddle with the categories. The categories you use need to describe your objectives and your practices accurately. For couples, it's important that the categories mean the same thing to both partners.

Be aware that money takes on the coloration of its intended use: the ten-dollar bill tossed around freely on a vacation is very different from the ten-dollar bill you spend in a supermarket. A budget plan that doesn't take this human element into account will be hard to follow. People who include restaurant meals in their food budget, for instance, can be setting themselves up for failure. It can be psychologically devastating when a dessert at a nice restaurant wipes out the savings gained in the food budget by three months of clipping cereal coupons.

Start with the categories provided in Figure 1-3, but amend and add to them freely. *Your* budget doesn't need to resemble anyone else's.

In setting categories, remember the decisions you made about the purposes of your budget plan. If you're on a "tight budget," you'll want categories that break out the specific items you can control. For instance, you may want to divide "food" into "meat," "groceries," "beverages," and "housewares" to track where your money is really going. You should also consider breaking down "credit card and charge accounts" so you can tell whether expenditures here represent clothing, home furnishings, tires, or other expenses that belong elsewhere in your budget. At the same time, to simplify things, you might well lump all your fixed housing costs into one item, since you can't make cuts there.

If you're using your budget to diagnose and control spending, remember that you're looking for things you can change, places where you can alter your habits to correct a problem or free up money for use elsewhere.

If your objective is to squeeze some more money out of your budget by hook or by crook, you might want to do some brainstorming to identify candidates for reduced spending. Then you can break them out and track them in your new budget.

Couples may want to settle on categories together, bouncing ideas off each other. This is better done early in the budget-writing process, before you get too deeply into specifics and the dulling effect of reality.

Here are some additional questions to help you examine and edit your budget.

First, can you find any leverage possibilities, items large enough that a 10 percent saving, say, would make a difference? Food, for example, is a big item, and for many people, it's the one where changes can produce the best results. Do you know how much you're really spending on edible groceries? Keep in mind that supermarket tabs can be distorted by cosmetics, hardware, household goods, and the like. How much goes for fast food and to convenience stores? To eating out? It could be that more data here could help you make better choices. If so, consider breaking out special subcategories.

Second, is there hidden spending you should examine more closely? Do you know how much you spend on cigars or cigarettes, for example? Would that be worth tracking for a few months? Do you know exactly how many dollars you spend on fitness and recreation? Have you ever added up *all* you spend on tennis, or golf? Fishing? Your roses? Your tomatoes?

Third, are there some relatively painless ways to get more out of your money? Are your gasoline bills too high simply because you don't bunch shopping trips? Are your last-minute trips to convenience stores running up your bill for food and miscellaneous items? Are your video rentals so high that you'd be better off buying cable (or vice versa)? Could you save on telephone expense by getting rid of extensions, buying rather than using the phone company's instruments, using weekends and late hours more for long-distance calls, switching to a cheaper long-distance service?

On the other hand, are there some things you've been doing that turn out to be more trouble than they're worth, and that you can now happily abandon? Are discount coupons worth the trouble? If you've been driving out of your way to use the cheapest filling station, do you save enough to justify the hassle? Does laying down your own fertilizer save that much over using a lawn-care service?

Based on these thoughts, modify or add categories to your budget to help you use it to track possibilities for change. You now have your own edited version of expense categories. Now we'll begin to spread money against them.

1. Use the budget planning sheet (Figure 1-3) and go to the column marked "Budget Year (Monthly)."

2. Where you already know, from last year, what the figure will be this year, enter the amount, taking into account whatever increase is predictable.

3. For lump sums (property tax, tires, etc.), make your best guess as to whether they are the kinds of expenses that are likely to recur (you won't need a new clutch again this year, surely, but other things can be expected to go wrong when your car reaches a certain stage in life). If an item is recurring, enter it, divided by 12 for the monthly increment, in the "Budget Year (Monthly)" column. If you think it was truly a freak expense, leave it off.

4. Scan other items from last year. Is there anything that you think isn't typical? If you had zero medical expense, are you likely to be so fortunate again this year? Put down a figure that seems most realistic. On the other hand, perhaps you spent a lot on clothes; was that mostly because your weight changed, and will that happen again? Adjust the numbers accordingly.

5. Think ahead: Is there anything big coming up this year that would be new? A wedding? A trip to your parents' anniversary party? Put down a figure for that, divided by 12.

6. Next, consider how much reserve you need. Maybe your money is so tight that allowing for reserves doesn't seem relevant. Even so, it's worthwhile to think about this, because you may well decide that your most important priority, once you get a few dollars ahead—more important than *any* purchase—is to create a buffer between you and disaster: à layoff or major medical problem.

7. Now it's time to fine-tune the totals. Make sure you have numbers in all the spaces of the Budget Year (Monthly) column. If there are any blanks, put in your best guess based on what you've spent in the past.

8. Add up the column.

9. Now go back to the income projection you made on your income Money Planner (Figure 1-1). Subtract the expenses you've budgeted from your income projection. If there is a surplus, you get to boost some categories. If your result is negative, you have the dismal job of distributing the shortage.

- If you have a surplus, go down the column and consider which items you'd like to increase. Put a plus sign next to them.
- If you have a negative result, go down the column and place a minus sign by the items you think you can reduce.

Couples who do this part of the exercise independently should then compare notes. Doing so can force clarity about your priorities and surface any differences in your perceptions.

10. To complete the job, give your pluses or minuses specific dollar assignments.

- If you have a surplus to distribute, put a few dollars here, a few dollars there, beside the plus items until the surplus is spent. You may want to prioritize here, assigning money first to the items you most want to increase and, if necessary, leaving some of the less important ones as they are.
- If you're dealing with a negative, go to the items marked with a minus for reduction, put down an amount you can realistically cut, a few dollars here and a few dollars there, until you've accounted for all the deficit. Begin with the items that are easiest to reduce or that you care the least about.

11. You may be wondering about those new tracking categories you created, the ones where you broke out "beer" or "convenience stores" or "cosmetics" so that you could see whether you're spending more than you realized. You didn't know how much you've spent in the past, so you don't know how much you'll spend in the future. (That's why you're doing the tracking.) How do you handle them?

The easiest way is to carry them as subtotals under a category for which you've allotted funds, and then begin recording how much you actually spend for the subcategories. You can put "beer" or "convenience stores" under "food," for example, and begin recording these expenditures separately for tracking purposes. Just don't double-count them when you reconcile your budget.

PUTTING YOUR BUDGET TO WORK

So now you have your new budget. Now comes the hard part— making the budget work. Let's review your objective: you wanted something that would:

- Direct your money to the places that give you the greatest satisfaction
- Make it as easy as possible for you to exercise discipline (stick to it)
- Ensure that money is there when you need it as bills arise

There are several tools you can use to make sure your budget achieves its objectives. Let's review them.

Bank Accounts Provide Records (and Can Pay Interest)

Bank accounts assist budget management through the records they generate—your check register and monthly statement, and the checks themselves. They can also pay interest: you can use a checking account to pay operating expenses that occur at least once a month, and use a regular savings or money market deposit account to get maximum interest on funds you set aside to pay periodic expenses, such as taxes and insurance premiums.

We discuss banking and accounts in greater detail in the next chapter, but here are some points to consider in using them as budget tools.

If you have free checking, use checks to help keep track of spending. Write separate checks for separate purchases, to the exact amount, and note the purpose on the "Memo" line. Avoid scooping in a little extra cash when you write checks for purchases.

Tracking cash withdrawals, especially with the convenience of automated tellers, is a special challenge. A few suggestions:

- Write down everything you spend cash on. Save receipts, or scribble notes. Date them and collect them in a box or an envelope set aside for that purpose. Especially for groceries, your records will help you decode spending patterns (and will be useful for price-comparison shopping).
- Set a schedule for cash withdrawals, say twice a month, with a set amount reflecting specific budget categories: groceries, gasoline, allowance, barber shop, and so on.
- You may decide to be selective. Maybe you won't bother to track what you pay for gasoline, because you've decided you won't change your driving habits on the basis of gasoline expenditures. But you do need to be sure you're not overspending on something big and discretionary, such as groceries. So do track those items carefully.

• When a special need arises, estimate what you'll specifically need, then draw out an amount that reflects that estimate rather than a generalized $25 or $50. When it's time to reconcile your budget, it will be easier to remember why you needed exact amounts like $37.50. And withdrawing the exact amount helps make sure you spend no more than the $37.50; with $50 in your pocket, you're tempted to spend it all.

As a further aid in controlling your budget, consider maintaining separate accounts for specific purposes. You may want to gather together all your fun categories—allowance, entertainment, recreation, vacation—in a single account so you can watch them more closely and be warned more quickly when you're running over (or feel good sooner when you're building a surplus). Even if separate accounts cost a little extra in maintenance fees, they can be worth it for some people.

Instead of having separate accounts, you can play a small game: divide up the money in an account and use separate checkpads and stubs or ledgers to record expenditures and balances. You can create a "car book," a "house book," and even a "fun book." You'll just need a little extra time to reconcile your bank statement.

The main disadvantage of using bank accounts to budget expenses is the attention required to record the activity in each account and balance your statements and checkbooks. Also, you generally are charged service fees for each checking account and for frequent withdrawals from a savings account. If you have an interest-paying checking account and you keep a low balance or write a large number of checks, the charges could exceed the interest you earn. Find out about the costs and procedures involved in the accounts you're considering before you make a choice.

Charge Accounts and Credit Cards Can Help

Some people use charge accounts and credit cards as budget-tending tools. Let's say you have a line of credit at a department store for which you budget $86 per month. You decide to make that your limit for home furnishings, including appliances. You can't buy a microwave oven, let's say, until you've paid off the dishwasher and that drops off the monthly bill. Using charge accounts this way can be expensive—the interest rates on store accounts approach 20 percent—but it's an option.

Be mindful, though, that using charge accounts as a general budget heading can cause you to lose track of where the money went. As mentioned earlier, your "clothing" budget can be misleading if your clothing purchases are disguised here. It's easy enough to counteract this problem: when you pay your credit card bill, charge the individual items against the specific budget category.

Consider the Simple Cash Box

Another way to monitor your budget is to set up a cash box with a number of envelopes, each marked according to the purpose for which the money will be spent. At the beginning of the planning period, you put the money you've budgeted into the appropriate envelopes; when payments are due, you withdraw the amounts you need. You can also keep receipts in the same envelopes.

The advantages to this system are its simplicity and control. There's little chance of using the money meant for one purpose for another. And you may be less likely to overspend, because you can see when you're out of funds.

But there are serious disadvantages to the cash box system as well, especially if you're working with large amounts. The main one is the risk in keeping cash at home: the money can be lost to fire or thieves. Or, because it's so accessible, you may be more tempted to spend it. Also, to use this system you need to make all your payments in cash or convert the cash to some other form of payment, which might entail a service charge.

Possibly the most useful and least dangerous kind of cash box system is one used only for small expenses—bus fare, weekday lunches, babysitters—that you normally pay in cash. To help track where the money went, especially if you lump all your cash together, do what companies do with their petty cash boxes: put in an IOU that tells how much you took, when, and why.

How You Can Set Aside Money and Track Cash Flow

It takes a bit of planning and some extra bookkeeping to make sure that money is there when a big bill—such as property taxes—comes in.

On the Money Planner Worksheet for expenses, there is an asterisk beside certain items and a footnote that identifies these as "Set-Aside Accounts." This reflects the special problem of planning for bills that aren't paid monthly and expenses that require saving for a few years, such as the down payment on a house.

In writing your budget, you provided for these items by creating an artificial monthly amount. That's fine, but that money can give a false sense of well-being in the budget as it accumulates. Also, there's a strong temptation to fudge on those accounts if it isn't quickly obvious that you're running behind. On the other hand, the funds may build up to an amount that really should be working for you by earning interest. Finally, there is a question of timing: in the first year, you need to make sure that you've built up money fast enough to meet the bills that arrive early in the year.

The solution is to create a separate Set-Aside accounting record—it doesn't need to be elaborate—in which you identify accounts you want to treat this way, and track the amounts you pay and the resulting balance. Your contributions to your Set-Aside accounts are subtracted from your monthly budget, and keeping a separate record of them will give you a truer picture of how you're doing.

To create your record, gather your Set-Aside expenses. Write down the amounts and the dates they come due, in sequence (see Figure 1-4). Add them up. Divide by 12 to get the monthly amount you need to budget for these accounts.

To make sure you have enough cash to meet bills as they come due, do this: show the cash you will accumulate month by month in the Projected Balance column until you hit the first bill. Enough there to cover it? Fine, subtract the projected expense from the running balance and continue to the next expense.

If at some point you won't have enough to cover an expense due, you'll need to go back and beef up monthly payments to make up the difference. But that's okay, because you'll be able to reduce payments for the rest of the year to compensate for that amount. Keep going down the calendar.

Now you have your pattern for the year (called a "cash-flow analysis"). Each month, pay yourself the monthly amount (or transfer it to a special account you establish for this purpose). Note any payments you make against this account as you make them. Check the actual balance against the projection. Okay? Good.

Do this with each of your Set-Asides. Oops! Running a little short on "car insurance" because the company raised its rates? Take a look at your other accounts. Are any of them running a little rich? Well, roof repairs are coming in a little lower than you feared, so overall you can handle it. But make a note to correct that car insurance figure for the future.

If you're running your Set-Aside accounts within the same account that handles your monthly expenses, you might want to protect yourself against false optimism. At the beginning of each month, compute your Set-Aside balance and subtract that figure from the current balance in your account to show how much money you really have available for the month.

You can use this same process to help you set specific spending goals. Let's say you want to pay special attention to clothing, and you set a budget of $900. Open up a Set-Aside record for clothing and track your expenditures and the running balance each month. This technique will help you stick to your target by warning you when you're running over (Figure 1-5).

You can decide how important it is to you to be sure of having funds set aside for when you need them. Maybe you're the kind who

Figure 1-4   Example of a Set Aside/Cash Flow Record

Month	Item	Expense	Projected In	Projected Out	Projected Balance	Actual In	Actual Out	Actual Balance
Jan.	Heating oil	250	404	250	154	404	243	161
Feb.			404		558	404		565
Mar.	Car insurance	500	404	500	462	404	530	439
Apr.	Heating oil	250	404	250	616	404	260	583
May	Roof repair	500	404	500	520	404	435	552
June	Vacation	700	404	700	224			
July			404		628			
Aug.			404		1,032			
Sept.	Home insurance	350	404	350	1,086			
Oct.			404		1,490			
Nov.			404		1,894			
Dec.	Property tax	2,300	404	2,300	(2)			
TOTAL		$4,850						

Divide by 12 = $404/month

List each expense according to the date when it comes due in the Expense column. Add up these expenses to get your annual total. Here, it's $4,850. Then divide by 12 for your monthly allocation. Here, that's $404 per month, rounded.

To see how much cash you'll have at any point, use the Projected column. Enter the monthly allocation (here, $404) each month, then subtract the projected expense, and list the balance, month by month. In this example, with no set-aside expenses in July or August, you build up a pretty good surplus; you lose a little paying the homeowners' insurance in September, but you have just enough (well, within two dollars) to cover property taxes in December.

Under Actual, pay yourself the $404 from your budget, then list what you actually spend. "Car insurance" was up a bit, but "roof repair" was lower than expected. So as of May you have a balance of $552, a little ahead of the $520 you projected.

says, "Oh well, if some big expense arises, I'll just take out a loan." Some people, in fact, deliberately finance their lump expenses. Rather than worry too much, they would just as soon borrow. Many people pay their taxes every year with a loan that they pay off just as the next bill arrives. It's true that they're paying interest all the time, whereas

Figure 1-5   A Set-Aside Account for Clothing

Budget: $900
Divide by 12 = $75/month

Month	Item	In	Out	Balance
Jan.		75		75
Feb.	Scarf	75	5	145
Mar.	Jacket	75	120	100
Apr.		75		175
May	Shoes	75	37	213
June		75		288

they could be *earning* interest if they simply got a year ahead. But if it's not that important to them, fair enough.

TRACK AND RECONCILE YOUR BUDGET

To make your budget work, you need to track what you actually spend, examine how your expenditures relate to the budget plan you set for yourself, and make necessary changes. That may sound obvious, but many people feel that once they've gone through the ritual of setting a budget, they've done their duty. Or they simply sit down now and then and adjust the budget to fit the spending they just did. And there are a *lot* of people who review their budget, see how badly they've missed it, then do nothing about it except feel rotten.

The object, of course, is to use the budget to guide your decisions about when you can buy something, how much you can spend for it, and when you have money free for saving, investment, or speculation purposes.

There are many ways to handle the actual reconciliation. A simple one is to create your own bookkeeping record by getting some column-ruled paper, a looseleaf notebook, and setting up pages with your categories, as illustrated in Figure 1-6. For simplicity, the figure shows just two categories, Entertainment and Transportation. Of course, you'll have as many categories as there are in the budget you set up earlier. Set up each category with In, Out, and Balance columns, as shown for cash-flow records earlier.

How Often? How Much Detail?

How often you sit down to reconcile your budget, and how much detail you want, is up to you. There's a logic to doing it every time you

Figure 1-6 Running Reconciliation of a Budget

Entertainment				Transportation			
Date	In	Out	Balance	Date	In	Out	Balance
3/1	150		150	3/1	170		170
3/3		70	80	3/8		11	159
				3/15		230	−71
4/1	150		230	3/20		12	−83
				3/25		7.50	−90.50
				4/1	170		79.50

Enter the budgeted amount as "In" each month. List expenditures under "Out" as they occur, subtracting them from the previous balance. The Balance column then shows whether at any given time you're ahead of budget or behind. In this example, "Entertainment" is doing fine: at the beginning of April, the budgeted amount of $150 added to the $80 carried over from March gives a balance of $230. "Transportation" ran behind during the month, but the April 1 infusion brought it back.

balance your checkbook, recording expenditures against budget allocations for the month. But many people get around to doing a full budget check only once a quarter, or even less often. They see that there's still a good balance in the checkbook, so what can be so bad?

Well, if they don't have a Set-Aside ledger or the equivalent, a temporary surplus in the checking account won't prevent unpleasant surprises. Also, the resolve to watch your spending can melt away if there's no reassuring proof of progress or no warning that you're about to slip.

Moreover, tracking these items through the year helps you to spot a change. If an expense is higher than you expected, did you guess poorly, or is there something going on that you can change? Does the unplanned expense mean that you may be cutting into other accounts before the year is out? Of course, you may also find that your estimate was high and have the happy problem of finding a new place for the money.

Even if you want it fast and simple, you'll need to take time to at least run spot checks on specific categories to be sure you aren't getting into trouble. If you're on a very tight budget, though, you can't afford the luxury of inattention. Check your budget progress every time the bank statement arrives.

You may prefer to strike a compromise by selecting specific accounts to track every month. A suggestion: include your Set-Aside accounts on this list, because they're your bad-surprise insurance.

Another suggestion: check the items where you've made changes since last year. Say you decided to make a cut in a certain category to free up money elsewhere. Are you sticking to the cut? And check the "elsewhere," too. Did you get carried away and overspend there?

In general, check the categories that should come in for special attention. Do you remember those questions you were asking yourself, back when you drew up the budget, about how to adjust your spending habits to get more pleasure out of your money? If you set up special categories to track certain spending habits, you'll want to monitor those.

Remember how you were speculating that maybe you were spending so much on video rentals that you'd be better off with cable? How has that turned out? And weren't you going to track your spending at convenience stores, to see whether that was a cash leak? How does it look, now that a couple of months have gone by? And how about the true cost of that second car?

Be Ready to Adjust the Plan

When you reconcile your budget, keep an eye out for adjustments. For example, inflation can affect your projections. To allow for its effects, you could pad your annual expense projections by an across-the-board increase equal to the rate of inflation. Otherwise, you may need to reallocate funds if you discover that inflation has skewed your projections.

Reexamine your goals and timetables occasionally to determine whether they're still realistic. It may be that your budget is squeezed because you've been trying to get too far too fast. If your original plan was to buy a home in three years, for instance, you've been saving a lot for the down payment every year. Is it too much? Or maybe your budget could be tighter, and the savings plan speeded up. Check out your original plan.

Also look at your "fixed" expenses. Could you pay off some credit accounts more quickly and save on finance charges? Are your income tax withholdings larger than necessary?

What If Ends Won't Meet?

A minor budget deficit once in a while generally shouldn't cause great concern, but if you regularly fall short by a wide margin, it may be time to take decisive action.

Check out the categories where you're consistently over budget. Examine in detail where the money went (remember those receipts you've saved?). Use that information to set a specific reduction target, and stick to it.

Make it harder for yourself to spend money. Ration your cash. Leave your credit cards at home, or cancel them. Cancel charge accounts at stores that have proved to be too appealing.

If your bills are overdue, act quickly to protect your credit rating. Organize your bills so that you know exactly how much you owe to whom, and the status of each account—current, past due, or delinquent. Next, write to your creditors to explain the situation and to ask whether they'd work with you to resolve it, perhaps by extending your repayment schedule.

You may find that your irreducible expenses—rent or house payments, car loan payments, and the like—simply consume so much of your income that there's no way you can afford the other things you want, or need. Finding that out isn't much fun, but not knowing it is worse: you could be slipping deeply and dangerously into debt. If you're faced with fixed expenses that are too high for your income, you can do one of two things:

- *Reduce fixed expenses.* Sell your car or refinance the loan. Refinance your mortgage. Get a roommate or housemate. If you must, find a less expensive place to live.

- *Increase income.* If you can't reduce outgo to match income, what are the options for increasing the money coming in? A second job? A different job? If the problem is relatively short-term, can you sell some things you don't need?

We'll talk in greater detail about managing debt in Chapter 5, but it's mentioned here because that's one service a budget performs: waving the red flag early to warn you of a serious mismatch between income and outgo. With credit cards and other forms of credit, it's all too easy to have a bad problem before you know it. If you begin now to manage your money with a carefully planned budget, you won't find yourself desperately trying to make ends meet later on. Better still, you may find that you *can* afford the things that are most important to you—because you've planned for them.

Chapter Two

Banks and Banking

You want a place to keep your money where it will be safe and easy for you to get. You also want a place to borrow and a place to save.

Never before have there been so many people so eager to provide these things for you, and never with such dazzling technology.

It used to be boring, but simple. Banks were the only place you could do banking, and they told you what you could do and couldn't do and what it would cost. Moreover, only banks could offer the service most people need—checking. Deregulation designed to foster competition has changed all that. Now savings and loans also offer checking accounts, and so do credit unions (where they're called "share-draft accounts"). In fact, deregulation has financial institutions falling over each other trying to get your business and offering a plethora of services to bring you in. It's a boon for the consumer and a delight to those who remember the banks of old, which made you feel your money belonged to them and that it was improper for you to ask any questions about it.

In this chapter and the next, we'll talk about ways to apply the enthusiastic solicitude of today's financial institutions to your particular money needs, whether that means mixing and matching a number of institutions or simply assuring that you make the best possible use of your own bank. We'll focus chiefly on the uses of banks for handling your "get-at-able money," reserving detailed treatment of saving, investment, and loans and credit to the chapters that specifically deal with those subjects.

From now on in this chapter, we will use the word "bank" broadly, to describe the place where you do your banking. That could be a "full-service bank," a savings and loan, or a credit union. Government regulations used to create clear distinctions among these types of institutions, spelling out which ones could offer which types of products and services. But much of that has changed. We'll deal with the distinctions where they're important.

NEW WAYS TO DO YOUR BANKING

A new, eager, marketing mind-set is only one of the big changes that has taken place in banking. Another is the use of computer technology and telecommunications to help you handle your money in new and more convenient ways.

The most conspicuous example of the electronic revolution in personal banking is the automated teller machine (ATM), which for many people has eliminated one of life's most mind-numbing quarter hours: waiting in line at the bank. In addition, networks of ATMs enable you to get at your money almost anywhere in the country you happen to be. We'll talk more about ATMs in a moment, but there are many other uses of the same basic technology:

- "Debit card" or "point of sale" (POS) cards are becoming more popular at filling stations, grocery stores, and other businesses, where they can replace cash. You simply run them through a machine similar to an ATM, and funds are transferred from your account to pay for your purchase. You may even be able to use your regular ATM card for this purpose. As with ATMs, though, point of sale cards deduct the amount immediately from your account; they don't provide a grace period before charging interest the way most credit cards do.

- "Home banking" lets you use your computer to pay bills, move money from account to account, look to see whether a particular check has been paid, verify your balance, track investments, and generally stay on top of your finances.

- You can arrange to have bills paid automatically from your account through electronic transfers. And, as seems only fair, you can have money paid automatically *to* you, through electronic deposits of paychecks, pension checks, and the like to your account.

- You can arrange to have funds moved automatically between accounts—from your checking account, say, to your savings or money fund account.

And that's not all. Technology, married to a marketing imagination that is pretty amazing when you consider the staid history of banks, has created a variety of other nifty services:

- Do you want to make sure that every extra dollar is working for you by earning interest? You can get a "sweep" account in which the computer watches your checking account balance, then when it rises above a certain level, grabs the first dollar over that amount and moves it into an interest-paying account.

- Do you need a quick, hassle-free loan? Your bank card can be tied electronically to an account that carries a credit line so that you can grant yourself a loan at the punch of a key. And those cards, along with cards issued by non-banks, also offer a spectrum of special services, such as travel insurance.

What all this means to you as a consumer is that you can find lots of help in managing your money. But because there is a wide variation in services, costs, and convenience, it pays to take the trouble to *shop*.

HOW TO SHOP FOR BANKING SERVICES

In shopping for banking services, you'll want to examine your own needs. You'll probably put location high on your list, selecting from banks that have branches and automated teller machine outlets handy to where you live or work. With ATMs scattered all around, you may feel free to select a bank whose offices aren't that close to you. That's OK, but it could be a problem if you're also thinking about building a relationship with the bank for future purposes. Your user-friendly ATM won't remember your face.

If your banking business consists almost exclusively of checking and savings accounts, and you don't foresee a need in the near future for loans or other services, you probably should shop for price. Look for the bank that, overall, offers the best numbers. We'll discuss this point more in the next chapter.

If you're just starting out, with a modest income that you'll routinely use up month by month, you want a bank that:

- Has the lowest charges for the minimal levels of activity you'll need

- Doesn't penalize mistakes—bouncing checks, for instance—too severely

- Is interested enough in small loans that it will help you build the kind of credit record you'll need when the time comes to buy a house or make other major purchases

If you have a mix of needs—loans, investments, perhaps foreign currency exchange—in addition to accounts, look for the organization that offers all the services you want. Not every bank does, and most emphasize certain service areas at the expense of others.

If you are fairly aggressive in your money management, you may want to assemble your own network of institutions, maintaining a checking account at one bank, short-term savings somewhere else that offers better interest rates, and perhaps high-interest certificates of deposit handled by mail through an institution in another state.

If you simply want the easiest way to handle all your financial needs, you can think in terms of developing a money-management relationship with a single bank. In that case you'll want a warm and personal place where you can get support, advice, and the satisfaction of continuity.

Many bankers argue for that last approach. They say you want your bank to be one that you are comfortable with, that makes it as easy and pleasant as possible to do some things that may not be inherently easy *or* pleasant: pay bills, exercise discipline, borrow money.

Moreover, they say that your personal bank can help you with information and that credit is easier and cheaper to obtain when you've had a long-term relationship with that institution. Since it costs money to bring in new customers, banks look for ways to get and keep your business, often with incentives such as preferential rates and special services for long-term customers. If your check bounces and the banker knows you, you may get a telephone call so you can cover it before it embarrasses you (if you haven't arranged for automatic overdraft protection, a special feature most banks offer). And at a bank where you're known, your chances of getting a loan may be better, and the banker may intervene to speed it along.

If the business you have with any one bank aggregates to some size, you may get loans a little cheaper and be paid higher interest on your savings. Thus, you may find that it's cheapest for you in the long run to get everything, including your certificates of deposit, your home mortgage, and your car loans, in one place, and it would obviously be more convenient than having your accounts scattered all over town. In addition, many banks use the concept of "personal banker," assigning a specific bank officer to service accounts above a certain level, sometimes as low as $10,000. With a personal banker, you have a name, a face, and a number to call.

Whichever institutions you consider, you'll probably want to satisfy yourself about the safety of your money by determining whether the institution is a member of the Federal Deposit Insurance Corporation (FDIC) or the Federal Savings and Loan Insurance Corporation (FSLIC). Both of these insure accounts up to $100,000. This insurance costs the institution money and subjects it to additional regulation. Some institutions elect not to join and may offer incentives to persuade you to go with them. Before you do, consider that your funds may not be insured.

WHAT SERVICES DO YOU NEED?

Let's scan the menu of banking services that are currently available. Keep in mind, though, that competition is forcing changes so rapidly that you'll want to check out all the options available at any given time. That applies whether you're looking for a new bank or whether you simply want to make sure you're taking advantage of everything available where you are now.

Select the Right Accounts

To most people, accounts—checking and savings—are the most important service and the basis for price shopping. We devote the next chapter to accounts, discussing how to shop for and select the right ones, as well as the mechanics of using them (including tips on balancing a checkbook). So for now we'll just mention the chief categories:

- *Regular checking:* You pay a monthly fee and possibly a charge per check and per ATM withdrawal. However, those fees and charges are reduced or eliminated if you maintain a certain minimum balance.

- *Interest checking:* Called NOW accounts ("negotiable order of withdrawal") when banking regulations changed, interest checking accounts pay a set interest rate. Banks vary as to the rates, minimum balances required, and fees.

- *Money market checking:* Called a Super NOW, this type of account pays an interest rate tied to current money market rates (typically higher than the NOW account). Usually these accounts require higher minimum balances than NOW accounts.

- *Regular savings:* These accounts pay interest. Withdrawals usually are limited, and you can't write a check on the account to pay someone else.

Look at Loans and Credit

Banks, savings and loans, and credit unions each have their own mixtures of loans and credit mechanisms, including the following:

- *Installment loans,* where you borrow a specific amount and contract to pay it back in installments over a specified time. Included are personal loans, home improvement loans, auto loans, and home mortgages. The interest rate on an installment loan may be fixed (a set percentage for the full life of the loan), or it may be variable (changing to reflect the cost of money).

- *Lines of credit,* where you can draw out what you need yourself—up to a predetermined limit—and pay interest only on the amount you're using at any time. Interest rates may be fixed or variable. Financial institutions can offer these directly; in addition, some credit cards provide lines of credit, backed by a bank.
- *Bank credit cards,* which are really a plastic version of a revolving line of credit. You pay interest (typically higher than with other forms of credit) on the money you've spent after a certain period. Usually there is an annual fee. You can carry a balance, paying it off over time. (There are also credit cards available from non-banks that expect you to pay in full each month. These were the original credit cards, created principally for travel and entertainment, and are still often called "T & E" (travel and entertainment) cards or "convenience" cards.

We'll discuss getting and using credit in greater detail in Chapter 4.

Do Your Investing at Your Bank?

You may want to handle investments through your bank, too. At this writing, regulations still restrict banks, savings and loans, and credit unions from selling you corporate stocks directly, but many institutions have an arrangement with firms that do provide this service, along with other investment options, for their customers. Of course, there are a number of other items you can buy directly from banks for your portfolio:

- *Certificates of deposit (CDs),* which pay a set interest rate for a specified length of time
- *Government investments,* including U.S. Treasury bills, notes, and bonds; municipal bonds; and federal-agency investments
- *Individual retirement accounts (IRAs),* offered at most institutions

These investments are discussed in greater detail in Chapter 7.

BANKING ELECTRONICALLY

Years ago, the expectation that electronic transactions would replace paper transactions led to talk of a "cashless society" and "checkless banking." While that hasn't happened yet, automation has made things a lot easier for bank customers. Through the use of electronics and telecommunication, you can:

- Set your own bankers' hours

- Avoid lines at the teller window (although there are can still be people backed up at the automatic teller)
- Make purchases with a card that automatically transfers money from your checking account to pay the merchant
- Go on vacation secure in the knowledge that your bills will be paid on time while you are gone
- Do your banking from your home computer

Behind the scenes, financial institutions have been making use of electronic technology for some time. You have, too, if you've arranged to have your paycheck automatically posted to your account or if you have bills that are automatically paid from your account for you.

The new electronic systems and services are easy to use. You don't need special training to take advantage of them. But you do need to be aware of the ways in which they are different from what you may be used to.

The most important difference is that electronic transactions are almost immediate. That makes it more important than ever for you to keep track of account balances. (At the same time, the new systems make it easier for you to do that.) The new technology also raises issues of privacy and security. You should know about these issues and what steps to take to protect yourself.

Let's review what's available, along with the safeguards you should be aware of.

Automated Teller Machines (ATMs)

ATMs are self-service machines you can use not only to obtain cash but to do most of the things you normally do with a human teller. When you sign up, you specify which accounts you wish to include. Full-service ATMs typically let you check your current balance, make deposits, transfer funds between accounts, receive cash advances from your credit card account, and otherwise keep your bank accounts current. Also, most will accept payments on credit cards and loans, saving you postage. Some banks have limited-service ATMs that provide only cash withdrawals, account information, and transfers between accounts.

Unlike human tellers, the automated variety can operate 24 hours a day, seven days a week, meaning you can do your banking whenever it suits you. In addition, most banks have networks of ATMs around town, so that you can bank almost wherever you want. ATMs are found at the branch offices of financial institutions, in shopping areas, and sometimes at airports. There are walk-up and drive-in versions.

Some financial institutions participate in shared networks that link you to other ATM systems across the country. These let you obtain cash and check your balance when you're away from home. Shared ATMs won't accept deposits or bill payments, though, and typically a fee is charged for each transaction on an ATM that isn't operated by your own bank.

People who are accustomed to dealing in cash and checks may feel less secure with intangible electronic transactions. ATM banking, though, is really no different than working through a human teller. When you go to a human teller window, the teller pushes some buttons on an electronic keyboard to do your business. With an ATM, you push the buttons yourself. You insert your card, which is magnetically encoded. Then you punch in your personal identification number. The bank's computer reads the information off your card as well as the personal number you've entered and checks its memory bank to see whether the two match up. That's how the system makes sure that only you can get at your accounts. (The system won't work without both elements—the information on the card and the associated number that you provide separately.) That "personal identification number" (PIN) is given to you by the financial institution. It is confidential, and you must protect it carefully.

After you enter your card and verify your identity with the PIN, the machine guides you through a simple procedure by means of instructions and questions displayed on a screen. It tells you step by step what to do, including how to correct a mistake or cancel a transaction. (What if it's the machine that fouls up? When you sign up for an ATM card, the financial institution will give you a number to call if a machine malfunctions.) When you're done, the machine gives you a slip of paper that shows the date, place, and amount of the transaction. Some transaction records also show your new account balance. If there is a charge, the record may show that as well.

Keep your transaction records for use in balancing your checkbook and reviewing your bank statement. If you find an error on the statement, tell your bank immediately, if possible, and definitely within 60 days. Special rules and protections that apply to electronic fund transfers are spelled out a little later in this chapter.

Remember that ATM transactions withdraw funds or credit your account immediately. Be sure to record what you did and then calculate your new balance. Keep in mind, though, that on electronic deposits, as with paper transactions, there is such a thing as a "hold"— the waiting period for uncollected or unverified funds. Your deposit will show up on the screen, and the new balance may reflect the amount you've deposited, but you may not be able to use the funds until your deposit is verified or, in the case of checks, until the bank collects the funds. That applies particularly to checks drawn on another bank, out-of-state checks, or third-party checks.

Point of Sale (POS) Transfers and Debit Cards

Some retailers let you pay for purchases by transferring funds directly from your account to the retailer's account. Such point of sale (POS) transfers can be faster and easier than writing checks or using credit cards. You may find POS machines at filling stations, supermarkets, convenience stores, and elsewhere.

POS transfers involve using a debit card at a terminal, very much as you use your ATM card. Some banks let you use the same card, with the same personal identification number.

Because POS withdrawals are immediate, you'll want to shop carefully. An error in the transaction or a problem with the purchase probably won't show up until the money has already been transferred from your account to the retailer's. Try to resolve any purchase problems on the spot, and keep track of your account balance.

Special Considerations in Using ATM and Debit Cards

Protect Yourself. To protect yourself against misuse of your ATM or debit card, hold onto it tightly and take special care with your personal identification number:

- Memorize it.
- If you must write it down, disguise it as an address or telephone number, or in some other way.
- *Don't* write it down on your card or keep it next to the card unless you've disguised it.

As an added protection, terminals usually allow you only a few tries to enter the proper code. If your attempts are unsuccessful, the terminal will prevent further use. An ATM machine may keep your card, in which case you'll need to contact your bank to get it back.

Don't carry your ATM or debit card in full view. After using it, be sure to take it from the machine and put it away with the transaction record immediately.

If you're planning to use an ATM machine when it's dark, take a friend along. Don't use one if you see anyone loitering nearby.

If you think your card has been lost or stolen, notify your financial institution immediately. Your liability increases the longer the delay.

Understand Your Rights and Responsibilities. The federal government has special rules concerning the protections and responsibilities involved in electronic fund transfer activity. The federal Electronic

Fund Transfer Act spells these out in Regulation E. You can obtain this information from your financial institution or by writing the Federal Trade Commission in Washington, D.C. Here are some of the questions addressed by the government:

Q: What should I do if my card or PIN is lost or stolen—or if someone makes an ATM transaction without my permission?

A: Notify your institution immediately. You can't lose any money as a result of unauthorized use that occurs *after* you have contacted your institution.

You'll limit your potential loss to $50 if you notify your institution within two business days of the time you learn of the loss, theft, or misuse.

Otherwise, you could lose $500 or more if the institution can prove that timely notification would have prevented the loss.

Immediately report any unauthorized transactions that appear on your statement. Unless you report them within 60 days, *you could lose all the money in your account*—plus any amount available through overdraft protection—as a result of unauthorized transactions that occur *after* that 60 days.

Q: What if I am unable to notify my institution within 60 days?

A: If there's a good reason, such as a long trip or a hospital stay, the limit may be extended.

Q: Who is liable for losses or damages if my financial institution doesn't complete a transaction as agreed?

A: In most cases, your financial institution is liable, but not if you didn't have enough money in your account to cover the transaction or if you knew the ATM wasn't working properly or if the problem was caused by a fire, flood, or other circumstance beyond the institution's control.

Q: What should I do if I suspect an error in an ATM transaction?

A: Notify your financial institution as soon as possible but no later than 60 days after you get the statement that shows the error.

Your financial institution must investigate and resolve the error within 45 days—or 90 days, in the case of point of sale services. But if it hasn't completed the investigation 10 days after receiving your written notification (20 for POS), your financial institution must temporarily add the money in question to your account until it's resolved.

Your financial institution must correct any error promptly. It may also deposit any interest due to your account and refund any charges or fees involved with the error.

Q: What if the institution determines that the fault was mine?

A: The financial institution must send you a written explanation within three days after completing its investigation. The amount temporarily added will be deducted, but the institution must honor certain checks you wrote before it sent you notice.

Preauthorized Transfers

Preauthorized transfers are regular, automatic transfers of funds to or from your account that you authorize in advance. You can use them to deposit money and to pay bills, saving postage and time, and eliminating the time lag between sender and receiver.

Some automatic electronic fund transfers are arranged within your financial institution: loan payments withdrawn from your deposit account or regular transfers from your deposit account to your savings account. You simply work the arrangements out with your bank, and the transfers happen automatically.

Where a third party is involved, such as the government, your employer, or a utility company, there's a little more to it. You may arrange for regular recurring transfers into your account: your paycheck, Social Security or pension check, dividends, annuities, and commissions. Similarly, you can arrange for routine payments—for instance, to your utility company or insurance companies. Of course, all these types of transfers involve the cooperation of the third party.

When you arrange for direct deposit of your paycheck, your employer will typically give you a statement telling you what your earnings were, showing the tax and other deductions, and stating the net deposit made in your account. With other parties, the arrangements differ. In some cases, the financial institution will notify you that a deposit has been made, or it may notify you only if one has *not* been made. You may be given a number to call in case you want to check whether a deposit has been made.

When you authorize automatic bill payments, you specify in advance a stated amount, or a range of amounts, to be withdrawn and paid to the parties you have designated. The record will show up on your bank statement.

You can stop any preauthorized payment by notifying your financial institution three days before the scheduled payment date. If you do this by telephone, you may need to confirm it in writing as well.

Banking from Your Home Computer

Some financial institutions offer a way for you to connect your home computer to their system in order to pay bills, make payments to businesses and services, get instant information on balances, and—with some systems—even send electronic mail messages. You can see what checks are still outstanding, what charges have accumulated on any credit cards you have through that bank, and how close you are to your credit limit.

Many systems also provide such things as access to stock market quotations, a way to conduct stock trades, and linkages with money-management software programs. They may also tie you into general computer databases offering airline schedules and other information services.

These systems require you to have your own computer with tele-communications software and a modem, a device that enables the computer to transmit and receive electronic messages via a telephone line. You'll also need a computer printer if you want a paper copy of the information. Typically, using a home banking system costs a monthly fee.

REMEMBER MORE TRADITIONAL WAYS TO HANDLE MONEY

Of course, there are a number of other tried-and-true ways of han-dling money that are still useful.

Traveler's Checks

Traveler's checks can be purchased at just about any financial in-stitution, as well as from a number of other outlets. Generally they are available in denominations of $20, $50, $100, and sometimes $500 and $1,000. When you buy traveler's checks, the issuer gives you a pur-chase receipt. If your checks are lost or stolen, this receipt helps speed and simplify refund or replacement of the checks.

At the time you buy your traveler's checks, you should sign each one. Although you may or may not be required to sign in the seller's presence, you should sign them before leaving the branch or office where you purchase them. Anyone can use unsigned traveler's checks that are lost or stolen. When you present your checks for cash or pay-ment, you're asked to sign them again so that your signatures can be compared. You also may be asked to show identification.

Domestic Money Orders

You can buy domestic money orders at financial institutions, post offices, and some stores. They typically are used to pay small bills and to purchase mail-order merchandise. How readily a domestic money order is accepted can vary, depending on the reputation of the issuer. For example, U.S. Postal Service money orders are usually accepted throughout the country, but bank money orders generally aren't as readily accepted outside the state in which they are issued.

International Money Orders

You can buy international money orders for limited amounts to send money abroad. They're available through financial institutions and the U.S. Postal Service.

Cashier's Checks

Financial institutions issue cashier's checks for use in the United States. Often they are more readily accepted than domestic money orders or personal checks because they are drawn by the bank against itself. Typically, cashier's checks are used to pay large amounts, such as a down payment on a home, but you also can use them to pay for smaller items.

Now that we've had an overview of banking services, let's take a close look at the services that are most people's highest banking priority—checking and savings accounts.

Chapter Three

Accounts: Checking, Savings, and Variations

When we move to a new town, one of the first things we do is line up a checking account. We feel lost without one, hampered in buying things and in handling money. Even with the temporary checks they give us to use until the printed ones arrive, we feel somewhat vagrant.

Bank accounts are clearly important to us, and they represent our most frequent contact with the banking system. They are the reason most of us select the place to keep the bulk of our money.

In this chapter, we'll discuss the different categories of accounts, how to decide which services best meet your special situation, and how to shop for them.

Much of the chapter is devoted specifically to checks and checking, which we'll talk about in the detail that a beginner needs to get started. Even if you've been writing checks for years, you may want to skim the headings, for you may find some useful information here. For instance:

- Do you know what your liability is when a check is forged on your account?
- If you endorse a check to a third party, and the writer of the check turns out not to be good for it, who gets stuck?
- What are the rules on stopping payment?

We'll also deal with the task of balancing a checkbook and offer some tips for catching errors.

TYPES OF CHECKING ACCOUNTS

Regular Checking

Regular checking accounts charge a monthly fee, and typically you pay for each check as well. This is the cheapest account for people who maintain low balances or who write few checks (or both). If you write 10 to 12 checks a month, regular checking will cost you about $6 a month, plus the cost of printed checks (two hundred for, say, $7.50).

If you're putting very little into your checking account and spending it all every month, regular checking is probably the cheapest way for you to get the minimum service. First, though, check with your employer to see whether the bank the company uses offers free checking to employees, a service that sometimes is tied to direct deposit of your paycheck. If you're a senior citizen with a low level of income, look for banks that offer you free checking. Many do, at age 62 or 65. (The age varies.) Also, watch for special promotions: banks often use free checking for a certain period, such as the first year, as an incentive to attract new customers.

You can shop for these accounts by telephone. First estimate how many checks you'll need to write in a typical month, concentrating on money you'll pay by mail: rent, utilities, credit card and loan payments. Cash withdrawals from the bank's automated teller machine are probably free (but inquire to be sure), so you can reduce the number of checks you need by using ATMs. (Make sure you set up a system for tracking this money, though; otherwise, depending on ATMs can sabotage your budget keeping. Cash is very easy to spend, and it's hard to remember where it went afterward.)

Then call around. Use the same estimate of number of checks per month with each bank and ask what the monthly fee is and how much the first set of two hundred checks will cost you. Note how helpful the bank representatives try to be; that can be important later when you need help with questions and as you graduate to additional services.

While regular checking accounts are the cheapest for people who maintain minimal balances, a case can be made that your very first investment—worth saving up for from the very beginning—should be enough money to create a minimum balance that gets you into a free checking account.

Regular checking accounts have other uses, by the way. For example, they offer a low-cost way to introduce youngsters to the banking world. They are also a way to create a special account as a device for managing a specific piece of your budget. Or you can use one as a place to squirrel away money for gifts so that your spouse won't know what you really spent.

Free Checking and Interest Checking

If have at least a small cushion of money in your account each month, you'll want to use an account where your balance nullifies charges and perhaps earns you some interest. Shopping for these accounts can get complicated because there are so many variables:

- Banks typically set a schedule of minimum balances. If your account falls below a given level at any time, a fee is imposed. Some banks have different fees, pegged to different minimums.

- Banks may instead use an average monthly balance as the basis for imposing a fee.

- Some banks use both a minimum *and* an average to compute the fee. Checking might be free, for instance, provided that the account average during the month is $1,500 and that it never drops below $750. If either happens, there's a charge.

- With accounts that pay interest, the rate you receive varies from bank to bank in a number of ways, including the rate itself and the base on which it applies. Some banks pay interest only on the amount above a certain balance; some use the average balance; others use the ending or beginning balance; and so on.

If you're going to shop around for the bank that gives you the best deal, be prepared to do some arithmetic and set aside enough time to gather and compare information from a number of sources. In fact, you may want to do some rough computation first to find out whether the likely savings are worth the trouble of doing a lot of comparison shopping.

To begin with, if you already have a checking account, review your past monthly balances and determine whether they are likely to be about the same in the future. To assess the possible advantages of an interest account, you might then create an index: what's the net return (that is, after fees are subtracted), given the numbers that reflect your own experience: so many checks per month, so many ATM transactions (remember, some banks charge for these), and your average monthly balance?

Ask your bank to help you review your options there. Is there another account that pays better than the one you have? Things may have changed since you opened your account. Use the best deal you can get at your own bank as your base for comparisons.

Then watch the ads and select the bank that seems to be pushing for business most aggressively. Present your situation to them and see what the net cost or return would be for the index you've compiled. Does it look as if the difference is worth worrying about—and worth ending whatever relationship you've developed where you are? If so, be sure to check out other fees, charges, and services that are important to you. For some people, they may override the potential advantage of changing accounts. For example:

- If you bounce checks now and then, compare how the banks handle them and what penalties they charge or what it costs to have overdraft protection.
- If you frequently use network ATMs (those that aren't the bank's), perhaps because you travel a lot, check differences in charges for these transactions.
- If you frequently want help checking your account status, balancing your checkbook, and so on, check out how readily you can get that assistance. Many banks now offer this service over the telephone on a 24-hour basis.

SAVINGS AND MONEY MARKET ACCOUNTS

Regular savings accounts typically have a low minimum and a low fee and may limit the number of withdrawals you can make during a certain period before a charge is assessed. You can't write a check on them to someone else. They are designed, as the name implies, for dormant money, not in-and-out stuff.

Many banks provide a system that will connect your savings account with your checking account: everything over a certain balance in your checking account is swept automatically into savings to receive the higher savings account interest rate.

An alternative to regular savings is a money market account. This type of account offers a return pegged to current money market rates, a return that is usually higher than savings account interest. Some money market accounts offer limited checking privileges as well. Usually, you can write only so many checks within a certain period before a fee (which may be sizable, as much as $5) is imposed on each check. Typically, the checks must be for at least a certain minimum (and fairly high) amount, typically $500. Of course, if you need less, it's easy enough to draw out the full $500, take what you need, then redeposit what's left over either in that account or in your checking account.

WRITING AND CASHING CHECKS

The remainder of this chapter deals with the specific mechanics of checks and checking accounts. It is addressed chiefly to people starting out, including those starting out relatively late in life because their money affairs used to be handled by someone for them. Even if you're more experienced, though, you may want to skim these pages as a refresher.

We'll talk about how to write checks, how to endorse them, and how to make deposits. Then we'll look at special situations, such as how to stop payment and how to handle bounces. Finally, we'll discuss how to balance your checkbook.

The Face of a Check

Regardless of the type of check, all checks have certain features in common. The following explanations are based on the sample personal check shown Figure 3-1.

A. "159." This is the sequential check number. The check number can be very useful: be sure to record it accurately along with the amount and date of the check for reconciliation purposes later. You may have three checks stubbed "Cash $20" but suspect you wrote four of them.

B. "August 20, 1989." It doesn't matter whether you write the date in full, as shown in our sample, or write it as "Aug. 20, '89," or "8-20-89," "8/20/89." As of the date you write—day, month, and year—the check is payable. If there isn't a date on the check, it's considered current and payable.

Some terms you should know about: A *postdated check* is one dated for some time in the future. If you receive or write a postdated check, the financial institution may refuse to honor it until the date shown. A *stale-dated* check usually is one that's six months older than the date

Figure 3-1 The Face of a Check

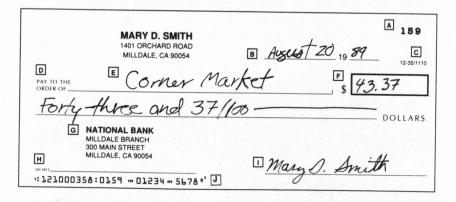

it carries. If a check becomes stale-dated more quickly, the stale date is specified on the face of the check in a phrase such as "Not Good after 60 Days." Financial institutions may not cash stale-dated checks. Checks drawn on the U.S. Treasury, such as Social Security checks, never become stale-dated. Checks that a financial institution draws on its own funds, such as cashier's checks and traveler's checks, might not become stale-dated either, depending on the institution's policy.

   C. *"12-35/1110."*   This is the ABA number, from a code developed by the American Bankers Association to indicate the financial institution on which the check is drawn.

   D. *"Pay to the Order of."*   Either this phrase or one of three others—"Payable to Bearer," "Payable to [name] or Bearer," or "Payable to [name] or Order"—must appear on the check to make it a legally negotiable item.

   E. *"Corner Market."*   This is the name of the *payee*—the person(s), business, or association that gets the money. If you're not sure how the payee wants the name written, it's a nice courtesy to ask. But don't leave the space blank for the payee to fill in, especially if you're mailing the check. Without the payee specified, the check is cash and the wrong person can redeem it.

   F. *"$43.37" and "Forty-three and 37/100 Dollars."*   You write the amount of the check in two ways—in numbers and in words—as a precaution against error. *If there's a difference between the two, the amount written in words is the legal amount of the check.* You can write the amount in various ways, as long as it's clear: for instance, $2225 can be written as "twenty-two hundred twenty-five and no/hundreds" or "two thousand two hundred twenty-five and no/hundreds." And no one cares if you use digits for the pennies ("and 00/00s"). Just be legible. Cross the 7's to distinguish them from 1's. As a precaution against alteration, fill up the line: if your writing doesn't do it, run a line through to the end.

   G. *National Bank, Milldale Branch.*   The name of your financial institution and your branch or office (called the *drawee*) are on the check so your account can be located and the check can be processed and paid.

   H. *Memo.*   Information here about the purpose of the check—"cash: gas, groceries"; "car insur. thru 6/30"; "Chris' birthday"; "Deduction: charity"—can assist you with record keeping.

I. "Mary D. Smith."   Your signature is kept on file at the branch or office of your financial institution where you have your account. Always sign your name as you did on the signature card when you opened your account. Variations may not be recognized, and your check may be returned unpaid.

J. Magnetic Code.   This is the line of magnetic ink that the computer uses to "read" your bank, branch, account number, and check number. You may be asked to read your account number from this line. If so, ask where you should start—how many digits from the end—and then read the symbols that are recognizable as numbers. If you use a counter check, you'll need to write in this number; get help to make sure you have it right.

Cashing Checks

Usually you can cash a check, whether your own or one made out to you, at the branch or office it's drawn on, provided that the check is good—that is, it's properly made out, you're known or you have acceptable identification, and the check is written against an account that has sufficient funds. A branch or office may cash checks drawn on another branch or office of the same financial institution or on other financial institutions, but it isn't obligated to.

Personal acquaintance is the best form of identification (ID). But because it's impossible for all employees to know every customer who walks into their financial institution, you need to carry identification cards or papers. In many cases, you'll be asked to show at least two forms of identification. Most financial institutions prefer that one of those IDs carries your picture or physical description.

In most states, acceptable forms of identification usually include a permanent driver's license or a state identification card (issued to nondrivers by the Department of Motor Vehicles), a passport, a check guarantee card, a nationally known credit card, an employee identification badge, a credit card from a well-known company, or a military ID card. Each must be current.

These forms of identification are acceptable because they commonly bear your signature and may include a physical description, your birth date, and your picture. All these IDs have a number that can be verified, and many have to be renewed at regular intervals.

Some financial institutions and merchants have incorporated the use of fingerprints, thumbprints, or picture-taking devices into their identification procedures to discourage someone from using your ID to cash your checks. Many financial institutions issue check guarantee cards to identify customers who have established a good financial relationship with them. Eligibility criteria and card privileges vary with the institution.

Financial institutions and merchants usually won't accept temporary driver's licenses, Social Security cards, non-local or unknown credit cards, library cards, birth certificates, savings passbooks, or checkbooks. These forms of identification are unacceptable because they are too easily obtained or don't firmly establish your identity. Some don't bear your signature. Any card that has expired or is altered or mutilated also is considered unacceptable for ID purposes.

If the employee at your financial institution isn't personally acquainted with you, the employee may compare the signature on the check you're cashing with the signature in the file and verify that you have enough money in your account to cover the check. In addition, you'll probably have to show an ID. At branches other than your own, the employee may call your branch to verify that the check is good.

You may find it difficult to get your check cashed at an institution where you don't have an account. Many institutions that cash non-customers' checks charge for doing so.

No matter where you cash your personal check, always sign it in the presence of the person who redeems it. He or she may want to see you sign your name before accepting your identification for signature comparison.

If a check made out to you is issued by a well-known, reputable organization, you shouldn't have a problem cashing it at your branch or office or at another branch or office of your financial institution. If the check is issued by a private party or an unfamiliar organization, however, you may have trouble cashing it anywhere but at your own branch. That's because other branches and other institutions may not have sufficient information to verify the check. You always have the option of cashing the check at the branch or office on which it's drawn, but if that's not convenient, your own branch or office is likely to give you the best service.

You may have problems with a two-party check, one that was originally made out to someone else, who in turn signed it over to you. In theory, a check can be endorsed and negotiated by any number of people. But in practice, institutions may be reluctant to cash a check with two or more endorsements. One reason is that in order to cash your check, the institution must endorse it; by doing so, it guarantees that prior endorsements are valid. If the institution can't verify the other signature(s) on the check, it may not want to make this guarantee. Typically, a bank will hold off payment until it can verify that the prior endorsement is valid.

In order to cash or deposit a check made out (or signed over) to you, you must endorse it (sign your name on the back). Endorse it as close to the top of the left side as possible. Many banks now have a line across the back to show where to write. When you endorse a check, you show rightful ownership of it. You also enter into a legally enforceable contract: your endorsement says you accept responsibility for making the check good, should it bounce—no matter who issued it. The fact that the financial institution may later guarantee the check by its endorsement doesn't relieve you of your responsibility.

How you endorse a check depends on the way it's made out:

- Endorse a check exactly as your name appears on it. If your name is misspelled, first sign it with the error and then sign correctly underneath.

- If a check is made out to "Mary Jones or John Brown," only one endorsement is necessary. The key word is "or."

- If a check is made out to "Mary Jones and John Brown"—note the "and"—then *both* endorsements must appear on the back of the check: one of you can't sign for both. An exception is made, however, for certain joint-tenancy accounts. If the other person has died or becomes incapacitated, you should ask the issuer to make out a new check in your name alone.

To sign a check over to someone else, you may endorse it in either of these ways:

- You can simply sign your name on the back. This is called a *blank endorsement*. It's important to note, however, that a check with a blank endorsement becomes payable to whoever holds it; it's like cash. If the check is lost or stolen, anyone may be able to cash it.

- You can write "Pay to the order of (the person's name)" and then sign your name. This is a *special endorsement*.

DEPOSITING MONEY

To be sure your money is deposited to the right account, fill out the deposit slip clearly and completely. An example of a preprinted deposit slip of the sort you receive with your customized checks is shown in Figure 3-2. Your branch or office and your account number are shown in a series of imprinted numbers in the magnetic code printed on the slip. On our sample deposit slip, these digits are the last ten in the code (A): 01234-5678. The first four of these numbers indicate the branch or office where your account is maintained. The last six numbers are your assigned account number. The arrangement of numbers can vary from institution to institution.

Figure 3-2 Sample Deposit Slip

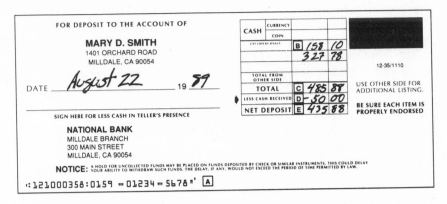

If you run out of preprinted slips, you may use blank forms provided by your financial institution. On these, you must fill in your name, branch or office, and account number. Be careful that you get your account number correct, lest you make an unintended surprise gift to some stranger.

Each check you deposit to your account should carry your endorsement. A *restrictive endorsement*—showing the words "For deposit only," followed by your account number and your signature—is a good safety measure when you bank by mail or endorse checks before you get to your institution. You also should use a restrictive endorsement when you deposit checks at an automated teller machine (ATM) or an "instant deposit" box.

With a partial deposit, you deposit part of a check and receive the rest in cash. This is also called a "less cash" transaction.

To make a partial deposit, first endorse the check by signing your name; don't use the phrase "For deposit only." On the deposit slip, enter the full amount of each check (B) plus any cash you're depositing. Record the total amount of all checks and cash in the section marked "Total" (C).

Enter the amount you want back in cash in the section "Less Cash Received" (D). Subtract the less cash amount from the total above, and enter the difference in the box marked Net Deposit (E).

To show that you've received some cash, you may be asked to sign the deposit slip in the presence of the employee who takes your deposit. You also may be required to show identification, since a partial deposit has the same effect as cashing a check.

Always be sure to get a receipt for your deposits. At an ATM, be sure to save the record slip the machine issues. When you make a deposit in person, make sure the record you get is legible and correct.

If you've deposited checks, the amount indicated on the receipt is subject to verification by the financial institution. For instance, if one of your deposited checks is returned because there's not enough money in the account on which it's drawn, the amount of that check will be deducted from your account balance.

Once you have a receipt for your deposit, in most cases you can begin to draw on that money immediately. The exception is when a hold is placed on your account for the uncollected funds (UCF). When your financial institution places a hold on your account for the amount of a check you deposit, you can't use those funds for a period of time specified by your institution. Your institution must notify you if a hold is placed on your account, whether you make the deposit in person, by mail, or through an instant deposit box or ATM.

New regulations that took effect in 1988 provide that government checks and the first $100 of any deposit must be available no later than the next business day after deposit. Beyond that, checks drawn on local banks must be available no later than the third business day. Checks from non-local banks must be available no later than seven business days after deposit.

Although you can't use the funds immediately, a hold doesn't necessarily prevent your funds from earning interest. (Whether or not a hold is placed on a check you deposit, the deposited funds may not start earning interest for up to two business days, under circumstances explained to you by your institution.) If the check is returned to your financial institution and interest has already been paid, the interest will be deducted from your account.

SPECIAL SITUATIONS

Lost Checks

If you lose any of your personal checks, even though they are unsigned, report the loss promptly to your financial institution. A warning will be placed on your account, and signatures on incoming checks will be carefully inspected for forgeries.

Stolen Checks

If you suspect that your checks have been stolen, first make a report to the police in the city or town where the theft took place. Then notify your financial institution of the time, date, and place the police report was made. A warning will be placed on your account. The institution may ask you to close your account and open a new one under a different number.

Forgeries

As long as you've reported your checks missing or stolen to the proper authorities, usually you won't be held responsible for losses due to forgery. The financial institution or merchant who accepted the forged check(s) is charged for the loss.

You would discover a forgery, of course, when you reconciled your bank statement and check stubs or register. Be sure to report a forgery to your financial institution promptly. If you fail to do so and the institution loses money, you may be held responsible for the loss. If you wait for more than a year after you receive your statement and canceled checks to report a forgery, you generally cannot recover the loss. Individual institutions are allowed to establish time limits that are shorter than a year. An officer at your financial institution can tell you its policy.

When you report a forgery to your institution, be prepared to back up your claim. You may be required to furnish a notarized affidavit that gives the details of the forgery. This document may be used to bring criminal charges against the forger.

Stop Payments

You can order a "stop payment" on a check if you don't want it paid because it was lost or stolen or for some other reason. (If it's because you've changed your mind about a purchase or some other transaction, the other party may have other recourse to obtain payment from you.)

To order a stop payment, you can go to your branch and fill out a stop payment form. You can also mail your branch a written request for a stop payment, or you may be able to arrange a stop payment by phone. In any case, you'll need to provide the date the check was made payable, the exact amount, the name of the payee, the check number, the name of the person who signed it, and the reason for the stop payment.

A stop payment won't go into effect until your branch or office verifies that the check hasn't been paid. If the check is presented at your institution for payment while the stop payment is in effect, the check will be returned unpaid to the person who presented it.

Most institutions charge for filing stop payments. The order stays in effect for six months. Usually you can renew the stop payment if necessary, often for an additional charge. Under certain circumstances, payment of a check can be enforced even though a stop payment order has been filed. Ask an officer at your institution about the limitations on stop payments.

Rejected Checks and Overdrafts

If you write a check for more money than you have in your account, that's an "overdraft." Your financial institution will either pay the check and overdraw your account, or reject (bounce) the check.

If your institution pays the check, the amount is deducted from your account, leaving it with a negative balance. You'll receive a notice of checks paid in this manner and the amount of the charge for the overdraft. You'll be expected to make a deposit to cover the overdraft and the additional charge.

If your institution rejects the check, it will be returned unpaid to the payee. You should notify the person or organization immediately of the date you'll have enough money in your account to cover the amount of the returned check. Financial institutions and many merchants charge for rejected checks. If the redeposited check bounces a second time, your institution again will charge you a fee; the merchant also may charge you again.

If a check you deposit is returned by the institution on which it's drawn, the amount of the check—and any interest paid on that amount, if you have an interest-earning account—will be subtracted from your account balance. The check will be returned to you.

Overdraft Protection

There are two types of overdraft protection financial institutions may offer to their customers. The first type involves automatic transfers from a savings account. If you authorize this service, funds are transferred automatically from your savings account to your checking account to cover any overdrafts.

The second type of overdraft protection service is backed by a credit card account or a personal line of credit established for this purpose. Money transferred into your checking account is charged against the credit card or line of credit, up to the limit of your available credit. The transferred funds may be subject to interest charges, according to the terms of your credit account agreement. Some plans also charge a fee each time a transfer is made.

With either type of overdraft protection, you'll find that qualification requirements, minimum transfer amounts, and transfer charges vary with the institution.

CHECKING TIPS

Here are some additional tips on handling your checks and checking account.

- Treat your checks as you would cash. Keep them as secure as possible. Destroy any blank checks you won't be using—for instance, leftover checks from an account you're closing.

- Don't make changes on the face of a check that is issued to you, and don't accept a check that looks as if it has been altered. Your financial institution may refuse to honor such checks.

- Avoid carrying checks made out to "Cash" or "Bearer," and never sign your personal check until you've filled in the amount and the payee. If such checks are lost or stolen, anyone can cash them.

- When writing a personal check for cash, make it payable to "Cash" or "Bearer." If you make it payable to yourself or the financial institution, you'll have to endorse it on the back. It's safest to write out such a check at the financial institution.

- Always inspect new check orders to make sure your name is spelled correctly, your address and phone number are listed accurately, and your account number is properly imprinted. Report any errors immediately.

- Take the time to balance your statement promptly. Doing so will help you avoid overdrafts and save a lot of time later if there's an error to trace.

Depending on the arrangements governing your account, your canceled checks may or may not be returned to you with your bank statement. If you have your canceled checks returned to you, compare them with your statement and your check register to make sure they all agree. If you're using a check safekeeping program (sometimes called *check truncation*), the financial institution doesn't return the original canceled checks. Instead, the checks usually are put on microfilm, which is stored by the institution for a number of years. With this program, copies of your canceled checks are available at your request when you need them for tax or other purposes, although there can be a charge for these copies. Either way, report any errors you find on your statement as soon as possible.

BALANCING YOUR CHECKBOOK

For some people, balancing a checkbook is one of life's most nagging irritations: it never comes out on the button. Usually, the problem is due to a small check you forgot to record or an error in arithmetic. Let's look at what you need to do to keep an accurate record of the money in your checking account.

Keeping Accurate Records

To begin with, you should keep an accurate, ongoing record of your checking account activity. Since you may not have your canceled checks, your checkbook register may be the only record you have to compare with your statement. Make that notation complete enough for use in budget allocations ($30 = groceries, $10 = beer), tax records ("charity"), and so on.

Record each check or deposit immediately. (Write down any ATM transaction as you would a check or deposit.) And don't postpone the arithmetic: subtract the amount of each check or other debit from your balance promptly, and add each deposit or transfer.

When you make a deposit, the bank adds it to your account at the end of the business day. When the checks you write reach the bank, they are subtracted from your account, canceled, and filed. Keep in mind that checks may not reach the bank in the order you wrote them.

With computers, banks process checks faster than ever. A check you cash today could be subtracted from your account tonight. You may risk an overdraft or a returned check if you count on using "float" to cover your checks with a deposit. (Float is the time it takes the check to travel to the institution on which it's drawn and where it will be paid.)

At about the same time each month, the bank prepares a statement showing all the activity in your account and sends it to you. As soon as possible after receiving your statement, compare it with your own check register or stubs and reconcile any differences. Of course, you may have made deposits or written checks since the date your statement was prepared, and therefore show a balance in your checkbook that's different from the one that appears on your statement. To reconcile your record and the bank's, you'll need to account for these transactions. (We'll show you how momentarily.) After you've balanced your checkbook, keep it up to date as you make deposits or withdrawals so you'll know how much money you have in your account at any time.

Your checking account statement is the bank's record of your checking activity, including deposits made to your account and checks paid from it. The statement also lists any automatic transfers you've authorized the bank to make regularly. These include both *debits* (subtractions), such as monthly service charges, loan payments, or transfers from checking to savings accounts, and *credits* (additions), such as payroll deposits or transfers to cover overdrafts.

Your statement also shows electronic fund transfer (EFT) transactions. These include deposits or withdrawals made at an automated teller machine; payments made to retailers with a card that debits your checking account; and transactions initiated with your personal computer, if you have that service. If you have an interest-earning checking account, your statement shows the interest you've earned.

As we've noted, if you use a check safekeeping program, your canceled checks are stored on microfilm by the bank, and copies are available at your request. Otherwise, your original checks will be returned with your statement.

By balancing your checkbook when you receive your statement, you can verify the amounts of checks, deposits, ATM transactions (keep any duplicate deposit slips and ATM transaction records), and other subtractions or additions. Correct any errors in your checkbook promptly, or ask the bank to correct any mistakes it may have made.

Unless you balance your checkbook regularly, you can't be sure how much money you have in your account. As a result, you may accidentally write a check that you don't have enough money to cover. In that case, the bank may "reject" (bounce) the check and return it, unpaid, to the payee, or the bank may create an overdraft by paying the check. How the bank handles this situation depends on the amount of the check, whether you have overdraft protection, and your past checking activity. Without overdraft protection (or if you exceed your credit limit), you'll probably pay a charge for the check, and suffer some embarrassment as well. Businesses that allow you check-cashing privileges also may charge you for unpaid checks the bank returns to them.

Understanding Your Bank Statement

Every bank has its own statement design, and happily for the consumer, banks compete at making theirs easier to use than their competitors'. (What IRS form designers need is a good competitor.)

We've created the specimen statement in Figure 3-3 to illustrate the specific kinds of information you'll typically find on bank statements. While your statement may not look exactly like this one, it will contain the same basic kinds of information.

A. "Services Summary."   If you have accounts other than your checking account listed on your statement, your statement will include a brief summary listing each account. The summary gives the account numbers, branch location, and account balances as of the statement date. For each account listed, your statement will include a separate section that provides more information about activity in the account.

B. "Checking."   This portion of your statement shows any activity in your checking account during the statement period. It is divided into five main areas (C through G in Figure 3-3).

Figure 3-3   Sample Bank Statement

```
National Bank                                      Statement
MILLDALE BRANCH NO. 0999
123 MILLDALE AVENUE
MILLDALE, CA  99999
PHONE 213-123-4567

DATE OF THIS STATEMENT   08-29-89

PAGE 1 OF 2                       CHARLES D. SMITH
E11                               MARY D. SMITH
              0999-PS22           1401 ORCHARD ROAD
                                  MILLDALE, CA 99999
[A]
SERVICES    SERVICE           ACCOUNT        BRANCH                    BALANCE
SUMMARY
            CHECKING          09991-02345    MILLDALE BRANCH            204.15
            REGULAR SAVINGS   09992-03456    MILLDALE BRANCH          1,609.50
[B]
CHECKING    09991-02345 CHECKING PLAN                      TAX ID  376-62-5160

SUMMARY     PREVIOUS STATEMENT BALANCE ON 07-31-89................................221.02
[C]
            TOTAL OF 2 DEPOSITS FOR......................................1,254.31
            TOTAL OF 1 OTHER CREDIT FOR....................................643.33

            TOTAL OF 11 CHECKS FOR......................................1,609.51
            TOTAL OF 5 OTHER DEBITS FOR....................................305.00

            STATEMENT BALANCE ON 08-29-89..................................204.15

            AVERAGE BALANCE THIS STATEMENT PERIOD...........................494.25

CHECKS/     CHECKS
OTHER
DEBITS             CHECK       DATE                   CHECK    DATE
[D]                NUMBER      POSTED    AMOUNT        NUMBER   POSTED    AMOUNT

                   1546        08-01      19.69        1553     08-18      36.35
                   1547        08-01     135.86        1554     08-20     150.00
                   1548        08-04      46.18        1555     08-25      78.12
                   1549        08-04     575.00        1557     08-26      69.50
                   1550        08-08      74.05        1559     08-29     107.76
                   1551        08-11     317.00

            OTHER DEBITS

            DATE          TRANSACTION
            POSTED        DESCRIPTION                                   AMOUNT

            08-01         AUTOMATED TELLER TRANS 123456 ON 08-01
                          CUSTOMER 792333469 AT TERMINAL 654321--PAYMENT
                          TO VISA 4019-1234-5678-9012...................40.00
            08-11         AUTOMATED TELLER TRANS 123456 ON 08-08
                          CUSTOMER 792333469 AT TERMINAL 654321--CASH
                          WITHDRAWAL...................................100.00
            08-18         AUTOMATED TELLER TRANS 123456 ON 08-18
                          CUSTOMER 792333469 AT TERMINAL 654321--CASH
                          WITHDRAWAL...................................100.00
            08-25         AUTOMATED TELLER TRANS 123456 ON 08-24
                          CUSTOMER 792333469 AT TERMINAL 654321--CASH
                          WITHDRAWAL....................................60.00
            08-29         SERVICE CHARGE (BASED ON MINIMUM DAILY BALANCE
                          OF 122.55 ON 08-11)............................5.00
```

C. "Summary."   The checking summary includes your previous balance, your current balance, and totals for the various checking transactions during the statement period. If you have overdraft protection, for instance, the summary will show you the total amount of funds available.

D. "Checks/Other Debits."   This section lists your checks and other debits subtracted from your account in the statement period. First, your checks are listed in numerical order. Any gap indicates a

Figure 3-3 (continued)

```
National Bank                                   Statement
MILLDALE BRANCH NO. 0999
123 MILLDALE AVENUE
MILLDALE, CA  99999
PHONE 213-123-4567

DATE OF THIS STATEMENT  08/29/89

PAGE 2 OF 2                    CHARLES D. SMITH
                              MARY D. SMITH


CHECKING    09991-02345 CHECKING PLAN  (CONTINUED)
─────────────────────────────────────────────────────────────────────
DEPOSITS/  DEPOSITS
OTHER
CREDITS                     DATE                          DATE
                            POSTED    AMOUNT              POSTED    AMOUNT
 E                          08-01     1,209.31            08-14     45.00

            OTHER CREDITS
            DATE        TRANSACTION
            POSTED      DESCRIPTION                                 AMOUNT
            08-18       PAYROLL XYZ CORPORATION.....................643.33
─────────────────────────────────────────────────────────────────────
DAILY       DATE      AMOUNT      DATE      AMOUNT      DATE      AMOUNT
BALANCE
 F          08-01     1,234.78    08-14     167.55      08-25     386.41
            08-04     613.60      08-18     674.53      08-26     316.91
            08-08     539.55      08-20     524.53      08-29     204.15
            08-11     122.55
─────────────────────────────────────────────────────────────────────
SERVICE     MONTHLY MAINTENANCE CHARGE...................................2.50
CHARGES     CHARGE FOR 3 CHECKS/DRAFTS 3 @ .50
 G              EXCEEDING 8 CHECKS/DRAFTS...............................1.50
            CHECK ENCLOSURE SERVICE CHARGE..............................1.00

            TOTAL SERVICE CHARGE......................................5.00
 H ─────────────────────────────────────────────────────────────────
REGULAR     09992-03456                        TAX ID 376-62-5160
SAVINGS
─────────────────────────────────────────────────────────────────────
SUMMARY     PREVIOUS STATEMENT BALANCE ON 07-31-89...................900.50
            TOTAL OF 1 DEPOSIT/CREDITS FOR...........................790.00
            STATEMENT BALANCE ON 08-29-89..........................1,690.50
            INTEREST PAID THIS YEAR...................................12.75

ACTIVITY    DATE        TRANSACTION
            POSTED      DESCRIPTION                                 AMOUNT
            08-04       DEPOSIT.......................................790.00
```

check still outstanding, or one you tore up. The "date posted" is the date the bank paid the checks. Next come electronic fund transfer (EFT) debits and automatic transfers from your account, as well as any subtractions the bank makes for special situations (such as a stop payment charge).

E. "Deposits/Other Credits." Deposits are listed first, in the order in which they were posted. Next, other credits are listed, such as EFT deposits, automatic transfers to your account (for instance, direct deposits of your paychecks), or a credit posted to your account after the bank finds a deposit error in your favor.

F. "Daily Balance."   Your statement may include the daily balance, reflecting changes in your checking account balance as credits and debits are posted throughout the statement period. It's good to glance at this section each time you receive your statement. Remember that day you wondered whether you dared write another check? Well, this tells you how close you came to an overdraft, or how close you came to slipping below the minimum of a fee bracket, where that applies. A gap between the dates means that the balance was unchanged for that period.

"Daily Interest Calculation Balance" (Not Shown).   If you have an interest-earning checking account, your statement will have a section showing your account balance and the interest rate for each day during the statement period. Entries appear only for those days when the interest rate changed. A gap between the dates means that the balance and the interest rate were unchanged for the period between those dates.

G. "Service Charges."   Your monthly maintenance charge and per-unit charges are listed here. Any monthly service charges will be subtracted from your account on the last day of your statement period.

H. "Regular Savings."   This section provides a detailed description of activity in your regular savings account.

Getting Down to Balancing Your Checkbook

Now comes the fun part. To balance your checkbook, you'll need your check register (or check stubs), your monthly statement, and any EFT transaction records you have. Follow the steps on the sample shown in Figure 3-4 to see how the procedure works. (Your own bank statement probably has a section very like the one shown.)

If you go through the balancing procedure described in Figure 3-4 and your checkbook still won't balance, the following steps may help you locate the error.

Transactions the Bank Makes.   Make sure you've added to or subtracted from your record any debits or credits the bank makes for you. You'll find them on your statement. These may include service charges or loan payments and other automatic money transfers.

Figure 3-4 Checkbook-Balancing Worksheet (from Sample Statement)

Statement

THIS WORKSHEET WILL HELP YOU IN BALANCING YOUR CHECKBOOK

You will need your checkbook record (register or check stubs) and your ATM transaction record.

STEP 1

In your checkbook record, mark all the checks and other debits (withdrawals such as service charges, automatic or ATM transactions) shown on your statement. Below, list any checks or other debits that are recorded in your checkbook, but do not appear on your statement.

STEP 2

Mark all deposits and other credits (additions such as interest payments, automatic or ATM transactions) shown on your statement. At right, list any deposits or other credits that are recorded in your checkbook, but do not appear on your statement.

DATE OF DEPOSIT/OTHER CREDITS	AMOUNT
TOTAL	

CHECKBOOK NUMBER OTHER DEBITS	AMOUNT
#1552	75 00
#1556	15 00
#1558	50 00
TOTAL	

STEP 3

Be sure your checkbook record is complete. It should include entries for all checks and other debits as well as all deposits and other credits that are shown on your statement.

To verify your statement balance, complete the arithmetic at right. Your statement balance (shown in the Summary section of the statement) is the balance as of the date of the statement.

Your current checkbook balance and your statement balance for this period should match. If these balances are different, check your addition and subtraction in your checkbook record and review each step in the balancing procedure.

If you find any errors, notify your bank immediately. If you don't report any errors, your account will be considered correct.

THIS STATEMENT'S BALANCE	$204.15
ADD DEPOSITS/OTHER CREDITS NOT YET CREDITED IN THIS STATEMENT	+ 0
SUBTOTAL	= $204.15
SUBTRACT CHECKS/ OTHER DEBITS NOT LISTED IN THIS STATEMENT	- $140.00
YOUR CURRENT CHECKBOOK BALANCE	= $64.15

EFT Transactions. It's important to record all deposits and withdrawals made through an automated teller machine and other EFT transactions at the time they are made. Keep all transaction records for reference. Compare your records carefully with the transactions listed on the statement.

Arithmetic. Doublecheck the additions and subtractions you've made in your checkbook and in the balancing procedure. Here are a couple of tips.

Doubling: If the difference between your balance and the bank's can be evenly divided by 2, the error could have been caused by adding—instead of subtracting—a check in your checkbook.

Transposing: Can the difference between your balance and the bank's be divided evenly by 9? If so, there's a good chance the error was caused by transposing numbers—for example, recording a $23 check for $32, or $5.17 as $7.15.

Recording Errors. Compare the check numbers and check amounts that you recorded in your checkbook with the check numbers and check amounts on your statement. If you receive your canceled checks with your statement, you should also compare the amounts and check numbers with your check register. The check amount the computer recorded is encoded on the bottom right corner of each check. The amount should be the same as the check amount you wrote and recorded.

Last Month's "Checks Outstanding." Make sure that any checks outstanding from last month's balancing that still have not been paid by the bank are included in this month's list of checks outstanding. You'll know they're still outstanding if they don't appear on your statement.

Balance Forward. In your checkbook, be sure that you carried forward the same balance from the bottom of one page to the top of the next page.

Unrecorded Checks and EFT Transactions. Have you recorded and subtracted from your checkbook balance all the checks and EFT transactions listed on your statement?

Missing Checks. Suppose there's a check missing from your checkbook record or from the numerical listing on your statement. If your record fails to show a check listed on the statement, did you forget to record a check you wrote? You may have saved a sales receipt that can help jog your memory. If a check you've recorded is not listed on the statement, it's probably still outstanding—or maybe you destroyed it.

"Less Cash" Deposits. When you deposit a check and withdraw part of your deposit in cash (in one transaction, using one deposit slip), you have a "less cash" deposit. Be sure you recorded correctly the amount that was actually added to your account. You should have a record you can use to check: either the teller's stamped entry on the Deposit Record page of your checkbook or your receipt (a stamped duplicate deposit slip).

Same Deposits. Do you and the bank show the same number of deposits, for the same amounts? Again, you should have a receipt or a stamped entry in your checkbook to verify each deposit you've made.

Matching Statement Balances. Be sure the "previous balance" shown on this month's statement is the same as the ending balance on last month's statement.

Still Won't Balance?   If you need more help, gather all your records—checkbook, deposit receipts, statement, check stubs or canceled checks (if you have them), and EFT transaction records—and visit the bank. Some banks have a special "statement window" to handle this problem.

Receiving "Today's Balance."   Here's an important point to remember: If you inquire at your bank to get today's balance, the amount reported to you may not necessarily be the true balance of your account, because it won't include checks you've written that have not yet reached the bank. You need to allow for these checks to keep from overdrawing your account.

Bringing Records Up to Date

As we've emphasized, reconciling your records with the bank's is much easier if you balance your checkbook promptly each month. If you haven't balanced your checkbook for several months, though, here are the steps to follow to bring your records up to date.

If you have a record of deposits and checks written:

- Balance your checkbook one statement at a time, beginning with the oldest statement. This makes it easier to locate and correct errors.

- Find the last check listed on that statement (the check with the highest number). In your checkbook, draw a line under the balance you recorded when you subtracted that check.

- Balance that statement to your checkbook balance on the line you just drew. Follow the procedure described in Figure 3-4, or use the worksheet provided on your own statement.

- Go to the next oldest statement. Repeat the procedure until your checkbook is balanced up to the current date.

If you *don't* have a record of deposits and checks written, visit your bank for help in reaching an accurate balance. Bring your checkbook, your bank statements, and any EFT transaction records. You may be charged a fee if the bank must assist in balancing several months' statements.

Once you've balanced your checkbook, keep your records updated so you'll know how much money you have in your checking account from day to day.

Good record-keeping habits can save you a lot of time and irritation. They're also useful in helping you manage credit, as we'll see in the next chapter.

Chapter Four

Getting and Using Credit

If you're like most people, you've acquired a lot of attitudes about borrowing money, most of which make you feel guilty when you do it.

Business people, however, have no such hang-ups; to them, money is something they buy when they need it—as cheaply as possible, of course, just like other raw materials. There are public-policy sanctions for credit, too. The uses of credit that have the highest level of social acceptance are those for home mortgages (we feel pretty emotional about The Home) and those for business investment (because that can create jobs). National policy endorses both by granting tax incentives for them.

The fact is, credit involves a kind of fantasy: it makes it possible for us to have things beyond our immediate ability to buy and, even deeper into fantasy, lets us reach into the future. That can add a valuable dimension to our financial management. It can also create the worst of financial nightmares.

WHY USE CREDIT?

For most people, the real reason for wanting credit is impatience. We all know we could save up first, but we don't want to wait. Besides, we'll be making more money later (or inflation will come along, or we'll win the lottery).

But there are other reasons, too. Let's look at them.

Purchases Too Big to Handle Any Other Way

Most people need credit for homes, cars, college, and other big items. There are also unusual circumstances that require more money than we have handy: weddings, funerals, medical emergencies.

Convenience

Using a charge account or credit card can be easier than carrying cash or a checkbook. Credit cards are more likely to be accepted than personal checks, especially out of state. They provide good records for budget reconciliation, reimbursement, and tax purposes. Also, credit cards facilitate mail-order and telephone purchases; they can save money by avoiding COD charges, and they make it easier to return merchandise and to stop payment when a deal isn't satisfactory.

Budget Management

For many people, credit works very effectively as a budget-management tool imposed from the outside. For instance, many people set a monthly maximum for their credit cards and their charge accounts, then let those maximums limit their purchases. They can decide that they will hold their account at a department store to $75 per month and that they won't make a new purchase there until something has been paid off and drops out. Some people use one credit card for all their entertainment and business expenses, another for household purchases, and an oil company card for automobile expenses.

Consumer counselors will argue that this use of credit is expensive, directly and indirectly: most credit cards charge annual fees, and the interest rates charged for both credit cards and charge accounts can add up. But if using credit this way works for you, and you know exactly what you're doing, it's your choice.

Inflation Hedge

When inflation is running high, many people feel that saving up today's dollars will leave them disadvantaged when they have to buy in tomorrow's inflated dollars. Why not buy now, and pay back when money is cheaper? This practice is not necessarily based on sound and rational economic analysis, but it's a popular reason some people give themselves.

Tax Avoidance

Before tax reform, the federal government carried a sizable portion of the cost of consumer credit for people in higher tax brackets by permitting taxpayers to deduct the interest charges from their income. The 1986 tax law changed all that, but home equity financing—credit obtained by borrowing against the value of your home—persists as a way to deduct interest costs. And interest on a home mortgage continues to be an important tax deduction for many people and one of the reasons (along with the deduction for property taxes) people most often give for buying a place to live, rather than renting.

FORMS OF CREDIT

The most common forms of credit are store charge accounts and charge cards, oil company charge cards, bank credit cards, installment credit, and the newly popular home equity credit.

Charge Accounts and Credit Cards

Charge accounts and credit cards come in two varieties: single-payment accounts and revolving accounts. With single-payment accounts, whether they are credit cards or charge accounts, you pay your bill in full each month. Most travel and entertainment cards operate this way. Usually, you don't have to pay a finance charge, so long as you pay on time, but you are charged an annual fee.

Revolving charge accounts, which also are available as credit cards and as store charge accounts, let you charge purchases up to a specified limit. You're not required to pay your bill in full each month, but you must make a minimum monthly payment (the minimum amount is based on your outstanding balance). You can pay more than the minimum amount if you wish, and reduce the interest you'll be charged on the unpaid balance. You may not be charged interest if you pay the account in full within a specified time, generally 24 to 30 days from the date of your statement.

Interest rates for revolving credit generally are higher than for some other forms of credit, such as loans from financial institutions. The longer you take to repay, the more you'll spend on interest. Many credit cards also have annual fees in addition to the finance charges.

Installment Credit

Installment credit, which you pay back in regular intervals over a fixed period of time, is available directly from lending institutions. Loans of this type usually are granted for a single, specified purpose, such as buying a car or taking a vacation. You also may be able to get installment credit through the seller of a product you're buying—from an auto dealer to finance the purchase of a car, for instance.

You must apply for installment credit each time you want to use it and, depending on what you're financing, you may be required to make a down payment. Interest rates for installment credit are often lower than those for revolving credit, especially if you pledge property such as a car or a savings account as collateral.

Home Equity Credit

Home equity credit—credit based on the value you have in your home—has become very popular because it's usually cheaper than other forms (the home offers good security to the lender) and interest is tax-deductible in most instances (tax reform is phasing out the deductibility of interest not involved with homes). This kind of credit is available either as an installment loan or as a line of credit (whereby you can borrow up to a certain limit and are charged interest only on the portion that's unpaid).

If you have high creditworthiness, lenders may let you have up to 80 percent of the current value of your home, minus the amount of your outstanding mortgage. You get at the money by writing a check on it, using a credit card, or both.

Its advantages aside, this type of credit *does* use your house as collateral and puts it at risk if you default. The relative ease with which you get the money can lure you into spending beyond your means, which can be particularly dangerous with loans that have relatively low monthly payments but then put big payments—called *balloon payments*—at the end. You may find you can't meet those large payments and so lose your home.

To find the best rates and also to find the combination of features that most suits you, you need to shop hard. There are lots of choices.

Interest rates can be a fixed percentage that lasts the life of the loan or, more typically, a variable percentage that changes according to some index, such as the rate on U.S. Treasury bills. Many have a cap; they will go only so high, no matter what the index does. Some permit you to convert to a fixed rate at a future date.

There can be significant other costs. Some home-equity lenders charge up-front costs comparable to the closing costs paid when you bought your house, including such things as application fee, title search, attorney fees, and points (a percentage of the amount you borrow). If you end up not using much of the credit line, that front-end cost can make the money you *do* use very expensive. Shop around, though. Lenders vary widely in their treatment of these closing costs. In addition, there may be an annual participation or membership fee, as well as transaction fees charged each time you tap the credit line.

Repayment may take the form of a fixed monthly charge that includes both interest and principal. Many plans have variable monthly payments that charge according to the current interest rate. Some collect only interest as you go, leaving the principal to be repaid as a big balloon payment at the end.

In the case of balloon note plans, you may want to get an agreement that permits you to refinance or extend that final payment if it turns out you can't make it. You'll want to be sure you know the penalties for late payment and the conditions under which the lender can consider you in default and foreclose on your property if you don't pay off the full amount.

The Federal Trade Commission (FTC) has developed a useful checklist to use in comparison shopping for home equity credit. The FTC suggests you ask each of several lenders the following questions to determine which plan is best for you:

1. How large a credit line will you extend to me?
2. How long can I take to repay?
3. What are the minimum and maximum withdrawals I can make?
4. Do I access the credit with checks or credit cards?
5. Does this loan have a fixed rate? If so, what is it? What is the annual percentage rate (APR)?
6. Does this loan have a variable interest rate? If so, what is it? What is the annual percentage rate (APR)? What is the highest this rate could go (cap)? How often can the rate change? What is the index? (Lenders use such things as the rates paid on six-month certificates of deposit or U.S. Treasury bills as a reflection of interest; the loan interest is tied to that index.) What is the margin? (Lenders charge a "margin" above the index interest rate to cover costs, loan-loss reserve, and profit.) Is this convertible to a fixed rate?
7. What are the total closing costs that I must pay? Points? Application fee? Title search? Appraisal? Attorney fees? Are there any other closing costs I pay?
8. Are there any continuing costs? Annual membership fees? Transaction fees?
9. Does this loan have a fixed monthly fee? How much?
10. Does it have a variable fee? How is it determined?
11. Do the monthly payments include both interest and principal?
12. Is there a final balloon payment? How much? Do I have the option of refinancing it? Do I have the option of extending the loan term?

13. Is there a penalty for late payment? What is it?
14. What are the default provisions?
15. Are there any terms that can be changed without my consent?
16. Is there a penalty for early repayment?

Other Forms of Credit

In addition to charge accounts, credit cards, installment loans, and home equity credit, there are second mortgages on a home (related to home equity loans), loans against an insurance policy, and loans against your retirement savings plan at work.

SOURCES OF CREDIT

The most common sources of credit include the following:

- Stores and oil companies, which offer credit as a way to facilitate sales
- Banks and savings and loans
- Credit unions
- Finance companies

In addition, your doctor, dentist, and other providers of professional services often extend credit of various kinds. This practice used to be casual—your friendly doctor would carry you at no interest for a while—but professional people increasingly use services to monitor and collect on accounts, and they now may impose finance charges on unpaid balances.

ESTABLISHING CREDIT

By law, your application for credit must be evaluated without regard to your race, color, religion, national origin, sex, marital status, receipt of income from public assistance programs, or age (provided you're 18 or otherwise capable of entering into legally binding contracts). The federal Equal Credit Opportunity Act also prohibits discrimination against anyone who, in good faith, has ever exercised any right under the Consumer Credit Protection Act, such as making a complaint of sex discrimination.

Within such legal guidelines, creditors may set their own standards. Based on the same information and financial situation, one creditor may extend credit, another may not.

Factors That Affect Credit

Creditors generally consider the following factors:

Age.   To get credit, typically you must be at least 18—the age at which you're legally bound to honor contracts you sign. Seniors should note that those over 62 cannot be denied credit because of age or because they cannot obtain credit insurance (an insurance policy that pays off the debt if you die or become disabled).

Stability.   In determining stability, creditors may look at how long you've lived in the area and at your present address; whether you rent or own your home; whether you own other property; and whether you have savings, insurance, or investments.

Income.   You'll probably be asked to provide information about your occupation and employer; how long you've worked at your present job; how much you earn and how you're paid (by salary, commission, or fee); and sources and amount of other income available for the payment of your debts, such as pensions, annuities, and dividends. You don't have to reveal in your application any income that comes from alimony, child support, or separate maintenance payments, unless you want creditors to consider this income in determining your creditworthiness.

If you're self-employed, you may be asked to provide tax returns as a way to verify your business income.

Expenses.   Your expenses relative to your income influence your ability to pay your debts. Creditors may request information regarding the number of your dependents; your financial obligations, such as alimony and child support; and your living expenses.

Debt Record.   Potential creditors may consider how much you already owe (your outstanding debts) and how promptly you pay your bills. They also may want to know how often you borrow and why; whether a creditor has had to take action to make you repay; whether items you've bought on credit have been repossessed; and whether you've ever filed for bankruptcy.

To evaluate your creditworthiness, creditors use the information you supply on applications and may consider any information contained in your file at consumer-credit reporting agencies, also known as credit bureaus. These are commercial organizations that collect information on how well people have managed their debts in the past to help creditors predict future creditworthiness. The kind of information that is likely to be in your credit report and your rights concerning this information are discussed in the box on page 68.

Getting Credit for the First Time

People just starting out are the ones who need credit the most. At the same time, they're the ones who have the most difficulty getting it.

But they aren't the only ones who have difficulty. Our attitudes about credit have caused many people to use cash or to avoid the use of credit in other ways. The result is that they don't have a credit history, or don't have it in their own name, when they need it. This can be a rude discovery to someone who loses a spouse by divorce or death, especially if the spouse was the breadwinner.

The best protection against being denied credit for lack of a credit history is to create credit experience in advance. You can do that without creating new spending and budgeting patterns and without paying very much in financing costs.

Here are some suggestions for creating a credit record, whether you're just out of school or a senior citizen. (Whether you actually get credit is a matter between you and the creditor.)

Recognize first that the lender is concerned with two things:

- Your ability to repay: do you have the income to pay off the debt, or collateral that can be tapped if you don't?
- Your trustworthiness: Given that you *can* repay; *will* you pay your bills reliably and on time?

Your ability to repay is easy to establish, if you've got it. Trustworthiness is tougher if you're just starting out or have never borrowed money in your own name. The lender has no place to turn to get a history of your past performance as a bill payer. You name won't be in the files of the credit bureaus lenders rely on. Here's how to remedy that.

1. Open a Charge Account or Take Out a Loan.   Open a small account and faithfully pay it off on time. Explain that you're building a credit rating, and make sure the store reports to the established credit bureaus. Most do, but if your store doesn't, it's less helpful to your cause. You can still use your payment record as a reference, but it's stronger if that information is in the records of the credit reporting agencies.

Another, similar tactic is to take out a small loan where you bank and pay it off promptly.

You are most likely to get credit if the amount you request is small and the business is local and familiar with you. Your banker or creditors doing business in your community are more likely to know you or your employer, so they can verify more readily the facts on your credit application.

2. *Get Checking and Savings Accounts and Handle Them Well.* A responsibly maintained checking or savings account in your name indicates good money management habits. Potential creditors check this out almost automatically from the information on your application.

Some financial institutions offer checking accounts that enable you to qualify for a credit card if you manage a small line of credit responsibly for a set period. Many institutions also allow responsible minors to open checking or savings accounts in their own names with parental consent.

3. *Get a "Secured Credit" Card.* With a secured credit card, you pledge an amount from your savings to back the card, and you can borrow up to that amount. Borrow some and repay quickly. That gets you into the system.

Other Ways to Get Credit. It will probably take a year of the kind of bill paying we've described before you'll finally have your credit established. If you need money sooner, you may need to consider some immediate options.

One option is to use layaway plans. Some stores that aren't willing to extend you credit will let you make payments on time while they hold on to the item you're purchasing. Once you've made regular payments, you may be allowed to open a charge account.

A second option is to use your savings or time deposit account as collateral. This helps get credit established and it can also be one of the least expensive ways to borrow, because your money continues to earn interest while it's pledged against your loan. Usually, you may not withdraw the amount pledged until the loan has been repaid.

A third option is to make a big down payment. Creditors may be more willing to lend you money to purchase a car, appliances, or furniture "on the installment plan" if you make a large down payment. The more of your own money you invest in an item, the more likely it is that you'll continue to pay on the amount owed.

Finally, you can get a cosigner. Until your credit qualifications are strong enough for you to get credit on your own, a creditor may agree to extend you a loan or charge account if you have a cosigner (also called a *comaker* or *guarantor*). This can be a parent, relative, or business associate who meets the creditor's credit standards and who agrees to pay your debt if you don't.

What's in Your Credit Record

A creditor usually will want to see your credit history report before deciding on your application. The first time you apply for credit, the information you supply is likely to be used to initiate a file on you at one or more consumer credit reporting agencies. Most creditors use the services of at least one agency to obtain information on credit applicants and to provide information on credit customers.

The Fair Credit Reporting Act protects your right of access to the information about you in credit reporting agencies' files. You can determine which agencies have files on you by contacting your various creditors and asking the name of the agency to which each one reports. You can also look in the Yellow Pages of the telephone directory under "Credit Reporting Agencies" for a list of the agencies in your area. Ask each agency what procedures you should follow to obtain the information you want.

A credit report about you usually includes the following:

- Identifying information: name, date of birth, Social Security number, current address, spouse's name, and the names of any dependents
- Employment information: occupation, current employer, and length of time on the job
- Financial data: other sources of income, credit accounts and available credit, and bill-paying history. Public record information: bankruptcies or lawsuits, for example
- Any inquiries received, usually within the past year, for credit information about you

Restrictions imposed by law and by the credit reporting process itself exclude certain kinds of information from your report. For instance, your credit report won't contain information about your reputation, character, and lifestyle. Also, federal law regulates how long negative information, such as an account sent to a collection agency, may be included. Usually it's no more than seven years, or ten years for bankruptcies.

Besides excluding certain kinds of information, your credit report may be missing portions of your credit history. This could happen because a credit application you filled out is incomplete— for instance, because you left out information necessary to locate your files at other credit reporting agencies or because some of your credit history was reported only in your spouse's name.

Information also may be left out of your report because your creditors report to different agencies that don't communicate with each other. You can help prevent any gaps in the information flow by telling your prospective creditor about your previous credit accounts—the names of past creditors, approximate opening and closing dates on the accounts, and your name and address during those times.

Your credit report won't recommend whether you should receive credit. Creditors evaluate your creditworthiness independently, according to their own standards.

Establish Your Own Credit Identity

Women who marry and change their names can lose the credit history they've built up under their given names. And when they are separated, divorced, or widowed, they can lose the benefit of a credit history developed in the name of their husband.

The Equal Credit Opportunity Act addresses this problem. It applies as well to men when a couple's credit is established in the wife's name.

If you're married, all credit accounts opened on or after June 1, 1977, that you shared with your spouse must be reported in both your and your spouse's names. Joint accounts established prior to June 1, 1977, however, may be on file in your spouse's name only. You can still have these accounts reported in your name as part of your credit history. If the accounts are still open, ask your creditors to add them to your credit bureau file.

You can also ask creditors to evaluate the credit history of any account you've used that's listed in your spouse's or former spouse's name, provided that you can show that the account reflects your willingness or ability to repay. It may help to show canceled checks with your signature for payments on credit accounts.

To ensure that you are protected after a spouse is gone, it is important to know what kinds of accounts you have. There are three basic kinds, with different effects:

- An individual account, opened in one person's name and based wholly on that person's income and assets
- A joint account, opened in the names of both partners, based on the income and assets of both, and with both partners contractually liable for any debts

• A user account, where two names may appear but the account is based on the income and assets of just one and only that one is legally liable for debts

If a spouse dies who was the legally responsible party in an individual account or user account, there is no protection for the surviving spouse. Only a joint account continues credit standing. Even there, while a creditor cannot close or change the terms of your joint account solely because of the death of your spouse, the creditor can ask you to reapply if there is reason to think your income will no longer support the credit level.

If you are concerned about maintaining your credit status, then, it can be wise to open one or more individual accounts in your own name to develop your own credit history.

Moving? Carry Your Credit Record with You

When you plan to move, get the names of the credit reporting agencies in your old community so you can give them to new creditors. You can get their names by asking your former creditors which agencies they reported to or by looking in the Yellow Pages under "Credit Reporting Agencies." When you apply for credit in your new area, the creditor will ask the former agency for your report.

You may find it helpful to transfer your checking and savings accounts to your new community so that you'll have a local bank reference. A bank or oil company credit card and a personal introduction to new creditors also may be useful.

Turned Down for Credit? Find Out Why

The federal Equal Credit Opportunity Act requires creditors to tell you within 30 days after they've received a completed application whether they've approved or denied the application. If a creditor denies your application, the creditor must tell you the specific reasons in writing.

If the denial was based on information received in a credit report from a consumer credit reporting agency, the federal Fair Credit Reporting Act requires creditors to tell you so and to give you the name and address of the agency. You then can obtain a copy of your credit file free of charge by writing or visiting the agency within 30 days after you receive written notice that you've been denied credit. (Even if you've never been denied credit, you have the right to see the information in your file. However, the agency may charge you a fee, usually about $10.)

You have the right to request an investigation of any incorrect or incomplete information and to have the wrong or unverified information deleted from your file. If the investigation doesn't resolve your dispute, you may write a brief statement to be placed in the credit file and included in future reports.

If information in your file is found to be inaccurate, at your request the agency must supply the correct information to anyone who received the inaccurate report within the past six months—or, if the report was used for employment purposes, within the past two years.

If you feel you were denied credit for one of the reasons that are not allowed under the Equal Credit Opportunity Act, you can complain to the government agency that regulates that particular creditor.

If you have specific questions or problems, you should contact the creditor or credit reporting agency involved or seek legal advice. For help with a problem concerning a credit reporting agency, you also can contact the Federal Trade Commission (FTC), which is responsible for enforcing the Fair Credit Reporting Act.

SHOPPING FOR CREDIT

You may decide to keep your credit choices simple. You can get charge cards at the stores you use most and oil company cards from the stations you use most or like best. Then you can rely on the place where you do your banking as the source of your credit card and any loans—mortgage, car, tuition—you need.

On the other hand, you may want to shop around aggressively, selecting your credit cards the way you do products and making a specific search for the best terms on each major loan. It all depends on what's important to you.

Shopping around will probably save you money. On something big, such as a home mortgage, it may save a lot: while the financial institution you're already using will have to be fairly competitive, and many give preferential rates to established customers, the range in actual costs can vary enough to be significant. (We discuss mortgage loans in greater detail in Chapter 10.) There can also be significant differences in the cost of credit for everyday purposes: credit card fees and interest rates, for instance, vary widely.

How Many Credit Cards?

One point to consider in shopping for credit is how many cards you need. There are some good reasons for carrying fewer rather than more. For one thing, each card represents an additional hazard. It's easier to lose one of many and not miss it. In addition, bill paying and record keeping time and trouble are multiplied by the number of cards you have. In terms of cost, credit cards typically charge an annual fee, and you'll want to consider why you want to pay for more than one.

For most people, though, the biggest problem with too many cards is that they make it that much easier to run up too many bills. Each card will have a spending limit, but the totals of several cards can put you in trouble before you know it.

On the other hand, having a variety of cards lets you shop more selectively: you can use the department store that has the best sale or the filling station whose prices are currently lowest. Too, as mentioned earlier, different accounts and cards can be dedicated to specific purposes as an aid to managing your budget—one for routine purchases, one for entertainment, one for business, one for him, one for her, and so on.

A final reason for having at least two credit cards is that you may want to dedicate one card with a deliberately low credit limit to mail-order and telephone purchases, since they involve giving out the card number—potentially the key to your account—to someone else.

Fees and Charges

Charge accounts are typically free if you pay the entire balance each month. Creditors vary in the percentage they charge for unpaid balances, however, and they can compute their charges in different ways. Ask what their grace period is (that is, how much time you have to pay before finance charges are applied), what interest they charge, and what balance they use as the base. Then compare.

Many issuers of credit cards will offer the first year free or provide some other kind of start-up incentive. Some provide a discount or rebates tied to purchases; see whether that realistically will make a difference in the cost of the card.

Consider your personal practices in determining what's important. If you'll be carrying a sizable balance and therefore incurring interest, you'll be more interested in a low interest rate than in the annual fee. But if you always pay your accounts off before you incur interest charges, you don't really care what rates they charge: you'll want the lowest fee.

Special Features

Credit cards are being promoted with great imagination these days, and many offer beneficial features. The one from your bank may tie in with your automated teller services and may provide other linkages to your accounts, including overdraft protection. If you want it to, your credit card account may automatically dip into another of your accounts to pay itself off.

Some cards automatically provide accident insurance if you use them to pay travel fares. Many provide access to emergency cash when you're away from home, at different fees. That may be an important feature to you, saving you the trouble of carrying "just in case" cash or traveler's checks. If features like these really make a difference to you, you will want to take them into account along with fees and interest charges indicating which card or cards best suit your needs.

Who Accepts Which Credit Cards?

The major credit cards all advertise as to how widely they are accepted nationally and internationally. In today's competitive marketplace, that changes. For you, all that's important is what cards work at the places where you're likely to use them. Any of the big national cards will be accepted at almost any hotel, motel, or restaurant (although, as you may have discovered to your embarrassment, some very expensive restaurants accept no cards at all). Probably more important to you is the practice of the local shops you frequent: they can be more selective about which cards they accept. Ask around.

MANAGING CREDIT

When you're almost out of cash or your checkbook balance is low, you know that you're nearing your spending limit. But if you use credit, you can overspend without realizing it—until the bills come in. That's why wise credit use requires planning and monitoring: planning how much credit your budget can handle, and monitoring your credit spending to make sure it stays within your established limits.

There's a limit to the amount of credit you can get on most credit accounts; but if you have many accounts, the total limit available may be more than you can handle. So it's up to you to establish your own personal credit limit—the most you'll allow yourself to carry on all of your accounts, including installment loans, credit cards, and charge accounts, at any given time.

How do you know when it's time to stop buying on credit? That depends on your individual circumstances, such as the size and stability of your income and your present and anticipated expenses.

One guideline is whether the percentage of your income that goes to pay your debts is higher than the limit used by creditors to evaluate loan requests. Although this limit varies, lenders generally agree that your total monthly debt payments and housing expenses together shouldn't exceed 30 to 40 percent of your gross monthly income (before deductions). To figure what percentage you're spending, divide your total monthly debt payments, including house payments or rent, by your monthly gross income.

Another rule of thumb often used by financial counselors is that you should stop charging whenever your credit payments alone (not including a mortgage) approach 15 to 20 percent of your take-home pay (what's left after income taxes, Social Security, and other deductions). Test yourself against this guideline by dividing the total of your monthly loan payments by your monthly take-home pay.

Remember to take your individual circumstances into account. For example, a family of four whose monthly gross income is $1,600 probably will have more difficulty handling a 40 percent debt load (which leaves $960 for all other living expenses) than a family of four whose monthly gross income is $2,400 (which leaves $1,440 a month for other expenses).

Setting Your Limit

Perhaps the most workable way to find your personal credit limit is to figure how much you can afford to pay each month for credit purchases. That may mean setting up a budget if you don't already have one. At the least, you'll need to evaluate your monthly cash flow—the money you receive and pay out. Although your focus is on the sum of your monthly credit payments, don't overlook the amount of your total debt outstanding. The higher it goes, the more your monthly payments will be.

Once you establish your personal credit limit, you must plan your credit spending so that the total of all your monthly credit payments doesn't exceed this amount. Suppose you set your personal credit limit at $500 a month. Imagine that you have monthly payments of $225 on your car, $50 on your bank card, and $60 a month on your oil company card (which you probably pay in full each month). In this case, you have a leeway of $165. You can apply this money to an existing debt—your bank card, for instance—so you can pay it off sooner and save on finance charges. Or you can put the extra money in savings, spend it, or take on additional debt.

Reevaluate your personal credit limit from time to time. Don't be too quick to increase it unless you honestly believe you can handle the extra debt—perhaps because of a raise in pay or some other change in your financial status.

Keeping Track

To make sure you stay within your personal credit limit, you need to keep track of your charge account and credit card purchases. This is fairly simple if you have only one or two accounts, but if you maintain a number of accounts, you may lose sight of your overall credit picture.

One tracking technique is a credit register like the one shown in Figure 4-1. It works much like your checkbook register, except that you

Figure 4-1   A Credit Register

Credit Cards ($500 Limit)			
Date	Item	Amount	Balance
2/1	Current Debt		$100.00
2/5	Shoes	$67.22	167.22
2/15	Bicycle	207.00	374.22
2/20	Finance Charge	3.26	377.48
3/3	Payment	(150.00)	227.48
3/11	Shirt	22.38	249.86

add credit purchases and finance charges to the balance and subtract monthly payments from it. (In the illustration, the payment is enclosed in parentheses to distinguish it from purchases and to indicate that it's subtracted from the balance.) The balance represents money you owe rather than money available to spend.

It's important to enter purchases and payments as you make them so that your credit register always reflects your current credit standing. Also, keep your credit register and your other financial records—such as your budget and installment loan records—in one place for quick reference when you want to review your overall credit picture.

If you prefer to keep less detailed records, you can modify the credit register. For example, rather than noting individual purchases as you make them, tally your charge slips each week and enter the weekly total for all your accounts.

You may be able to keep track of your credit spending simply by examining your monthly statements or by regularly reviewing your charge slips. But bear in mind that the more closely you track your credit spending, the clearer your credit picture will be.

Remember, too, the value of charging credit card purchases to specific budget categories, as we discussed in Chapter 1 If you want to know how much you're spending on clothes in order to keep that part of your budget under control, you'll need to make sure all those purchases are recorded together somewhere.

Other Disciplines

There are three other steps you might consider to help you manage your use of credit.

- Except in cases of emergency, make it a practice to postpone a credit purchase until you've thought it over for a few days.

- Borrow only the amount you need, and make as large a down payment as you can. If you're using a credit card or charge account, you may want to pay for a portion of the purchase in cash.
- Combine your credit use with a savings plan. After you pay off a revolving or installment debt, put the amount of that monthly payment into a savings account.

WHAT TO DO WHEN DEBT PILES UP

Even the best-laid plans can be upset by an emergency expense, a sudden loss of income, or an impulsive purchase. You may take on several "easy payment" loans when your income still meets your expenses, and then you find yourself slipping into deep trouble.

You may be tempted to ignore overdue notices on your bills and calls from collection agencies, hoping things will eventually straighten out. But if you don't act now to get your finances back in order, you may be jeopardizing your peace of mind as well as your credit rating.

Danger Signals

Here are some clear signals that you're getting overextended. Any one of them can indicate potential difficulty; several together are cause for real concern.

- Juggling payments—that is, stalling one creditor to pay another
- Receiving past-due notices in credit billing statements
- Failing to save even a little money each month, or dipping into savings for normal living expenses
- Charging more each month than you make in payments to your accounts
- Taking longer and longer to pay off credit account balances
- Running out of money before payday
- Using cash advances on your credit card to cover everyday living expenses or to make payments on other credit accounts

If you're sinking into debt, don't despair. There are some steps you can take. We'll talk about working with creditors, understanding your rights and responsibilities, seeking financial counseling, and getting a new start.

Find Out Where You Stand

The first step in taking charge of your debts is to know exactly where you stand. Make a personal financial statement that lists the following:

- Monthly income after taxes and other deductions
- Everyday living expenses such as mortgage payments or rent, food, utilities, transportation, and child care
- Periodic expenses you must plan for, such as property taxes and insurance
- Required monthly payments for loans, credit cards, and charge accounts

The next step is to see whether you can reduce your debt load by trimming other expenses and applying the money to your debts. If you haven't been tracking where your money goes, use the information in your financial statement to prepare a budget (refer to Chapter 1 on budget preparation).

In addition, don't take on any more debts. You may want to stop carrying your credit cards for a while, or even cut them up and cancel your accounts.

In some cases, reducing your spending and monitoring your finances may be all that's needed to bring your bills back in line. But your debts may be so large that even these measures aren't enough. In this case, it's time to talk to your creditors.

Contact Your Creditors

You may hesitate to approach your creditors because you're not sure how they'll receive you. However, if you contact them as soon as you run into financial problems, and if you've paid your bills regularly in the past, most creditors will appreciate your taking the initiative and will want to help. Explain the reason for your financial bind, whether it's because you lost your job, had large medical bills, or just overspent. Your creditors will need to know why you can't pay your debts so they can help you with possible alternatives.

Creditors generally handle payment problems on a case-by-case basis. What an individual creditor would be willing or able to do for you depends on the creditor's policies; the type of debt (installment loan, home loan, bank card, or retail charge account); your financial situation; the reason for your account problems; and the way you've handled your payments in the past. The following are some of the possibilities.

Extension.   If you're suffering a temporary financial squeeze—caused, for example, by unexpected medical expenses or a brief layoff from your job—a creditor might give you an extension (extra time to make your required payment). A typical extension would be 30 days, although in some instances it could be more.

While some creditors may require no payment at all during an extension, others may want partial payments or ask you to keep paying the interest or service charges. An extension may mean that your creditor won't report your account as delinquent to a consumer credit reporting agency, but you should ask to be sure. If the account is reported as delinquent, you may want to file a statement with the agency yourself, giving the reasons why you're late and explaining that you're working with the creditor to bring your payments up to date.

An extension most often is granted when your creditor has good reason to believe that you'll soon be able to make your regular payments again. Interest or service charges (and, in some cases, late charges) usually continue to accrue. Some lenders may charge an additional fee.

Loan Revision.   If you're having trouble making payments on an installment loan, your lender may be willing to lower your monthly payments by revising the loan for a longer term. Your lender will decide whether to revise the loan at the original or current interest rate. When your loan is revised, you may pay more in interest, but the lower installments should enable you to make your payments on time. Some lenders may charge an additional fee.

Loan Refinance.   If it seems as if your payment problems are going to be lengthy and you need a dramatic change in the terms of your loan, your lender may consider refinancing your loan. Refinancing is different from an extension or a revision because it is a new loan, not just a revision to the original terms. The new loan will have a new interest rate, reflecting the current market rates, and a new payment schedule. Refinancing fees usually are a percentage of the loan balance, plus other closing charges, such as appraisal and title fees.

Consolidation Loan.   In talking over your problems with a creditor, you may be asked if you would be interested in a debt consolidation loan designed to pay off a number of existing debts. The monthly payment is generally lower than the total amount you are paying on the bills you consolidate. That's because you'll be extending your payments over a longer period of time.

A consolidation loan can enable you to pay your bills before they become delinquent. However, there are some big disadvantages. One of the greatest dangers is that the lower monthly payments might lead you to think you have extra money, prompting you to take on new credit obligations. In addition, the longer repayment term may end up costing you considerably more in finance charges, and you may be required to pledge collateral as security for the loan.

CREDITORS' RIGHTS AND LIMITATIONS

When you take out a loan, open a charge account, or receive a credit card, you enter into a legally binding agreement with the creditor. If you don't meet the terms by paying your debts as agreed, the agreement specifies steps your creditor can take to recover the money you owe.

Acceleration Clause

If your agreement has an acceleration clause, a creditor has the right to demand the entire amount you owe if you don't adhere to the terms of your contract. Most creditors exercise this right only after other attempts to resolve a payment problem have failed. But you should be aware that, under some circumstances (such as a poor payment history), a creditor can demand the total amount owed if you miss only one payment.

Additional Charges

If you miss a payment, don't pay on time, or don't pay at all, a lender may assess a late charge. This is usually a percentage of the payment due, which you must pay along with your regular payment. In addition, if you exceed your credit limit, your lender may assess an over-limit charge until you bring the balance back below your limit.

Blocking Your Credit

If you don't pay your bills, or if you exceed your assigned credit limit, your creditor may notify you to stop charging on that account or using your line of credit checks and ask you to return or destroy your cards or checks. If you use your credit card or line of credit after you've been notified to stop, your creditor may warn merchants not to accept your card or checks.

Right of Setoff

Suppose you have missed payments on an installment loan. If you also have a checking or savings account with your lender, the lender may, under certain circumstances, withdraw money from your account to cover your past due amounts. Usually, a setoff can be done without advance notice, but you will be advised when the transaction occurs.

Repossession

When you finance the purchase of property with an installment loan, that property generally serves as collateral to ensure that you'll repay the loan as agreed. If you don't, your creditor can take the property held as collateral, sell it, and apply the proceeds toward the balance you owe. If you refuse to give up the property, your lender may obtain a court order forcing you to turn it over. Because repossessions become part of your credit history, you may want to sell the property yourself and pay off the lender before it's repossessed.

Under some state laws, you must be sent a notice that the repossessed property will be sold. Such a notice will tell you your rights regarding redemption of your property. In most cases, you have several days to redeem the property by paying the seller the full amount due. In some cases, you also could reclaim the property and reinstate your loan by bringing your loan payments up to date and paying any late charges, collection charges, repossession charges, and storage costs.

Repossession won't always clear you of any further liability for the debt. For example, suppose a creditor sells a repossessed vehicle and receives less for it than you still owe. You may have to pay the difference (called a *deficiency*), plus some of the creditor's other costs, such as storage and repair. State laws vary on this point. In some states, if the creditor is going to hold you liable for the deficiency, you must be notified that the creditor intends to sell the vehicle. However, if the vehicle is sold for more than you owe, you're entitled to the surplus funds.

Court Action

Even if a loan is secured by personal property, in most cases a creditor can choose not to claim that collateral and can sue you instead for the entire amount you owe, plus costs.

If a creditor wins a lawsuit against you, that creditor can levy against your property. This means your creditor can attach your property, sell it, then apply the proceeds toward the balance you owe. Some items, such as necessary household furnishings, appliances, and clothes, are exempt from levy.

Rather than seize your property, a creditor may ask the court's permission to take part of your wages (an action known as *garnishment*). If permission is granted, your employer must send a portion of your pay to the county sheriff, who sends it to your creditor.

By law, you can't be fired if your wages have been garnished for a single debt. But depending on your employer's policies, two or more garnishments could jeopardize your employment. Employers' policies should be clearly stated in the employment agreement.

If You're Sued.   In nearly all cases, your wages cannot be garnished and your property cannot be attached unless a court judgment gives the creditor the right to take this action. However, property that is serving as collateral for a loan or an installment purchase contract may be repossessed without court action.

Losing by Default.   You can lose a case merely by not showing up in court; that is, you can lose by default. Legally, a creditor must serve you with a formal notice of an impending lawsuit. However, some unscrupulous creditors may never deliver the notice to you. Or a creditor may file suit in a court so far from where you live that it's difficult or impossible for you to get there.

If you didn't appear in court because you didn't receive notice of the hearing, or if it's too far away, contact your local legal services program or bar association for referral to a lawyer. You should complain to the court where the case was decided.

Debt Collection

State and federal laws specify what creditors and collection agencies may and may not do when attempting to collect a debt. Generally, collection agencies are *not* allowed to do any of the following:

- Call you late at night or make a series of calls, one right after the other. (They can call you at reasonable hours and intervals, both at work and at home.)
- Tell your employer, neighbors, or friends about your debts, or publish your name in a list of delinquent debtors.
- Pretend to be from a consumer credit reporting agency, governmental agency, or attorney's office.
- Threaten to take you to court unless they actually intend to do so.
- Send you written forms that are made to look like legal documents.
- Force you to pay more on a debt than you legally owe.

IF YOU NEED HELP

Sometimes you may need counseling to help straighten out your financial affairs. Loan officers in some financial institutions may suggest some action steps to take, or you may be referred to a nonprofit organization for counseling.

Consumer Credit Counselors (CCC) is a nonprofit organization, supported by contributions from the business and professional community, that specializes in counseling individuals with debt problems. It has more than 200 offices in 44 states where there are people who will help you set up a plan acceptable to you and your creditors.

These services are provided at little or no charge to you. When you contact CCC for help, you'll receive a budget form for listing all your expenses, debts, and income. You'll need to complete this form for your first meeting, so that a counselor can help you analyze your financial situation. The counselor may find areas where you could cut back, freeing enough money to pay off your debts.

Debt Management

If budget trimming alone won't enable you to meet your obligations, CCC may recommend that you enter its debt management program. Under this program, CCC works out a repayment plan and contacts your creditors. CCC may ask them to extend your payments, accept partial payments, and drop interest charges.

If your creditors and you agree to the plan, you'll sign an agreement allowing CCC to administer your payments. You'll pay CCC a set amount each month, and the payments will be distributed to your creditors. When your debts are paid, CCC will provide you with letters to major credit reporting agencies stating that you've successfully completed the program. This information could help you reestablish a good credit rating.

To enter the debt management program, you must usually turn over your credit cards to CCC and agree not to take on any more debts. Any counseling sessions you have are free. If CCC administers the program, they'll charge you a nominal monthly fee, unless yours is a hardship case.

For more information, contact the Consumer Credit Counselors office listed in the white pages of your telephone directory. Or, to get the location of the CCC office nearest you, write:

The National Foundation for Consumer Credit, Inc.
Suite 601
8701 Georgia Ave.
Silver Spring, MD 20910

Be Wary of Some "Help"

Take care if you're contacted by a "credit counselor" who is in business for profit. Like CCC, these "debt consolidators" or "proraters" take part of your pay and allocate it to your creditors. Unlike CCC, they charge a fee for their services that can amount to 20 percent or more of your salary. A few disreputable firms may simply pocket the fee and never pay your creditors. Many of these services operate by mail; typically, you'll receive a letter promising relief from debt by letting the debt counselor handle your creditors.

You also should be cautious of "credit repair clinics" that promise to restore your good credit rating and help you obtain new credit or credit cards. Many of these clinics charge a large fee for results you can obtain yourself by investigating your credit record.

Before you sign up with a debt consolidator or credit repair clinic, get advice from a nonprofit credit counselor or your financial adviser. Also contact the Better Business Bureau or the state or local Department of Consumer Affairs to see if there have been any complaints against the firm you're considering.

EXTREME CASES: THREE KINDS OF BANKRUPTCY

If your situation seems hopeless, you may be considering voluntary bankruptcy. Before you file, think it over very carefully; bankruptcy is not the easy way out some claim it to be. Bankruptcy stays on your credit report for up to ten years.

Here are some essential points to know about the three kinds of bankruptcy.

Bankruptcy: Chapter 7

To file bankruptcy under Chapter 7 of the federal bankruptcy law, you or your attorney draws up a petition listing your assets (everything you own) and your liabilities (everything you owe others). You submit your petition to a U.S. bankruptcy court and pay a filing fee. Your assets, except for certain exempt items, may be collected and sold by the court. If so, the proceeds from the sale will be distributed among those creditors who have filed a claim against you. The court then will discharge the debts not paid from the proceeds.

Understand the Consequences.   Although the procedure appears relatively simple, the bankruptcy law is complex. You should consult an attorney before you file to make sure you fully understand the consequences.

Declaring bankruptcy can have long-term personal and financial repercussions. You may be forced to give up important possessions and change your style of living. With bankruptcy staying on your credit record for up to ten years, you may find that you can obtain credit only at high interest rates or by putting up a large amount of collateral. If you ever need a substantial loan—to buy a home, for example—you may have difficulty obtaining it. In addition, employment that requires you to be bonded may be more difficult to obtain.

Moreover, declaring bankruptcy doesn't discharge all your debts. Those you must still pay include

- Alimony and child support
- Most state and federal taxes owed in the three years before you filed
- Most student loans
- Any debts not listed on your bankruptcy petition, unless the creditor has filed a claim
- Most debt created 90 days or less prior to filing bankruptcy

Bankruptcy: Chapter 13

An alternative to Chapter 7, Chapter 13 of the federal bankruptcy law provides a means of paying your debts while protecting you from harassment and lawsuits. An attorney's advice would be useful in deciding whether to take this alternative.

To file under Chapter 13, you draw up a plan to repay your existing debts within three years (or five years, with the court's permission). While you can prepare this plan yourself, it's best to work with an attorney. Depending on your circumstances, you could draw up an extension plan that pays your debts in full. Or you could prepare a composition (reduction) plan under which you pay a percentage of every dollar you owe. Either way, the court must approve your plan.

When you file, the court issues a restraining order stopping your creditors' collection efforts, repossessions, foreclosures, and other legal proceedings. In some cases, interest and late charges also are suspended at the time you file.

Making Payments. If your payment plan is approved, you'll make monthly payments to a court-appointed trustee, who serves as a representative to your creditors. The trustee distributes the payments to the creditors and responds to their questions. As long as you're under the plan, the court will exercise some control over your finances. For example, if you can't make your payments because of illness or unemployment, your payments may be extended or reduced. However, if you've been taking on new debts, the court may end the plan entirely.

Costs for filing Chapter 13 include a filing fee, a trustee's fee (approximately 10 percent of your monthly payment), and any attorney's fees. As long as you make your payments, you can keep your assets. If you successfully complete the plan, the remainder of your debts are discharged. Be sure to keep good records of your payments as proof to future creditors that your debts were paid according to the plan.

Bankruptcy: Chapter 11

Chapter 11 bankruptcy is used almost exclusively by businesses and usually is very costly. Under Chapter 11 of the federal bankruptcy code, you draw up a long-term plan for reorganizing your business that meets with the approval of your creditors. As with other forms of bankruptcy, you should consult with an attorney before you decide to file.

A Fresh Start

Once you've paid off your debts, you're ready to start over. First, make sure your credit record is up to date. Contact the consumer credit reporting agencies in your area (look in the Yellow Pages of the telephone directory under "Credit Reporting Agencies") and ask to see your credit file. By law, you have a right to see your file, although in some cases you may have to pay a small fee.

Although most credit information can be kept on record for seven years or more, your creditors may be willing to add that you did pay them. If a creditor refuses, you can place a letter in your file explaining the circumstances.

Rebuild Your Credit Rating.   You can reestablish your creditworthiness by showing that you're willing and able to pay your debts. When applying for a loan, be candid about your past problems so that they won't come as an unpleasant surprise if your lender finds out about them later.

For a while, you may have to pay more for the credit you do obtain. To get a loan, you'll probably need a creditworthy cosigner, or you may be required to provide collateral, or both. A retail store may let you buy something on an installment plan, and if you maintain a good payment record, the store may consider giving you a charge card.

Change Your Financial Habits.   Changing your financial habits is the most effective way to avoid problems in the future. Make a budget and stick to it. Hold family discussions about spending priorities and goals. Regularly set aside money in a savings account as a cushion against unexpected expenses. Limit yourself to two or three credit cards, and keep track of purchases each time you charge. If you're married, both you and your spouse should pay the bills so you both know where your money is going.

The other chapters in this book should assist you as you establish more effective financial practices. You know it already, but we'll say it anyhow: an ounce of prevention is worth a pound of cure. In the next chapter we'll discuss not only how to prevent problems but how to plan for a prosperous future.

Home Loan Troubles

Your home loan is usually the largest debt you have. With substantial monthly payments extending over 30 years or more, it can be very hard to catch up if you miss payments. While most lenders will try to help you keep your home, the farther you fall behind, the more they are limited in what they can do.

Contact your lender as soon as you run into trouble. Depending on your credit standing and the reason for your missed payments, your lender may reduce or suspend your regular payments for a specified time. For example, your lender may accept reduced payments for a year and then add a portion of the overdue amount to each of your regular payments. You would then pay higher monthly payments until the overdue amount was paid. Or your lender may be able to extend the length of your loan and add the missed payments at the end.

A lender's policies and certain legal requirements may restrict what can be done. Your lender might consider suspending the principal portion of your home loan payment, but still require that your payments cover interest, taxes, and insurance. If you've had your loan only a few years, this requirement would result in only a very small reduction in your monthly payments because of the large amount that is going toward interest in the early part of a 30-year loan.

Foreclosure

Your situation can become serious if you continue to miss payments on your home loan or on credit secured by your home, such as a home improvement or home equity loan or a home equity line of credit. Your lender will tell you how much you must pay to bring your loan current and how long you have to work out an arrangement for paying the past due amount. If you still don't pay, your lender may begin foreclosure proceedings, and your home could be sold to pay your lender the amount you still owe.

In a judicial foreclosure, a court orders the sale of your property, which is then carried out by a sheriff or court-appointed commissioner.

In a foreclosure under power of sale, your property is sold by the trustee named in your deed of trust. The way that operates in one state, California, is illustrative. The trustee records a notice of default in the county recorder's office where your home is located. You then have until five days before the foreclosure sale to reinstate the loan. Reinstatement involves paying the installments you missed and any late charges, foreclosure costs, and advances made by your lender (to cover taxes, for example). Three months after the notice of default, the trustee will place a notice of an auction to sell your home in a general circulation newspaper covering the area where your home is located. In most cases, you also must be mailed a copy of the notice at least 20 days before the sale. Slightly different notice and sale requirements apply if your home is serving as security in a contract for goods and services, such as a home remodeling contract. If any money is left over after the claims against you have been satisfied, you receive the surplus funds.

Selling Your Home

If you're sure you can't continue your payments, you may want to protect your equity (the current value of your home minus the debts against it) by selling the home yourself. You may earn enough from the sale to pay off your debts and have some cash left over. In addition, you'll avoid having a foreclosure become part of your credit history. Don't wait until the foreclosure proceedings have started, or you'll be forced to sell quickly and may have to accept a greatly reduced price.

If You Have an FHA Mortgage

If your mortgage is insured by the Federal Housing Administration (FHA), you or your lender can ask the Department of Housing and Urban Development (HUD) to become your lender. For HUD to take over your mortgage, you must have missed at least three consecutive monthly payments due to events beyond your control, such as an illness or a layoff. You also must have some prospect of being able to make regular mortgage payments again within a reasonable time.

If HUD takes over your mortgage, a counselor will work out a new repayment schedule that reduces or suspends your loan payments for a period of up to 36 months. You'll also be given a list of HUD-approved agencies that will give you financial counseling and try to help you avoid foreclosure. For further information, contact your local HUD office, listed in the telephone directory under "United States Government."

Chapter Five

Planning Your Future

These two things can be said about personal financial planning as it arises as a topic at a neighborhood party:

1. Everybody agrees it's a great idea.
2. Virtually nobody does it.

Certainly, not nearly as many as should, which is everyone.

Financial planning is hard work. And plans often don't turn out the way they're supposed to. At least, that's the way it seems.

Still, without some kind of plan, some vision for the future, you may let momentum carry you someplace you didn't want to go. You put yourself at risk for disasters. And when the time comes for something that's very important to you—college for the kids, retirement—you're likely to discover that you're not able to handle it properly.

In this chapter, we'll try to convince you not only to plan your financial future, but to do so in the broad context of all the things that make for a satisfying life.

Many a financially successful executive fully intended to spend a chunk of his life with his boy in Little League. But suddenly, the organ is playing "Lohengrin" at his son's wedding.

Oops.

And how many retirees discover, early in a second career, "Hey, *this* is what I want to be when I grow up"?

The key is to determine the few, big goals that really matter. Get them firmly in mind.

Then, as you face important decisions along the way, test them with the question: which course is most likely to get me where I really want to go?

Asking this question encourages you to think about the purposes you want your financial plan to serve.

The point is, what you're looking for is not "financial success"; it's a satisfying life. Your financial efforts are merely one of the ways you're going about fashioning one. Making money, then spending, saving, and investing it, are means to an end.

In this chapter, we'll encourage you to think creatively what that end is, so that you can make financial decisions strategically. We'll look at goals and contingencies. In later chapters we'll deal with implementing saving, investing, retirement, etc.

Accordingly, we'll begin by asking you to consider, in an organized way, what's really important to you: all your wants and needs, not just salaries and budgets. Then we'll ask you to think about worries, bad things that could happen—including things that may require money, but that money alone won't necessarily fix—and what you should do about them. In later chapters, we'll get into the specifics of saving money and planning for education, home, and retirement.

IMPORTANT WANTS AND NEEDS

To develop a fresh mind-set toward the subject of financial planning, we'll use the process of brainstorming.

A Brainstorming Exercise on Wants and Needs

Take out a pad of paper. Write at the top: *Things I Want and Need Most*. Then, quickly and freely, write down whatever comes to mind (brief phrases will do). You're looking to collect all the things that most contribute to your personal satisfaction, now and in the future.

Couples should both do this exercise at the same time, but recording your ideas separately.* That is, don't stop to discuss your listings or censor each other's choices. Afterward you can compare results and see what conflicts and areas of agreement surface, and what kinds of accommodation may be needed.

---

*It can be an even livelier exercise if you create a joint writing surface where you can do the exercise together, striking intellectual sparks off each other. Tape some large sheets of paper to the wall—masking tape won't damage most surfaces—and write on the sheets with a big felt marker. Ask for "easel pad" at your local art or office supply store. (A 50-sheet pad costs about $10.) Get a roll of 3/4" masking tape and some washable markers. Put several layers of paper on the area where you'll write. As you fill each sheet, move it to another surface where you can still see it.

Don't prejudge or censor what comes to mind. The idea is to dig below the surface, to get at feelings and desires that are important but that you may have pushed to the back of your mind for some reason. Don't attempt to structure your thoughts in any way. If one item makes you think of something else that seemingly is unrelated, write that down quickly. Remember, you're not restricted to money matters.

Figures 5-1 and 5-2 (pp. 92–93) show examples of completed lists for one couple, Harry and Harriet. Try to get going on your own before you read them, so they don't bias you. You want to know what's lodged in *your* head, not someone else's. You'll get the most out of this chapter if you go ahead and do the brainstorming exercise before reading further.

Analyzing Your List

When you've completed the exercise, read the examples in Figures 5-1 and 5-2. Did you mix apples and oranges, the way Harry and Harriet did? Fine. Did you also use some highly imprecise terms ("Nice house"; "Good car")? That's also fine. The less polished your lists, the more you were engaging in open and creative brainstorming.

Your lists probably have apparent duplications (if not, you were editing your thoughts). That can be instructive, as we'll discuss in a moment.

There are systematic ways to organize and evaluate lists like the one you've just created. We'll use a fairly simple procedure, one that is nonetheless powerful.

Step 1.   Link items up and number them. If two or more items seem to duplicate, link them, giving them the same number, but keep them separate. In Harry's list (Figure 5-1), "lots of money" can be linked with "good pay" farther down the list, but note that these aren't exactly the same thing. Using the procedure illustrated in the figure, work through your list. Don't worry about being extremely precise. Link the ideas that immediately seem to go together, and move on.

Step 2.   Divide the number of your last item by 3. The result indicates how many votes you get to select your really crucial needs. (The choice of the number 3 isn't capricious; people who have worked for years at this process have found it works.) In Harry's case, for example, after duplications are linked, the total number of items is 24. Dividing by 3 yields 8 votes. (See Figure 5-3.)

Step 3.   Now review your list, selecting the items that are really crucial to you. Put a check mark by as many as you have "votes." The point, of course, is to think about differences, and to make choices.

Figure 5-1   Harry's Brainstorming List of Important Things in Life

Things I Want and Need Most

Lots of money
Good boss
Good job
Good cash cushion
Nice car
Nice community
More education: an MBA
Good family life
Good health
Nice house
Good pay
Good retirement income
Time to do the things I like
Golf
College for kids
Travel
Congenial work environment
Be respected / admired
Boating
Reading
Tennis
Challenging work
Minimum stress, conflict, hassle
Financial security
Friends
Inheritance for kids
Start my own business

Figure 5-2 Harriet's Brainstorming List of Important Things in Life

Things I Want and Need Most

Good assured income
Safe, attractive town
Access to mountains, skiing
Family togetherness
Friendly neighbors
Excellent local schools
Good marriage
Big house
Significant job
Good church, spiritual opportunities
Health
Active family life
Close friends
Active social life, parties, etc.
Vacations to Europe
Cultural life: music, theatre
Good books
Tennis
Swimming pool or swim club
College tuition fund
Good retirement income
Gifts and inheritance for children
Good cash cushion
Nice jewelry
Be near family
Be able to help kids
Be able to help parents

Figure 5-3   Harry's List Showing Linkages and Number of Votes

Things I Want and Need Most

① Lots of money
② Good boss
③ Good job
④ Good cash cushion
⑤ Nice car
⑥ Nice community
⑦ More education: an MBA
⑧ Good family life
⑨ Good health
⑩ Nice house
③ Good pay
⑪ Good retirement income
⑫ Time to do the things I like
⑬ Golf
⑭ College for kids
⑮ Travel
③ Congenial work environment
⑯ Be respected / admired
⑰ Boating
⑱ Reading
⑲ Tennis
③ Challenging work
⑳ Minimum stress, conflict, hassle
㉑ Financial security
㉒ Friends
㉓ Inheritance for kids
㉔ Start my own business

24 ÷ 3 = 8 votes

Step 4.   To further force choices, rank-order your checked items using the letters A for most important, B next most, C, D (etc.).

Pause for a moment to do an "eyeball" analysis: stare at your list for a few minutes to see what jumps out at you.

Note the linkages. Did the same subject come up in a variety of ways? That can tell you something about how significant that area of life is to you. Also, these different versions of the same thought can help define what is significant *about* that area. In Harry's case, for example, "good job" begins to be defined by the specific characteristics that popped into mind when he brainstormed his list.

Here are some "eyeball" observations that Harry and Harriet might make.

Harry: "Hmm, an awful lot of mine seem to be job-related. Apparently that's what's really important to me. . . . I seem to have some conflicts here. I'm not sure 'job security' and 'good pay' go together, and I'm not sure either fits with 'good family life' or 'time to do the things I like.' "

Harriet: "Wow, all I seem to be thinking of is family and the kids. What do I want for myself?"

If you have a spouse, compare lists. Any serious conflicts? Surprises? ("I have 'good marriage' as the most important thing, and you don't even have it on your list!")

When Harry reviewed his annotated list, he was surprised to realize that "start my own business" didn't make the cut. When he first put that down, he thought it was pretty important. Also, he realized that "minimum stress, conflict, hassle" wasn't as important to him as, for instance, "challenging work." "Lots of money" doesn't end up high, but "good pay" does. That gave him pause, but he figured it out after the next step.

Step 5.   Now examine how well your priorities relate to the way you're actually handling your life.

Go back to the items you've checked. To the right of each on, write one of the following:

- OK (meaning you're satisfied with the way things are with respect to this item, or at least satisfied that you're on track)
- Needs Work, or Not OK

Figure 5-4 shows how Harry completed his list. After looking it over, Harry decided that most of the lifestyle items seemed to be in pretty good shape, but a lot of work was needed to plug money into the right places for the future. ("It's a good thing 'inheritance for kids' ranked last in priority; at this rate, it doesn't look like there'll be any.")

Figure 5-4   Harry's Completed List of Important Wants and Needs

Things I Want and Need Most

1. Lots of money ✓ Ⓑ - needs work
2. Good boss
3. Good job ✓ Ⓐ
4. Good cash cushion
5. Nice car
6. Nice community
7. More education: an MBA
8. Good family life ✓ Ⓓ ok
9. Good health ✓ Ⓔ ok
10. Nice house
⑬ Good pay ✓ Ⓕ - needs work
11. Good retirement income Ⓘ - needs work
12. Time to do the things I like
13. Golf
14. College for kids ✓ Ⓖ - needs work
15. Travel
⑬ Congenial work environment
16. Be respected / admired
17. Boating
18. Reading
19. Tennis
③ Challenging work
20. Minimum stress, conflict, hassle
21. Financial security ✓ Ⓒ - needs work
22. Friends
23. Inheritance for kids ✓ Ⓗ - needs work
24. Start my own business

24 ÷ 3 = 8 votes

Harry also thinks that he now understands why he ranked "good pay" higher than "lots of money." When he wrote "good pay," he was thinking "fair," "reasonable," and "comparing favorably with other people." That is by no means the same thing as "lots of money," and perhaps, judging from the items that need work, "lots of money" is really what Harry needs.

Deciding on Action

OK, so what do you do with all this?

Look hard at the "Needs Work" and "Not OK" items, and begin brainstorming what you could do about them. Be as creatively flexible and nonjudgmental in doing this as you were in generating the list itself. For example, recognize that you have a certain amount of control over how you make your money, how much time and attention you devote to doing it, and how much money you make. Similarly, while there may be trade-offs involved, you have control over where you live and over the way you use your time.

In short, approach this part of the exercise with the idea that *you* are in charge of putting the parts of your life together in the way that works best for you.

Some case histories may suggest ways you can do this:

• A man loves his job, but it doesn't allow him time for much of anything else. It's not really an option for him to slow down; the nature of the work doesn't lend itself to that, his boss wouldn't like it, and he wouldn't know how to do it. So he resolves his conflict by setting a firm date to retire early and establishing an income and saving plan to assure he can. He's happy working full-blast until then.

Here are three responses to the challenge of college tuition:

• A couple determine that they both want the best schools for their children. They project the costs and determine that their overriding consideration in job selection must be income, even though this requires a career change for one partner.

• A couple look at future college tuition costs and resolve to move to one of the states they identify as offering good state-supported schools with affordable resident tuition.

• A man decided to abandon his well-paid but unsatisfying career for a position as a college teacher that brought with it free tuition for the kids as a job benefit. What's more, he now has more time for the family and himself, as well as access to a fine library and cultural activities—important wants that he realizes he'd been neglecting.

A vacation/travel case history:

- A woman who likes to travel and also likes to write arranged with the local paper to do travel articles on a freelance basis. Her vacations are almost all research/writing trips. She enjoys her vacations more, makes some money, and gets some tax benefits.

The point is, there are many ways to mix and match your different needs.

Fine, you say, I'll be creative and try to conjure ideas of my own. But at the moment, all my imagination sees is dollar signs. My wants require a lot of money, and what I need is a system for saving up for them.

In succeeding chapters, we go at that directly. We'll describe plans that you can use for those needs you've identified that have a money dimension. You'll see how to develop a schedule for savings so that your money will be there when you need it. (You're still the one who has to come up with the money, however; we try to be creative, but there are limits.)

For now we'll leave this part of planning and move on. Collect your lists of wants and needs, and your ideas for how to meet them. We suggest that you return to them periodically so that you can monitor your progress toward your own most-important goals: are you actually doing the work that your "needs work" items require?

The next exercise is not always pleasant, but it's an equally important part of planning for the future.

SERIOUS THINGS TO WORRY ABOUT

Planning, unfortunately, involves more than accounting for the things you want to have happen. You also need to be prepared for the things most people don't want to think about happening.

A Brainstorming Exercise on Serious Worries

On a new sheet of paper, write the heading "Serious Things to Worry About." Start listing all the concerns—possible problems, worries, disasters—that come to mind. Try not to think about their likelihood or unpleasantness or whether they are immediate or far in the future. Just write down whatever comes to mind, as freely as you can.

Your objective in this brainstorming exercise is to get everything out on the table so you can deal with it. For couples, this can be especially instructive. Both need to know what fears and worries the other has, and they need to jointly assess the likelihood of worrisome happenings, their possible effects, and the protective action they need to take.

Couples should recognize, however, that people vary in the amount of unpleasant reality they can confront comfortably. If one partner's aversion is extreme, that partner may need to delegate the major responsibility and authority for dealing with future threats to the other partner.

You may want to skim the following examples quickly, just to get you started. Of course, you want your list to be your own.

At work . . .

Lose job.

Company reorganized: I'm squeezed out.

Health . . .

I have heart attack.

I'm disabled. Temporary? Permanent?

I die.

It's got to be on the list if you have anyone depending on you.

Economic . . .

Stock market slumps badly.

Bad recession.

This isn't much fun, is it? But hang in there. Think about events that have already happened that might augur future troubles (when the air-conditioner repairman was here, he said it wouldn't be too long . . .).

Air conditioning goes out.

Furnace goes out.

Car conks out.

Mentally wander around your house, visualizing things that could go wrong.

Fireplace clogs, burns.

House burns down.

Think about the people in your life. This is difficult to do, but it's necessary.

One of the kids gets hurt or gets bad disease.

Spouse dies.

Parent dies.

Think about things that have happened to people you know.

Divorce.

Get sued for malpractice.

Die in car wreck.

Analyzing Your Worries List

When you have completed your list, with about as many of these things as you can stand, you'll want to organize and analyze it as you did your needs and wants list, with some variations.

First go through and line out items you decide, on reflection, simply won't happen. Then work through the following steps:

1. Number all the items, linking up apparent duplicates.
2. Get your Biggest Worries number by dividing the last number on the list by 3.
3. Consider which of the items on your list are your Biggest Worries, the ones most deserving of your concern. Check as many as your Biggest Worries number. You don't need to rank-order them.
4. By the items that you've checked, put one of the following:
   • OK (meaning you're doing all that needs to be done, or can be done; add a note indicating what that action is— "insurance," "wrote will," etc.)

   • Not OK, Needs Action (and note the desired action, if that's clear to you)

What Action Plans Are Needed?

Look over your completed list, and consider the actions— changes, decisions, discussions, fact-finding—that seem to be needed.

Some people, when they go through an exercise like this, get a warm, reassuring feeling that they are doing things right and should simply stay the course.

Others are pulled up short. They decide they need to rethink the way they're doing things or the plans they've been making. Some get a sudden sense of urgency about plans they've let slip, such as making a will or developing a good retirement-investment plan.

Many people find that, at the very least, there are many contingencies they need to think about. Couples often find that there are subjects they need to discuss a lot more fully. Harry, for example, was surprised to realize that, while he had bought life insurance, he hadn't considered the possibility of disability or stroke. And that got him thinking about health. He also realized that he needed to discuss these contingencies with his wife.

It's important to consider at this point the extent to which you can do something about your biggest worries. You probably have more control than you realize. You may be able to prevent some negative events from happening; failing that, you can modify their effects if you plan ahead.

In industry, there are people called "issue managers," whose responsibility it is to anticipate bad things that can happen to a company. They use the terms *early warning* and *environmental scanning* to describe the processes they use to identify potential issues.

They also talk about *proactive issue management.* By that they mean trying to head off threats—for example, working to defeat adverse legislative proposals or identifying and eliminating potential safety hazards in the workplace *before* a serious accident occurs. They also mean trying to change the direction or shape of the threat (proposing substitute legislation, initiating voluntary safety-control programs). Finally, they discuss *damage control*, or how to minimize the impact of the unavoidable.

There are lessons in these concepts that we can apply to our personal lives. Take proactive issue management, for example: Even better than planning what to do if you get fired is planning what you can do to make sure you don't. If real estate values are threatened by plans to build an incinerator nearby, you can do more than prepare for the worst: you can try to get your homeowners' association to act. You can't, by yourself, prevent a recession, but you *can* spread the money you invest in a way to cushion a recession's effect on you.

Let's look at some common serious concerns, and think through what can be done to anticipate them and either change them or cushion their impact.

Lose Job.   You've identified the threat of a takeover or reorganization at work. How likely is that, really? Is there anything you should do to strengthen your own early-warning system? What would be the telltale signs?

How vulnerable are you, specifically? Anything you should be doing at work—in setting your project priorities, in your relationships—to strengthen your position? Should you be preparing a fallback position: making quiet inquiries about opportunities elsewhere, refreshing your network, brushing up on some skills or adding others (maybe taking some night courses)?

If a takeover *is* somewhat likely, and you *are* vulnerable, how bad would that really be? Maybe you wouldn't mind changing jobs, and if your inquiries suggest that another job would be fairly easy for you to get, then perhaps you're not so bad off. But consider all the angles:

- How does your spouse feel? How would a change of jobs affect his or her plans, especially if a change might mean moving to another town?

- If you're not yet vested in the pension plan, you'd lose that completely. Maybe you want to give high priority to staying on at least until you're vested and can take that with you.
- What would the effects be on income? When salary stops, so do some other costs—commuting, lunches. On the other hand, there will be job-hunting expenses (which are tax-deductible, by the way; doesn't that cheer you up?). Pull out your budget and see which items would be affected.
- Should you reconsider any financial decisions that would add to monthly costs—avoiding new time payments, reevaluating plans to buy some investment property?
- Do you know where you stand on severance and unemployment compensation? What are the cash withdrawal options in the company savings and retirement program, and what are the tax consequences?
- How long would your life and medical insurance continue?

These are complicated issues, and being clear about them in advance can be important if indeed you are let go. You'll probably have emotional reactions then that can interfere with good judgment. Many people, caught by surprise and hurt, merely want to get the trauma over with quickly and get away. They miss an opportunity to negotiate optimum severance conditions at a time when the boss is feeling guilty over having to do this to them.

Facing up to these issues in advance may also suggest some things you should do now. For example:

- If your only life insurance is the policy you have through the company, should you see about converting it, or lining up something else?
- If you do have to move, should you be improving the house to make it easier to sell? Or should you be postponing planned improvements if there's a question whether you'll get the benefit of them?

Couples who discuss all the possibilities in advance can be more supportive, and can clarify expectations more readily, than those who are under the pressure of an actual event. How would a partner who now stays at home feel about going to work for a while? Are there some preparations to think about now? In each spouse's mind, what would be the worst thing that could happen?

Dealing with Death.   Harry and Harriet decide that, as grim as it is, they need to confront what will happen when one of them dies.

They decide to have a long talk. Harry has a bit of trouble with this subject, so Harriet takes it upon herself to make notes afterward:

> We discussed life insurance. Do we have enough? Decided to reexamine that in light of rising college tuitions. I'll contact our agent to see whether we should reconsider the amount he recommended originally.
>
> Noted that most of Harry's coverage is a five-year term policy that will keep going up. Agreed to check whether budget reflects that. Reexamined the decision to carry policies on both of us; decided to continue.
>
> Decided this might be a good time to reconsider my going back to work, to make sure of a fallback income. Decided I would move earlier on plans to take courses, etc.
>
> Discussed inheritances and the will we drew up several years ago; took the will out and reviewed it. Decided to make sure brother John is still agreeable to being executor. Reexamined the question whether to divide up the estate equally among the children or to take relative need into consideration. Decided to stick with "equal," but agreed to reexamine that later.
>
> Decided it was still too early to think about bequeathing specific items, but agreed to reconsider this later.
>
> Reviewed inheritance taxes. Decided we don't have enough yet for this to be a big issue (federal tax law allows us to pass along up to $600,000 tax-free).
>
> Discussed how we want to help out the children when they are young and need it most. Decided on a plan to have some money to help with their first homes, when they get to that point. Each parent can make gifts of up to $10,000 a year to each child, without incurring federal gift taxes; we're not in much danger of exceeding that. Considered arrangements whereby we could be joint owners or partners in buying a residence so we would enjoy some tax benefits at the same time. Decided to adjust saving and investment plans accordingly.
>
> Made sure we both knew where all financial and other key papers are kept. Decided we would both be involved in future decisions involving investments. Checked to make sure that Harry's pension had a survivor benefit.
>
> Discussed the fact that we sometimes travel together, without the children. Decided to write a note summarizing where key papers are and to leave it where it could easily be found.
>
> Discussed each other's burial wishes. Discussed each other's views regarding artificial means of sustaining life; we both decided to sign a "living will" provision not to use them. A grim subject—but *not* discussing it in advance could mean a terrible emotional and maybe financial burden on whichever of us is the survivor.
>
> We both decided to sign organ donor authorizations. And pledged to quit smoking. I think we mean it this time.

As you can see, a conversation that was originally meant to be on the subject of death became a wide-ranging discussion of important planning wishes, with a number of productive results.

Something Happening to a Parent.   As another example, one of the items on your list might be something happening to a parent— becoming seriously ill, being put into a nursing home, dying.

How likely is each event? Maybe you want to talk to them, determine how they really are, see whether there's something you should be doing for them:

- Are they taking care of their health? Anything you should do?
- Are they handling their finances OK? If one partner dies, does the other know how finances stand?
- Do they have wills?
- Have they considered a "living will" provision to state their preference regarding artificial life support?
- Do you know their preferences regarding burial?
- Do they have adequate health insurance?
- If nursing care is in the offing, what will it cost? What would be your role?
- Should you discuss all this now with your siblings and other relatives?
- If something happens to one parent, might you want to provide space for the other in your home? If so, what planning does that entail now?

Maybe you'll conclude that all you can do right now about the eventuality of something happening to a parent is to make sure you have plane fare if you must suddenly fly to them. And you may find that just providing for that much of a plan means that you're less anxious about this area of your life.

For couples, talking together about both sets of parents can help reassure both partners that neither's parents will be neglected. One partner may not have been sure how the other felt about helping out, adding to anxiety. Having discussed contingencies for both sets of parents in the abstract, the couple will have a better context for dealing with a real-life situation when it arises.

Additional Examples.   Here are some other "action" items that can come from this kind of exercise.

For health and medical disability:

- A designer decides not to continue playing in the softball league, as much as he likes it, because of the chance he could hurt his hands.
- One person's new action list:

  Get checkup

  Budget more money, time for exercise; join health club

  Learn a sport that's good exercise

  Eat better, diet

  Quit smoking

  Cut down drinking (quit?)

  Do some study about genetics, nutrition

For legal liability:

- A woman who runs a small business at home selling cookies becomes concerned about what would happen if she were sued by a customer. It's possible, and it could put everything she owns, including things she owns jointly with her husband, in jeopardy. Coverage is expensive though, so she decides it's cheaper to incorporate, in order to limit liability.
- A man serving on the board of an association begins worrying whether he is legally liable if there is an antitrust suit or some other suit against the group. He checks whether his own insurance covers him; it doesn't. He asks whether the association has adequate directors' and officers' coverage. It does. Otherwise, he would have quit.

For the possibility of fire:

- A man checks his insurance against fire and finds it adequate. But the exercise starts him thinking about personal safety questions. He increases the number of smoke alarms in the house. Conducting a family space drill, he discovers that some windows are too hard to open wide enough, and fixes them. He decides to get a fireproof safe for personal memorabilia and to rent a safe-deposit box for valuables.

Insurance and Wills

As you work down your list of concerns, you'll develop your own set of action items. As unpleasant as it may be to contemplate those distressing events, there is comfort in feeling that you've faced the worst and know its limits, and that you're doing all you can about it.

It can also be reassuring to discover that many of these concerns can be cushioned by two instruments specifically designed to deal with unhappy contingencies: insurance and wills. Let's take a moment to examine these.

Insurance.   To determine how much life insurance you really need, start by estimating what it would cost to maintain the people you want to protect at about their present level.

First identify all sources of income that will be available: return on savings and investments, survivor benefits in your pension, Social Security, the survivors' own income, proceeds from the sale of assets, and so on. Calculate the total income per year, in today's dollars.

Next, take your present budget and determine how expenses would be reduced or increased if you were gone. What is the shortfall between that total and the annual income you've calculated? You'll need enough insurance to generate that much annual income.

Add an amount of money for the cash that would be required immediately for funeral, burial, and inheritance-tax costs. Also, add amounts as necessary for college or other future needs not reflected in your current budget. You may decide to add enough to pay off the home mortgage, but that's not necessary if the budget you're preserving takes care of housing.

In addition to life insurance, you'll also want to make sure you and others are protected by disability and health and medical insurance against catastrophic illness, to the extent possible.

Special liability insurance is something else to consider in a disaster plan, in light of the size of awards in the last decade. If you have developed a net worth of any consequence, and a jury thinks you're rich, you run the risk of losing it all.

Will.   If you have a net worth of any consequence, it's important to make at least a simple will to ensure that your estate goes to the right people, doesn't get hung up for months in probate, and isn't eroded unnecessarily by fees and taxes. A will can cost several hundred dollars, but a good will lawyer will force you to think through and resolve a lot of important questions.

In this chapter we've encouraged you to think of financial planning in the broad context of the needs, wants, and worries that are most important to you—a unique individual. If you have done the exercises presented, review your lists from time to time. Monitor your progress toward your own goals—and get back in touch with them. Remember, it's not just a question of making the most of your money; it's a question of making the most of your life.

Chapter Six

Saving for Security and Satisfaction

For some people, saving is a pleasure. They enjoy the process of accumulating money, as well as the fact of having it. For others, saving goes against every instinct they have; one of these probably originated the bumper sticker that says "LIFE IS UNCERTAIN—EAT DESSERT FIRST."

Knowing yourself and the special characteristics of your own personality and situation will make it easier for you to decide how much to save and how to go about it.

For some, the reasons for saving are very clear — as vivid as their nightmares of the wolf at the door. If you have a powerful need for security, saving is a lot easier for you than it is for other people. Your motivation is very high, and you quickly find rewards in saving. In fact, you may be very anxious until you've established a saving pattern that promises the cushion you consider necessary. If there is no immediate prospect of reaching that goal, your comfort level may require that you take special steps — for instance, to adjust "fixed expenses" in your budget or to find ways of adding income. You may then find pleasure in holding back spending, building your cushion, and then padding it. The process itself is satisfying to you, and having the money in place is a continuing comfort.

Other people use the saving process to take control of their financial lives. It's where they inventory contingencies, draw a wish list, set priorities, make plans, and make sure they are getting the most satisfaction and peace of mind, over time, from their income.

If you're like most people, however, saving may seem to be in direct conflict with other personal priorities: buying luxuries to run up the score of visible success or to make life more fun; spending money with friends. In that case, you may find saving difficult at best, though doable as a device for meeting clearly visible future needs. And you may need to create incentives and rewards to meet saving goals you set for yourself.

Almost anyone must develop effective savings plans to have any hope of meeting such major long-term financial needs as these:

- Buying a car
- Going on vacations
- Accumulating the down payment on a house
- Paying for college tuition
- Planning for retirement

Couples need to understand how each partner feels about saving and the different motivations and pressures that go along with these views. Saving means self-denial, postponing gratification, and maintaining discipline, and that's a potential source of dangerous tension unless each partner understands and respects what the other is going through.

For people just starting out, saving suffers from a special impediment: nothing to do it with. In fact, you may feel you're doing the opposite — borrowing. But take heart, for a loan is forced saving. If you manage that well, making the payments steadily and paying it off, you'll have established the process that you can later apply to creating a nice savings account.

SET SAVINGS TARGETS

How do you determine how much to save? For many people — probably most — the process is simple, but badly flawed: figure out how much you want to spend and if there is anything left over, that's what you save. Usually, with that approach, there isn't, so you don't.

To set your savings targets, you can consider the guidance of experts. They say you should have a minimum of two to six months' take-home pay in your savings. Investment advisers say you should have six to twelve months' salary in liquid savings before you consider investing in such things as the stock market.

But since saving requires you to make sometimes painful decisions to postpone purchases, it can help to make your target very specific to your situation. It can strengthen your resolve if you have an explicit picture of the bad things you are determined to protect against and the good things you can look forward to enjoying in the future if you save a certain amount on a regular basis. In the last chapter, we discussed ways to spell out your worries and wants. Revisit them whenever your discipline falters.

THE SAVING PROCESS

You've heard it before and you'll hear it again: save regularly. You can reach your savings goal, one payday at a time, by developing a savings habit. Budget for savings each month, just as you do for rent, insurance, or loan payments. Decide to save a targeted dollar amount, or simply set a percentage of your income — 2 percent, 5 percent, 10 percent, or whatever you can — and stick to your decision.

Also, look for ways to make your savings automatic. For instance, you may be able to have funds from your paycheck deposited automatically into a savings account or have a specific amount transferred on a regular basis from a non-interest-earning account into an interest-earning account. You may also authorize a mutual fund to make regular transfers from your bank account into the fund for an amount you choose.

Choosing an Account

To choose a financial institution and a savings account that are right for you, you'll first need to think realistically about yourself — your financial situation, your goals, and how soon you want to reach them. Keep these major considerations in mind:

Security: The safety of your savings. The more secure your savings account is, the lower your risk of loss from bankruptcy of an uninsured financial institution, and the smaller the likelihood that your account will fail to pay interest or return your principal.

Access, or liquidity: The ease with which you can obtain your money without financial penalty.

Convenience: The ease with which you can manage your savings plan. Take into account the location of the financial institution where you save and the kind and quality of service. The discipline of regular saving is hard enough; at least make the mechanics as easy as possible.

Expense: The maintenance charges and service fees associated with the account. These costs can reduce the interest you've earned as well as the funds remaining on deposit. Because no single type of account is likely to measure up to all your financial requirements, you might use a combination of savings methods. For instance, you could invest a portion of your savings in a certificate of deposit (CD) and keep the rest in a regular savings account. The CD probably would bring a higher return, while the savings account would offer greater access.

Return: The amount your savings can earn, expressed as an annual interest rate and an annual yield. It's important to understand the meaning of these two terms.

The amount of interest that you receive over a one-year period is expressed as a percentage called the *annual interest rate*. This rate may be a fixed rate, or it may be a variable rate that increases or decreases at specified intervals (such as daily or weekly) depending on market conditions. Many financial institutions offer accounts that pay different rates of interest depending on the size of your balance.

The annual interest rate is only one of several factors that determine how much you'll earn on the funds in your account. A different percentage figure — annual yield — usually is a more accurate expression of your interest earnings. Annual yield is calculated on the assumption that deposits and interest stay in the account for one full year.

Annual yield also reflects the method of calculating interest. With the *simple interest* method, interest is calculated on your balance — that is, your deposits plus any interest that has been paid to your account. If your account pays 5 percent simple annual interest, your annual yield also is 5 percent. Thus, a deposit of $100 would earn $5 in simple interest in one year.

With the *compound interest* method, interest is calculated on your balance, plus any interest you've earned that hasn't yet been paid to your account. In other words, you earn interest on your interest. Compounding increases your interest earnings even though the annual interest rate remains the same. If your account pays 5 percent annual interest, compounded daily, your annual yield is 5.12 percent. An account with a balance of $100 earning 5 percent interest, compounded daily, would earn $5.12 in interest during one year.

Balance Computation

Every deposit or withdrawal you make affects your interest earnings. With the most common method of balance computation —date of deposit to date of withdrawal — you earn interest on the exact amount in your account each day. However, financial institutions can use other methods of balance computation that aren't as favorable for you. With the low balance method, for instance, interest is paid only on the lowest balance in your account during the statement period.

Make sure you understand how the balance is calculated before you choose an account. Further, many accounts don't credit (pay) interest daily. Some pay interest at the end of each calendar month or quarter. The less frequently interest is paid, the less you earn.

PLACES TO SAVE

A number of types of financial institutions offer savings accounts. You may want to choose a single institution for all your accounts on the basis of the combination of services available. Or you might want to look for the best deals on the accounts you're considering, and distribute your money among several different institutions.

Banks

You can receive a wide range of financial services at a bank. These include regular savings accounts; regular and interest-bearing checking accounts; certificates of deposit (CDs); money market deposit accounts; Individual Retirement Accounts (IRAs); consumer, business, and real estate loans; and trust, investment, international, and business services. Deposits in member banks are insured for up to $100,000 by the Federal Deposit Insurance Corporation (FDIC).

Savings and Loan Associations (S&Ls)

Savings and loan institutions provide much of the money used to finance homes in the United States. Other services S&Ls can offer include savings and interest-bearing checking accounts, CDs, money market deposit accounts, IRAs, consumer loans, and trust services. Deposits in member institutions are insured for up to $100,000 by the Federal Savings and Loan Insurance Corporation (FSLIC).

Credit Unions

Credit unions are nonprofit savings and lending organizations that provide services to members. Members must have a common bond through employment at the same firm, residence in the same community, or participation in the same group. Credit unions can offer a variety of services, including savings and share draft accounts (similar to interest-bearing checking accounts), CDs, money market deposit accounts, IRAs, consumer and real estate loans, and certain investment services. Deposits in federal- and state-chartered credit unions are insured for up to $100,000 through the National Credit Union Administration.

Loan Companies

Loan companies are a type of finance company that offers savings accounts. Besides making consumer and real estate loans, these companies issue investment certificates similar to regular savings accounts. Certificates are protected for up to $50,000 through the Thrift Guarantee Corporation.

Other Financial Institutions

Brokerage houses, mutual fund companies, finance companies, and other institutions may offer a wide variety of financial services, including such savings plans as CDs and money market funds.

TYPES OF SAVINGS

Savings accounts are a basic component of most savings programs. They provide a high degree of convenience and security and, usually, a predictable rate of return.

You may choose from many types of savings accounts, from low-yielding regular savings accounts to higher-yielding CDs and money market accounts. Each type has its own rules on deposits, withdrawals, payment of interest, and charges.

Regular Savings Accounts

Sometimes called a *passbook account*, a regular savings account is the most basic and flexible type of savings account. It's a good way to start a savings program because of the low opening deposit requirement, though the annual interest rate typically is lower than for accounts with higher minimums.

You can use this account to accumulate funds to meet the deposit requirements of accounts that pay higher interest. Regular savings accounts can be of value, too, as a place for emergency and short-term savings, since there's no penalty for early withdrawal.

Some institutions may limit the number of withdrawals you can make during a given period without charge. Some institutions also may impose service charges if your balance falls below a specified amount. If you close your account before an interest payment date, some institutions may not pay the interest you've earned for that payment period.

Certificates of Deposit (CDs)

With a CD or time deposit account, you agree to leave your money on deposit until the end of a specified period, called the *term* or *maturity* period. In exchange, you receive an interest rate that's usually higher than the rate on regular savings accounts. A CD is a good place to put your money if you don't need immediate access to it.

Because CDs are available for a wide range of terms, you can choose a term that matches your financial timetable. Terms range from seven days to ten years. With most CDs, the term begins on the day of deposit. The minimum deposit varies widely, from $100 to $5,000 or more.

The annual interest rate generally depends on the term and the minimum deposit. Rates may be fixed for the maturity period, or they may vary daily or weekly.

Additional Deposits.   Many CD accounts won't allow you to make additional deposits. Instead, you must open a new account with its own term. Your account may stop earning interest on the maturity date. Some accounts do allow you to add funds, sometimes at the same rate as your initial deposit. However, a minimum additional deposit may be required, and you may have to make the deposit during a specified period at the end of the term.

Typically, after the maturity date your funds are reinvested unless you withdraw them within a certain number of days. During this time, you also may be allowed to withdraw some of your funds without penalty. Generally, the funds left on deposit will be reinvested on the day of the withdrawal.

Early Withdrawal Penalties.   If you make a withdrawal from a CD before the end of the term, financial institutions generally impose a substantial interest penalty on the amount withdrawn. In some cases, the penalty may exceed the interest you've earned and even include some of the principal. Make sure you understand the penalties involved before you deposit your money.

Money Market Deposit Accounts

Money market accounts combine variable rates, easy access, and the safety of federal insurance. You may want to open one if you can meet the minimum deposit requirement — typically $1,000. Most financial institutions penalize you if your balance falls below the minimum deposit. A money market deposit account pays a variable rate of interest.

As with a regular savings account, you generally can withdraw your money without an early withdrawal penalty. You can make as many withdrawals as you wish in person, by mail, or at automated teller machines (ATMs). However, during each statement period, you can make a total of six transfers — including three checking or point-of-sale (POS) transactions — to another person or organization, or to an account you have at another financial institution. (For more information on ATMs, POS, and other electronic fund transfer services, see Chapter 2.)

Interest-Bearing Checking Accounts

If you regularly maintain a high checking balance, you may want to consider an interest-bearing checking account. This account pays either a variable or fixed rate of interest that's usually slightly lower than the rate on a money market deposit account at the same institution. The advantage is that you may write as many checks as you wish. Some interest-bearing checking accounts pay different rates of interest depending on the balance *lever,* or tier.

Another type of interest-bearing checking plan is the credit union share draft account. A share draft functions like a check except that you usually write it against a savings account instead of a checking account.

With most interest-bearing checking accounts, you need to consider the current interest rate, the balance you plan to maintain during a statement period, and the minimum average balance required (which may be as high as $5,000) to avoid monthly service charges. The interest you earn may be offset by your monthly service charges. Shop carefully for this and other interest-bearing checking accounts and be sure you understand the terms and conditions involved.

SPECIAL PURPOSE ACCOUNTS

Many financial institutions offer accounts tailored to certain goals, such as meeting holiday expenses, administering funds for another person, or generating retirement income.

Christmas Club Accounts

The purpose of these accounts, whether they're called Christmas Club or by some other name, is to help you save for year-end or holiday expenses. You agree to make deposits in equal amounts at regular intervals over a year's time.

Generally, you can't withdraw your money until a year has passed. Some accounts pay no interest; others may pay the same rate as a regular savings account.

Under most plans, you either set the total savings goal for the year or the amount of your regular deposit. Depending on the plan, you may have deposits transferred automatically from your checking or savings account, or you may receive a book of dated coupons to send in with your deposits.

Custodial and Informal Trust Accounts

These accounts are designed to benefit someone other than yourself, such as a child. They're available in the form of savings accounts and CDs, money market deposit accounts, and regular and interest-bearing checking accounts.

As an adult, you can open a custodial account for a minor. The child is considered the legal owner of the funds, and there are restrictions regarding deposits and withdrawals you can make. This type of account usually is opened under the advice of an attorney.

With an informal trust account, you're considered the legal owner of the deposited funds. After your death, funds in the account automatically belong to the person you named as beneficiary. Alternatively, you can sign a pay-on-death agreement designating a beneficiary. As with an informal trust account, the funds are released automatically to your beneficiary when you die.

SAVING OR INVESTING?

The line between saving and investing isn't always clear. You can think in terms of preservation (savings) versus growth (investment).

With savings, you want to make sure that a certain amount of money is there when you need it, and that means you don't want to risk any of it. If you sock away $1,000, you want all $1,000 to be there, plus maybe some interest, when you need it. As we will discuss in Chapter 7, that can be a little illusory because of inflation; the dollars are there, safe and sound, but they may not be worth as much, so you have lost spending power.

If you buy a bond and keep it to maturity, your capital will be preserved. If you need to sell that bond before maturity, however, the price you get will be affected by what people see happening to inflation as of that time. If your bond pays low interest and inflation is high, you could get less for it than you paid.

We'll discuss investments further in Chapter 7. Here we will mention some investments and programs that relate to many individuals' savings programs.

U.S. Savings Bonds

United States Savings Bonds are among the most convenient securities to use for saving. Your money remains accessible and is extremely safe, and interest earnings aren't subject to state or local income tax.

The most popular are the Series EE bonds, available in denominations of $50 to $10,000. However, they're sold at a discount — less than face value. You purchase an EE bond for 50 percent of its face value and redeem it for its full value at maturity. The maturity period is determined by how long it takes to accumulate enough interest to double the issue value of the bond. Federal income taxes on your interest earnings are deferred until you redeem the bond.

Series EE bonds that you purchase now and hold at least five years pay a variable rate tied to the rates for U.S. Treasury notes. When you redeem the bonds, you receive an average for the term; you're guaranteed a minimum of 6 percent, compounded annually. Interest is paid to you when you redeem your bonds; you can do so any time after six months from the issue date.

For the current interest rate and approximate maturity period, contact your financial institution. You can buy Series EE bonds at most financial institutions or through a payroll deduction plan if your employer offers one.

Thrift Plan/Long-range Savings Plan

Your employer may offer a thrift plan, sometimes called a *matching fund investment plan*. In general, in these plans you're offered a choice of investments ranging from the company's stock to a fund that invests in a variety of other stocks. After you choose, you contribute a percentage of your gross pay each month, usually between 1 and 6 percent. Your employer may match your contribution, typically with either 50 cents or one dollar for each dollar you invest, up to a certain limit.

If you leave the firm, you get your money back, plus any earned interest. You also may be entitled to your employer's contributions; plans vary in how long you must be with the company or participate in the plan before the company's contributions belong to you.

If the plan is one that the federal government certifies as a qualified retirement plan, no tax is due on your employer's contributions or on earnings contributions until you receive the funds.

IRA, Keogh, and SEP-IRA Plans

Another way to defer taxes on your savings is through Individual Retirement Accounts (IRAs) and, if you're self-employed, Keogh plans and Simplified Employee Pension (SEP) IRAs.

With these plans, the federal government prescribes a way you can put away a certain amount each year and avoid taxation on that income, as well as the interest, until you take it out at the age of 59 1/2 or older.

If you (and your spouse, if you're married) aren't considered an active participant in a company-sponsored retirement plan, you can deduct annual contributions of up to $2,000 (or 100 percent of annual earned income, whichever is less) on your federal tax return. If your spouse earned less than $250, you can deduct annual contributions of up to $2,250, or 100 percent of your annual earned income, to IRAs for you and your spouse. Even if your tax-deductible contribution is limited, you defer tax on the interest for any investment you make in an IRA.

IRAs are available in a wide range of investment choices. With certain exceptions, you must pay interest and tax penalties if you withdraw funds from your IRA before you reach age 59 1/2.

These plans were created to encourage saving for retirement, and we'll discuss them more fully in Chapter 9, on retirement planning. However, you can use their tax benefits for any purpose; you just can't get at the money without penalty until you're 59 1/2. When you do take money out, you pay income tax on it at your tax rate at that time.

The Tax Reform Act of 1986 substantially affected many of the plans discussed here, and tax law is always subject to revision. You should direct any questions you may have about tax changes or setting up retirement savings plans to your attorney or tax adviser.

Now that we've discussed how to preserve money through savings, let's turn to how to make money grow through investing.

Chapter Seven

Investing for
the Future

Investing can be a satisfying way to translate your financial goals into realities. The trick is to select the mixture of investments that will suit your purposes and your personality.

EXAMINE YOUR GOALS AND STYLE

To choose appropriate investments, you need to decide what your goals are—in particular, whether you're out to produce income now or are building up savings for the future. You also need to look at your own style, including your attitude toward risk and your willingness to roll up your sleeves and get involved.

Review Your Goals

Targeted Savings.   If you're like many people, investing is the long-range element in your saving plan: you have specific expenses planned in the future, with specific dollars and dates assigned to them—retirement, college tuition for the kids, a new home (those three goals were ranked first, second, and third in a survey by the International Association for Financial Planning).

To invest for the purpose of saving to meet targeted expenses, decide how much you'll need for each expense and when you'll need it. Then lay aside funds systematically for these purposes, using such vehicles as interest-bearing accounts, certificates of deposit, stocks, taxable and tax-exempt bonds, and zero-coupon bonds.

Generating Money for Current Income.   You may want regular dividends and interest payments to meet daily bills or to pay for the extras that make your standard of living more pleasurable. Use the same options as above, with the additions of corporate bonds and preferred stock.

Changing Your Life.   For some people, investing has another role: it's their bid for a different and better life: a new career, a business, a new place to live, early retirement.

Many of us have at least a little of this objective floating through our investment thinking. We enjoy toying with the idea of striking it rich. We may even have a list of places to spend the money (we developed it listening for our number in the lottery).

If your investment goal is to move to a new and different plane, you'll need to be willing to work very hard to make as much money as possible, then work very hard at finding ways to multiply that money. You'll very likely want to get much more deeply involved in the process than you would if you were investing for savings or supplementary income. You may well be willing to take big risks, with an all-or-nothing psychology. And you'll probably think about putting your money in places considerably more speculative than most of the ones we discuss here: you may look at franchises, part ownership of a business, rental property, commodity futures, stock options, puts and calls.

Reducing Income Taxes.   Finally, you may be looking for vehicles to shelter income, generate tax-exempt income, or defer taxes. Tax laws are too complex and change too often for anything but passing discussion here. You'll want to consult a tax adviser if this dimension is very important to you.

Look at Your Style

In addition to being clear about goals, you need to consider two dimensions of personal style that affect your choices of places to invest your money and ways to handle your investments.

How Hard Do You Want to Work at This?   Some investment plans take a lot of attention to succeed. If you have the time and you enjoy working with your investments, the process can be rewarding. You can save yourself money in commissions and other transaction costs.

Are You a Risk Taker?   This question will come into play no matter what goal you're pursuing, and it significantly influences the options you should consider.

Most stockbrokers open a conversation with a new client by asking questions about attitudes toward risk. It's important for you to know your attitudes—and for couples to know each other's—before you get very deep into investing.

The stock market plunge of October 19, 1987, affected people in varying ways, but the differences in their reactions are probably not differences of expertise. Those who had deliberately taken big risks, and who lost big, could shrug it off; they had known what they were doing and felt they'd make it back. Those who knew themselves to be risk-averse had stayed with bonds and fixed-income investments during the dizzying rise of common stocks in the preceding months. They had deliberately sacrificed extra gains in exchange for the advantage of not worrying about the very thing that eventually happened. Those who had ignored their cautious instincts and taken risks—thinking only of possible big gains—probably suffered pain out of proportion to any dollar loss. And the people who were *most* unhappy were those who had misjudged their own dispositions *and* also misunderstood where specific investments stood on the spectrum of risk.

Psychologists tell us that our attitudes toward risk taking have to do with such personal characteristics as our need for security, our feeling of self-worth, our confidence in our own ability to make things turn out the way we want, and the extent to which we take direction from inside ourselves as opposed to looking to outside forces to direct our actions.

They also explain that many people operate quite comfortably at what appear to be opposite ends of the risk scale: they put most of their money in the bank, but they also spend a great deal on lottery tickets. What's going on? Bank deposits are safe and recognized as such by everyone. If you use them, you're supported by public opinion. You don't "win" much, but you aren't expected to. The lottery, on the other hand, is a long shot, and everyone knows that. If you lose, no one will criticize you. So neither course of action puts you at odds with what society sees as a sensible attitude toward risk. You're not putting your ego on the line, just money.

Psychologists say we probably know our basic tendencies in regard to risk pretty well; that is, we know where we stand on the spectrum of low-risk, medium-risk, or high-risk people. We shouldn't let anyone force us to violate our comfort level, at whichever point on the spectrum it rests.

Investment strategies typically build a base of low-risk investments, with layers of higher-risk, higher-return investments, working up the pyramid to a cap of speculation. You determine the shape of the pyramid by deciding what percentage of your investment money goes to each level. Over time, as circumstances change, you may reassemble the pyramid; what started out as something very flat, with no cap of speculation, may rise to a sheer Alpine peak as you get more money or more confidence.

SOME CRUCIAL TERMS

To make sense of your investment options, you need a basic vocabulary of important terms. Here they are.

Risk

There are three types of investment risk:

- *Capital risk* is the possibility that your investment will sell at a lower price than you paid for it. This risk applies to common stocks, but can apply as well to real estate and the money you invest in Uncle Charlie's business.
- *Interest rate risk* is the possibility your interest-earning investment will lose value as a result of changes in general interest rates. This applies particularly to bonds. As interest rates go up, bond prices typically decline. Likewise, when rates go down, bond prices can be expected to rise.
- *Inflation risk* is the possibility that inflation will increase to a level greater than the return on your investment.

Return, Yield, and Total Return

Return is the amount you earn on your investment, expressed as a percentage of the amount invested. You'll need to be careful here to make sure you're hearing what you think you're hearing. "Return" is expressed in a variety of ways.

Yield is the term used most often. It describes the income an investment generates in relation to what it cost.

Let's consider the case of bonds first. For bonds, yield boils down a number of factors: the interest paid, the current selling price, and the time remaining until maturity. Annual yield is what you'll get in interest each year if you buy that bond and keep it until you cash it in. If you buy a bond for $1,000 that comes due in five years and the yield at the time you buy it is 10 percent, you'll get $100 each year until you cash in the bond for the $1,000 you paid for it. That's perfectly sure and safe, unless the organization that issued the bond defaults.

Now, to see how interest risk operates and affects yields, let's say interest rates rise suddenly the year after you purchase your bond to a point where people can get a return of 11 percent on a new bond (as opposed to 10 percent at the time of your purchase). The market adjusts. For the bond you hold to yield 11 percent to a new investor, the price of the bond has to drop to $900. So if you sell it at that point, that's all you can get for it, even though you paid $1,000 to buy it.

So, there are three important points to note here:

1. With bonds, you can know precisely what your return will be in dollars and can count on that *if* you keep the bond to maturity.
2. "Yield" goes up when the price of the bond goes down, even though that sounds wrong when you first hear it.
3. You can lose money on a "fixed" investment in terms of inflation, and you can actually end up with fewer dollars than you started with if you sell a fixed investment early.

Now let's look at common stocks. For stocks, "yield" represents the annual dividend divided by the price of the stock. Thus, a stock that costs you $60 and that pays quarterly dividends of $1.50 ($6 per year) would have an annual yield of 10 percent.

Suppose that the stock rises in price the next year by $10, to $70 a share, and the dividend stays at $1.50. In that case the yield would fall to 8.5 percent. But if you sold the stock, you would have gained the $6 dividend plus the extra $10 in value, for a total of $16—a gain of more than 26 percent. *That* figure, combining dividend and the appreciation in value, is referred to as *total return*.

Here are two more important things to note:

1. If you're buying common stock for current income, then high yield is what you want to look for, as with a bond. Stock tables in your newspaper normally list this figure with each day's price quote, in the column headed "Yld."
2. If you're buying stock to hold in order to have money at some future date, you're more interested in total return than in yield. This figure is not routinely published. Ask your broker for it when you are considering a specific stock or fund.

When you're sure you're using the term that measures what's important to you, you can compare investments more effectively. But remember, the figures you see reflect past performance, which may or not predict the future (but it's the better way to bet).

Liquidity

Liquidity refers to how easily you can get at your money—for an emergency, for another investment, to buy a car, or for some other purpose. Money in a money market account is available anytime; that's liquidity. But money invested in rental property is not liquid; it can take months to sell it so you can get your money out.

Diversification

Diversification is a golden word in investment. It refers to spreading your capital across different investments, a strategy that can reduce your capital risk (risk to the money you put in) by preventing large losses from any one investment.

Diversification has other advantages, too:

- Mixing categories of investment can help smooth out the effects of the ups and downs of the general economy.
- You can protect against inflation risk by buying things that usually go up with inflation, such as real estate.
- You can give yourself liquidity by staggering the dates that investments come due, so that not all your funds are tied up for the same period of time.

Some investments offer built-in diversification; that's a big appeal of mutual funds. As in anything else, though, if you hedge all your bets, you're not likely to win big. You'll sleep well, but maybe not on silk sheets.

LOOK AT PLACES TO PUT YOUR MONEY

Deposit Accounts and CDs

We've already talked about the types of accounts available at financial institutions: regular savings accounts, money market deposit accounts, and certificates of deposit (CDs).

All three of these have low capital risk. (Another term is *preservation of capital;* that is, will you end up with less money than you started with?) Deposits won't go down, and you'll get at least the full original value of your deposit, unless the institution goes under. Even then, insurance will come to the rescue as long as the institution is insured.

Money market deposit accounts and variable-rate CDs offer interest-rate protection because their return usually follows general interest rates (note: in both directions).

Regular savings and money market accounts provide high liquidity: you can get at your money readily. CDs almost always have an early-withdrawal penalty, but these aren't as forbidding as they may appear. Let's say the penalty is 90 days' interest. Suppose that an emergency forced you to cash in a $10,000, five-year CD paying 8 percent interest two years early. Your penalty would come to about $200. By that time, though, you would have earned $2,400. In effect, the penalty would reduce your annual return from 8 percent to 7.3 percent.

If you anticipate that you *might* need to cash a CD early, you may be able to reduce the early-withdrawal penalty by breaking up the investment. If you bought five CDs for $2,000 each, instead of one for $10,000, then you could cash only as many as you needed and pay the penalty only on that amount. (Of course, you may get a lower rate of interest on your $2,000 CDs than you would have received on the $10,000 one.)

Another way to improve liquidity is to stagger due dates. For instance, you could invest $2,000 in a CD with a one-year term, another $2,000 in a CD with a two-year term, and so on, reinvesting each one as it matures if you don't need the cash at that point. You'll probably sacrifice some interest, though, compared to longer-term CDs.

Investments in deposit accounts and CDs lay a solid base for almost any investment plan. They require little expertise to make or to manage. You don't need a broker, and you don't pay any commissions or fees.

Fixed Income Securities

U.S. Treasury Issues. The Treasury Department issues three types of securities: notes, bonds, and bills. These are considered among the safest investments you can make because they're backed by the U.S. government. Interest earnings are exempt from state and local income taxes.

Treasury notes have maturities of 1 to 10 years; bonds have maturities of 10 to 30 years. These securities accrue interest semiannually and are redeemed at maturity. Usually, notes with maturities of less than four years are issued in denominations of $5,000. Treasury notes with longer maturities and Treasury bonds are available for $1,000 or more.

Treasury bills, or T-bills, have maturities of 13, 26, or 52 weeks. They are sold at a discount and redeemed for their face value at maturity. The minimum denomination is $10,000.

You can buy T-bills through a broker or commercial bank, or directly from a Federal Reserve Bank. The bills are held for you in a safekeeping account rather than issued in paper form.

Federal Agency Issues. These securities represent the debt of various federal agencies that administer selected lending programs of the U.S. government. Agency securities offer the advantage of a generally higher return than you can receive on U.S. Treasury issues. Minimum denominations vary with each agency. Some are as low as $1,000, but a $5,000 minimum is typical. Maturities range from a few days to 30 years.

Most agency securities must be held in safekeeping for you by a bank or broker; you'll be charged for this service.

Certificates issued by the Government National Mortgage Association (GNMA), also known as Ginnie Maes, are popular, low-risk investments. The government guarantees the principal and guarantees that interest will be paid monthly, but does not guarantee how much the interest will be (an illustration of the two kinds of risk: there is virtually no capital risk, but interest rises or falls with general interest rates).

Municipal Bonds and Notes.   These are the debt obligations of state or local governments or state agencies. Typically, municipal bonds and notes are issued in denominations of $5,000.

These investments are popular with those in higher income tax brackets because the interest earned on them generally is exempt from both federal income tax and state and local taxes in the state in which they're issued. Depending on your tax bracket, the tax exemptions can increase your return by a sizable amount.

When buying bonds or notes, consider the issuer's creditworthiness. Several independent services provide credit ratings using a standardized system. Reports by two such services, Moody's and Standard & Poor's, are available at most public libraries. Bonds and notes with a good credit rating generally will provide you with greater investment security, but those with lower ratings frequently offer higher interest rates.

Corporate Bonds and Notes.   These represent the borrowings of corporations. Minimum denominations vary with each company but typically start at $1,000. Some bonds and notes, inelegantly called "junk bonds," are backed only by the company's promise to pay. Others are backed by specific assets; if the company can't meet the interest payments, the property can be sold to repay the investors.

Corporate bonds usually pay a higher interest rate than U.S. government bonds or tax-free municipal bonds with the same credit rating, but your interest earnings are taxable. As with municipal bonds and notes, you should consider the issuer's credit rating before you buy.

Zero Coupon Bonds.   This investment option is available on many obligations of the federal government and municipalities. You purchase a "zero" (or "strip") at a deep discount and redeem it at maturity for full value.

If held until maturity, zeros provide a predictable return. There typically is a market for these if you have to sell early, but there is interest risk: you may get less than you paid if interest rates are rising. The reverse is also true if interest rates drop.

The interest that accrues on a municipal zero is generally free from taxation. On federal government obligations, you will typically be subject to taxation year by year on the "imputed" interest, even though you don't get the money until the maturity date. You can defer paying taxes on the accrued interest if the zero is part of your Individual Retirement Account or Keogh plan and you allow the interest to accumulate (it isn't taxed until you start making withdrawals).

STOCKS

Stocks represent an ownership interest in a business or corporation. Investing in them can be one way to achieve long-term growth and balance for your investment portfolio.

Stocks can provide income by paying dividends related to the company's profits (income stocks) or by increasing in value so that you realize a capital gain when you sell them (growth stocks). Stocks typically provide both dividends and rising value (over time), but you pick them more for one than the other.

Historically, stocks have provided a higher return than bonds or money market investments, especially when the rise in selling price is combined with dividends. Stocks can also drop, of course; if yours happen to be down when you need the cash, the long-term averages, or prospects for future long-term growth, offer chilly comfort.

Still, if you're striving for a future goal that requires a large sum of money—college tuition or retirement, say—you may decide that you simply can't reach the necessary amount without at least some common stocks in the mix of your investments, and accept the risk that implies. Stocks can also help to provide protection against inflation.

Individual Company Stocks

You may well want to buy a specific stock or even construct your own portfolio of individual stocks. Many people buy shares in the company where they work, especially where there is a stock-purchase plan for employees. In that circumstance you have direct knowledge of the company's management, performance against competitors, earnings record, and dividend history, as well as the prospects in the company's industry. Those are the factors you'll want to investigate for any company whose stock you consider buying.

If income is your objective, look for stocks with good dividend records; utility stocks are commonly favored for this purpose. If you're looking for growth stocks—stocks you'll hold in the expectation that their price will rise—look for such things as strong prospects for new products, position in a growth industry, and willingness to plow money into research and development.

Stockbroker Fees and Commissions

The fees involved in buying and selling stocks can be an important consideration in your investment activity. You can easily spend 5 to 8 percent off the top of an investment, which could cancel your return for the first year. And if you go in and out often with small purchases, commissions—which are charged both times—can eat an investment away.

You can minimize your costs if you understand how they work. On stocks, charges are proportional to the size of the order. The percentage charge for purchases in lots of less than 100 shares ("odd lots") is much higher than the charge for "round lots" of 100 shares.

Percentage charges vary from broker to broker, and they can be negotiable on big orders. Here is a typical schedule of fees from one major full-service house on transactions of 100 shares or more:

100 shares of a stock selling at $5 = $35 fee (7.0 %)

100 shares of a stock selling at $20 = $66 fee (3.3 %)

100 shares of a stock selling at $30 = $83 fee (2.8 %)

100 shares of a stock selling at $40 = $97 fee (2.4 %)

500 shares of a stock selling at $40 = $345 fee (1.7 %)

2500 shares of a stock selling at $40 = $971 fee (0.9 %)

There is typically a minimum charge of $30 to $35.

"Discount brokers" may charge less than half the amount that full-service brokers charge. They give less advice, if any, and typically they charge minimums: on small transactions, they may not be cheaper than a full-service broker. But on large orders, where you know exactly what you want, the savings offered by a discount broker can be significant.

Some other charges and fees: U.S. Treasury bills and notes may cost only $25 each to buy, whatever the denomination. Certificates of deposit can be purchased from a broker with no fee (as is true when you buy them from the bank). Sophisticated investments such as limited partnerships—to be discussed momentarily—carry the highest fees: 5–8 percent.

There are various service charges: most brokerage houses will bill you $25 per year to defray administrative charges for handling your

IRA account in addition to the fees charged on the specific investments in that account.

A good way to understand these costs is to ask your broker, for each investment transaction you are considering (buying or selling): what dollar amounts will be subtracted from my investment now or at any other time? Are there any choices I can make that will affect those amounts?

MUTUAL FUNDS

A popular way to obtain the benefits of buying common stocks or bonds is to invest in a mutual fund. Here you buy shares in a portfolio of securities that is set up and managed for you and the other investors in the fund.

Mutual funds are professionally managed, so they can offer investment expertise you might not otherwise be able to afford. They also feature diversification, convenience, and high liquidity. You can buy fund shares directly from mutual fund corporations or through brokers and some large banks.

Some funds specialize in only one kind of security or industry; most offer a variety and, therefore, a way to minimize risk. If your fund belongs to a mutual fund family that offers several types of funds, you can switch from one fund to another to take advantage of changing market conditions. This can often be done in a way that minimizes the commission and other fees.

To choose the mutual fund that's right for you, consider your goals.

Some funds are designed for maximum growth over time, and are well suited for attaining a future dollar target. These are composed of companies whose stocks are expected to rise in value faster than average, perhaps because they are plowing earnings into research and development for greater future benefits. These funds will typically pay less in dividends and have lower yields, and the risk can be higher.

If you need money now—living expenses, let's say—you may select an income fund. These funds are composed of stocks of companies that regularly pay good dividends. The dividend payments can come to you as a regular check.

If you want a little of both, there are balanced funds, many with "Income and Growth" in their name.

Whatever your goal, you probably can find a mutual fund with the same aim. A fund's objectives usually are discussed on the first page of the *prospectus*. The prospectus is a description of a company's financial position, required by the U.S. Securities and Exchange Commission (SEC) and available on request. Before you invest, read the prospectus carefully and examine the fund's performance. Your local library may carry magazines that report on the past performance of mutual funds.

In addition to mutual funds that consist chiefly of common stocks, there are also bond mutual funds. These usually provide steadier returns and have a lower capital risk, but historically they've generally returned less over the long term.

Another popular type of mutual fund is a money market fund, which invests in U.S. government and government agency securities, CDs, and other debt obligations. Usually, you can withdraw a minimum amount at any time without penalty. Because a money market fund offers a high degree of liquidity, it can be good place to keep your cash assets.

Understanding Mutual Fund Fees

The sales commission on a mutual fund, called *load*, can be 5–8 percent. In addition, management fees can range anywhere from 0.4 to 3 percent annually.

There can also be something called a *12b-1 plan* that authorizes deductions to recoup marketing and distribution costs. That can be another 1 percent. It's typically taken before proceeds are distributed, so you don't see it.

Some funds have exit fees; that is, you pay when you take your money out. Many have a step-down system of charges: no fee going in, then a 5 percent exit fee if you leave in the first year, going down 1 percent a year until there is no exit fee at all. But there will still be annual management fees, and perhaps other costs, along the way.

With a "no load" fund, there is no commission when you buy, though management and other fees can be significant. Funds that impose their fee when you sell—called a *back-end load*—can no longer advertise themselves as "no load." Overall, no-load funds generally have lower total transaction costs than other mutual funds.

Stockbrokers will argue that the "load" you pay a broker actually buys you valuable advice and quick service (particularly when you need it most, in time of trouble). They say that "load" is a one-time charge and that a mutual fund should be approached as a long-term investment.

If you are trading in mutual funds actively, going in and out often, and you know what you're doing (you'd better, or you shouldn't be doing this), you'll probably save transaction money by using no-load funds. Remember though, that transaction costs are less important than performance. You buy a fund based on how well you think it will do the investment job you want done—growth, income, or a mix of the two. When you have narrowed your list to a few that meet your criteria, then look at transaction costs and consider going with the one that costs you least.

Before you buy into a fund, ask these questions:

• What dollar amounts will be subtracted from my investment now or at any time?

• What will it cost me when I sell?

• Are there choices I can make that will affect those costs?

LIMITED PARTNERSHIPS

Limited partnerships are investment structures that allow investors to pool capital to purchase an asset such as real estate or oil and gas property. Ownership of a share in a limited partnership limits the investor's legal liability.

These are typically long-term, developmental investments and were particularly popular as tax shelters before the Tax Reform Act of 1986 sharply limited their use for tax losses. Limited partnerships are typically purchased through a stockbroker.

Unlike a stock or bond, where prices are determined by action in the marketplace, the value and return from a limited partnership are based on the performance of the rental property, oil well, or whatever was purchased. If an enterprise makes a profit and pays off, the proceeds are distributed among the partners. When the property is sold, the partnership is liquidated, and the proceeds from the sale are distributed to the partners.

ANNUITIES

Another form of investment, one that is particularly appropriate when income is the goal, is an annuity. Annuities are purchased from a life insurance company in a single payment or several payments over a period of time. The annuity provides you with regular income for a period you select beginning with a date you establish. As with other insurance policies, rates, fees, and terms for annuities vary greatly.

You don't pay any taxes on the earnings accumulating in an annuity until you start receiving the distributions. If payments to you are based either on a fixed period or your life expectancy, you will receive back the amount you paid for the annuity tax-free, prorated over the period you receive distributions. Unless you're over 59½ or disabled, a 10 percent penalty generally applies if you receive distributions before the starting date in the annuity contract. If your employer contributes to the purchase of an annuity, generally you're not taxed on your employer's portion of the contribution until you begin receiving the distributions.

A *fixed annuity* offers a specified rate for a short period, typically one year or less. After that, the rate changes with market conditions and at the insurer's discretion. The rate for a fixed annuity won't fall below a minimum amount, usually about 4 percent.

With a *variable annuity*, your money is invested in a fund chosen by either you or by the insurance company. Your return depends entirely on the performance of the fund.

Because sales and administrative fees and early withdrawal penalties can take a big bite out of your annuity investment, you probably should consider a tax-deferred annuity only if you intend to keep it for its entire term.

LIFE INSURANCE

Life insurance belongs in a discussion of investment for two reasons: (1) it's an alternative way to contribute to your estate; (2) it's a vehicle for developing savings for use later. Its best use, though, is still its most common one: to support a survivor by replacing your income if something happens to you.

One type of policy for this purpose is a *whole life* policy (also called *straight life* or *ordinary life*). Before retirement, you pay regular premiums. Part of the premium goes toward providing a survivor's benefit; the rest accumulates in a savings fund. After retirement, you can use the cash surrender value—the amount your policy is worth at any given time—to buy an annuity that will make regular payments to you. Or you can have the cash surrender value paid to you in a lump sum for investment elsewhere.

As an alternative to whole life insurance, some companies offer *variable life* and *universal life* policies. Like whole life, these contain built-in savings features:

- With variable life, you have a choice of portfolios. Your return depends on how the investments in your portfolio perform.

- With universal life, your money goes into a portfolio that the insurance company manages; you're guaranteed a minimum return. Universal life also lets you vary the amount and the timing of your premiums.

Insurance companies charge a sales commission and an annual administration fee. Rates, fee, and commissions vary widely from company to company.

REAL ESTATE

Real estate has several advantages as an investment. Historically, it has provided a means of staying ahead of inflation. It can also offer good "leverage": that is, you may be able to borrow money to buy real estate, increasing your potential return in proportion to your actual investment.

The interest you pay on a real estate loan and certain expenses involved in managing real estate may be deductible from your income for tax purposes. This can be an important feature, but you'll want to work with a tax adviser: the deductibility of interest is determined under different rules for different types of investments—residence, rental property, or undeveloped land.

EMPLOYER INVESTMENT PROGRAMS

For many people, the highest return on any investment they can make is through participation in a company program where the employer matches the employee's contribution in whole or in part.

These programs are usually designed and administered as long-range, retirement savings plans, and some young people reject them out of hand for that reason. That's probably a mistake. Many provide for withdrawals before retirement under specified conditions or allow you to take out a loan against your account at lower interest rates than are allowed elsewhere.

Many employer programs allow you to direct the investment of your share, letting you divide it among stocks, bonds, and money market funds and perhaps allowing you to make changes in these allocations from time to time during the year.

If your employer matches 50 percent of your investment, which is not uncommon, that means you're getting $1.55, $1.60, or more (counting the return from the investment itself) the first year for each dollar you put in. From then on, the return on your dollar is based on that combined figure, so a 10 percent return, say, pays you 16 cents. Hard to beat.

There are early-withdrawal penalties and tax aspects to consider, but even if you're not working on retirement, these programs bear looking into.

REVIEWING GOALS AND STYLES

At the beginning of this chapter, we discussed different goals for investment—targeted savings, or income. We also talked about differences in style regarding involvement and risk. Let's look at these personal factors again in light of the information covered in the chapter.

Goals

Targeted Savings. To accumulate money for specific future purposes—retirement, college tuitions, and the like—you'll want to take advantage of your long-term perspective in selecting your investments.

You can afford to tie up money for predictable periods, so you can exact a premium for that. You can target higher interest certificates of deposit and long-term bonds to come due on or about the dates when you'll need the money.

Also because you have a long timetable, you may feel you can afford to ride the stock market, putting some of your funds in growth stocks (individually or through a mutual fund). You can search out stocks, mutual funds, or limited partnerships that key to high-technology explorations and other investments where you can afford to wait out the development period. You also have the option of real estate limited partnerships or other investments that take time to begin paying off.

Finally, you may want to examine direct investments, such as real estate.

Investing for Income. If your investment goal is income, the issue of attitudes toward risk comes sharply into focus. You don't want to endanger the principal that will generate income. Still, you want some growth to protect against inflation.

So you make some choices. If you can handle some ups and downs in income, you may aim for higher return through common stocks, maybe some that are more volatile than the average. But you may prefer to adjust your standard of living to the level of income that can be produced by an investment strategy of maximum safety: bonds, money funds. If you want certainty above all else, you might look at fixed annuities.

Style: Low Involvement or High?

One option in establishing your degree of involvement is to experiment. In particular, you could handle your first investments directly, since they'll probably be low-risk items, such as CDs.

Low Involvement. If your style is low involvement, you may want to use a stockbroker or financial planner to lay out a long-term plan that requires little of your attention (or theirs). Commissions are based on the one-time purchases, spread out over the years, so they don't amount to much (assuming you make sure you don't get into a fund with heavy management and administrative fees).

You'll want to make sure you know from your broker what the checkpoints are for reviewing your investments. What marketplace factors could cause you to reexamine your investment plan? You also want to set up a procedure for reexamining your own needs and sharing any changes with your broker to see whether they affect investment strategies.

It's a good idea to talk through some scenarios: What if the market drops? How do we react, and what do I do? What if real estate (or some other sector of the economy that figures importantly in your portfolio) goes sour? How will we know, and what will we do? Once you're content that all the bases are covered, you can relax.

High Involvement. If your style is high involvement, you can take the trouble to seek out the highest paying investments and attempt to outguess the market (and the laid-back people who opted out in the last section). You can shop for CDs, buying out of town if necessary to get the best rates. You can shop for mutual funds, seeking the ones with the best records and lowest transaction costs.

You can take the trouble to develop arrangements with brokers that best suit your purpose, maybe using a full-service house for your more complex requirements and a discount broker to execute your buy and sell orders.

You can give yourself liquidity to take advantage of market opportunities that arise by staggering CD investments and making fresh decisions as they come due. For instance, you can take a chunk of money, divide it into fourths, and spread it over time. Put a fourth of it in a money market fund against which you can write checks for quick access. Put the rest in CDs that compound daily and automatically reinvest the interest:

- A fourth for CDs that mature in 12 months
- A fourth in CDs that mature in 24 months
- And the final fourth in CDs that mature in 36 months

Each year, when one CD matures, look around and see whether there's a better place for it. If not, buy a new 36-month CD with that money.

In this way you're always within 12 months of half your money. Your return will reflect a blending of four different rates—the money fund's and those of the different CDs. As interest rates change, up or down, so will your blend.

At this point you should have a fairly solid grasp of your general investment options. The next two chapters zero in on two long-term financial goals that most of us need to account for in our savings and investment plans: providing for a college education and planning for retirement.

Chapter Eight

Providing for a College Education

The biggest and most perplexing financial challenge many families face is how to provide for college for the kids. It differs from other challenges both in size (it's one of the biggest) and character (it's much more complex).

A four-year education costs anywhere from $23,000 to $45,000—up to $80,000 at an Ivy League or other expensive school—and the costs keep rising. Heading into the 1990s, The College Board lists the average cost of one year of education, including room and board, as almost $6,000 at a public four-year school and about $11,300 at a private school. The difference is mostly in tuition and fees, which averaged about $1,500 for public schools nationally and $6,500 for private schools.

College is such a large expense that you need to get it into your financial planning as early as possible. As with other large expenditures, you want to spread your saving task over as many years as you can. You can benefit from the elapsed time to marshal the power of compound interest and gain equity appreciation. That's especially important in coping with the fact that college costs seem persistently to rise faster than inflation.

The tax techniques that used to help a little, chiefly by putting money in the future student's name, have largely been eliminated by the Tax Reform Act of 1986. Still, you should explore tax implications with whoever provides your tax and investment advice.

Determining the amount of money you'll need involves a number of variables we'll discuss later in this chapter, but the process of raising the money is not essentially different from raising money for other purposes. You may want to review the information about savings and investments presented in other chapters.

The size of your savings task will be influenced by factors we're about to discuss. You may have a changing target over the years, larger or smaller, as you consider the variables.

A SPECIAL PURCHASING DECISION

A college education is a complex purchasing decision with sub-decisions that can alter dollar needs by a factor of 200 percent:

- Expensive, prestigious private school versus resident-tuition state school
- Four-year versus two-year school
- Away versus home; far away versus nearby

If freshman year is years off, you can use the time to pursue a continuing task of determining what suits your child, your financial resources, and your preconceived notions.

It's a decision you should try to make as objectively as you make decisions about cars and washing machines. It is likely to be a major sacrifice for you, whatever you decide, and you want to be sure you're not buying more than you can afford or less than you need.

For some parents, it's an article of faith that they should give their children the best education they can possibly afford. And to some, that means the most expensive and prestigious school. This decision about the category of school is the one with the greatest dollar leverage; there's an enormous difference between Harvard at $80,000 and a state school at $23,000.

"Shop" colleges by talking to people who went to the prestige schools. Ask what benefits they received that they felt they could not have received elsewhere. Talk to graduates of other schools, and compare answers. For instance:

- A Princeton physics graduate feels that the quality of instruction was the key; he feels that few other schools had such excellent teachers, but he concedes that's not necessarily true.
- A Yale liberal arts graduate says that the intellectual stimulation gained from being with a select group of highly motivated classmates was what was most valuable to her. She feels that this probably is available only from really good schools.
- An accounting graduate of the University of North Carolina feels education is mostly a matter of how you apply yourself. His

school let him go as far as fast as he wanted. He feels he got at least as good an education as friends who spent far more.

That's the kind of conversation you'll want to pursue, to equip you to make your own choice as knowledgeably as possible. As your assessment takes shape, you may decide to change your saving and investment strategies, up or down.

The other high-leverage question is the choice between a two-year community college (about $3,000 a year, according to the College Board survey) versus a four-year institution. A compromise can significantly reduce total college costs: the student spends the first two years at a two-year school, then transfers to a four-year school to finish a degree.

Less significant financially are the questions whether to live at home and whether to select a school that's far away. Still, these have money implications, and you'll want to add them to the subjects you explore systematically as the time for filing applications approaches.

PARTICIPATORY DECISION MAKING

You also have a decision to make about the decision process itself: how you want the child to participate in the decision, and how early. That's partly a financial matter, but it's broader than that.

In some families, it's made clear very early that decisions about vacations, Christmas gifts, and home improvements are all conditioned by the college fund. Birthday checks from grandmother go there. So do earnings from summer jobs.

Beyond the effect this practice can have in making funds available for college, it can significantly shape the child's attitudes toward money generally and toward education. That can be character building and a good learning experience. It can also create resentment and unrealistic expectations about what effects the education will ultimately have. A college education does not inevitably produce a higher income and a better station in life, no matter what dad told you.

When a child approaches college age, there are other issues of participation. As your children get involved in picking a school, they need to understand clearly from you what the financial options are. Early on, you'll want a full discussion of the role they are to play in paying part of the costs. If you expect their savings to help pay the first year's tuition, and they're thinking of quite a different use for it (quite possibly beach-oriented), there's a potential for conflict. You'll also want to be sure you're together in your expectations regarding part-time work, summer jobs, or work-study programs. You might want to make the student responsible for researching financial aid. That's a major assignment that can help make participation in the decision process meaningful.

It's also good to clarify some other expectations ahead of time. Some kids get a car for college graduation. If you have no intention of making such a gift, say so. Go on record early with your intentions regarding postgraduate expenses, too. It's common for parents to say: We pay undergraduate expenses; you pay everything beyond. That's not an arbitrary distinction. After graduation, the student may be able to get aid not available before, because the student's income, not yours, is the basis for determining financial need. If the student realizes how much good grades affect the chances of a fellowship or other financial help in graduate school, that can be an additional incentive to perform well as an undergraduate.

EXPLORE COST-CUTTING POSSIBILITIES

If you plan ahead, you may be able to take advantage of ways of reducing your total college costs. Here are two to consider.

Save Money through Advanced Placement

Before your child reaches junior year in high school, talk about the use of advanced placement courses and other ways of reducing total college time. (Yale in three years is a lot cheaper than Yale in four.)

The College Board's Advanced Placement program gives high school students the opportunity to receive college credit in major subjects based on scores achieved on advanced placement exams. These are administered in conjunction with the more general Scholastic Aptitude Tests.

Once students are in college, the College-Level Examination Program (CLEP) allows them to receive college credit for knowledge gained outside formal educational settings, based on the proficiency they show on exams. The College Board offers CLEP tests in major subjects covered during the first two years of undergraduate study.

Consider ROTC or Military Service

The military also offers options that, among other things, can significantly affect college costs. The Army, Navy, Air Force, and Marine Corps ROTC college scholarship programs pay full undergraduate tuition for up to four years of study. ROTC scholarship students also receive $100 monthly for living expenses. After graduation, the student must serve at least four years on active duty as a commissioned officer.

There is also the possibility of going into military service first to get help on college costs. As the 1990s begin, here's how things stand: Anyone who enlists in one of the military services can save up to

$10,800 for future college or training costs, and the government will contribute $8 for every dollar the individual saves. The Army will add up to $14,400 to that amount for enlistees in certain jobs. Also, the military services will pay 75 percent—up to 90 percent in some cases—of tuition costs for approved courses taken while on active duty.

SEEKING FINANCIAL AID

Unlike most other big expenses, with college costs there's the possibility of getting some help. Opportunities for financial aid of various kinds—including loans, scholarships, grants, and work-study programs—are offered by the government, private organizations, and the schools themselves.

In most cases, financial aid administered by schools is based on need. The school provides you with an application in which you detail your financial resources, and an independent organization reviews the information you submit. The firms that provide this service use a standard formula developed by the U.S. Department of Education to determine how much the student and the family will be expected to contribute. The assessment takes into account the number of children, particularly the number who are in college simultaneously. Since your financial picture is likely to change from year to year, you'll be asked for new information each year you want to receive aid.

The organization supplies the information to the school, which then determines what aid, if any, to offer. The school looks at all the costs involved: tuition, fees, room and board, books, supplies, and transportation. If the total exceeds what the need-assessment firm deems to be the "family contribution" you can make, the overage is the "need" the school uses in deciding on any aid.

You're more likely to show need and thus be eligible for aid at a more expensive school, simply because there's a greater disparity between what you can pay and what the school costs. Also, "independent students" may get aid more easily, because they report only their own income (including that of a spouse) on their aid application; they aren't required to include the parents' resources as well.

For federal financial aid programs, students at least 24 years old by January 1 of their award year are considered independent. Students under age 24 are considered independent if they fall into any one of several categories:

- Veterans
- Orphans
- Students with dependents other than a spouse

- Single undergraduates who have not been claimed as dependents on their parents' tax returns for two prior years and who had an income of at least $4,000 each of those years
- Married students not claimed as dependents on their parents' tax returns
- Graduate or professional students not claimed as dependents on their parents' tax return

State requirements vary. For California financial aid programs, for instance, a child is considered independent if all of the following apply:

- The child did not live with the parents more than six weeks in any of the prior three years.
- The parents did not claim an income tax exemption for the child in the aid year.
- The child did not receive more than $750 each year from the family.

TYPES AND SOURCES OF AID

Three basic types of financial aid are scholarships and grants, loans, and work-study. The aid package may include any or all of these.

Each school determines the size and makeup of the aid package it offers, depending on student need and the resources available to the school. In determining awards, many schools will assign a certain level of "self-help" aid (loans or work-study) before awarding aid in the form of grants or scholarships.

The federal and state governments are the two largest providers of student aid. Federal student assistance alone has totaled $18 billion or more annually in recent years.

Government assistance is subject to change, so it's important to seek out the most recent information. Here we'll summarize the categories available in 1989, together with some illustrative dollar amounts. We'll look at both government programs and financial aid available from other sources.

Federal Government Programs

There are four major financial aid programs offered by the U.S. government: Pell Grants, Supplemental Educational Opportunity Grants (SEOG), Perkins Loans, and College Work-Study (CWS).

Pell Grants are offered directly to the student by the government, and the amount of the award will be the same no matter what school is selected. SEOG, Perkins Loans, and CWS are all "campus-based" programs. This means that they are awarded and administered individually by the schools, and the amount of the award is determined by each school.

Pell Grants.   Pell Grants are based solely on need and are available to low-income students who do not have a bachelor's degree and will attend school at least half-time. The grants may be used at two-year schools, including vocational schools, or four-year institutions. For the 1988–89 school year, Pell Grants for full-time students ranged from $200 to $2,200.

Supplemental Educational Opportunity Grants (SEOG). Undergraduate students eligible for SEOGs may receive a $100 to $4,000 grant each academic year, depending on the availability of SEOG funds at the school and the student's need.

Perkins Loans.   Formerly known as National Direct Student Loans (NDSL), Perkins Loans are low-interest (5 percent) loans made to vocational, undergraduate, and graduate students, based on need and the availability of funds at the school.

As of 1989, the student may borrow up to $4,500 for the first two years of study, a total of $9,000 for undergraduate education, and a total of $18,000 for undergraduate and graduate work combined. The student must begin repayment six months after leaving school or dropping below half-time status. Students may be allowed up to ten years to repay the loan.

College Work-Study (CWS).   Based on the availability of funds, the CWS program provides jobs for undergraduate and graduate students who need financial aid. The student will be paid at least the federal minimum wage for work at a public or nonprofit organization, either on- or off-campus. The school determines the amount of work-study and handles the arrangements.

Government-Guaranteed Loans

Government-guaranteed loans are administered jointly by the U.S. Department of Education and a state student loan program. They include Stafford Student Loans, Supplementary Loans for Students (SLS), and Parent Loans for Students (PLUS). Many banks, credit unions, savings and loans, and other lenders offer these. To be eligible, the student must be attending a degree or certificate program at a college or vocational school on at least a half-time basis.

Stafford Student Loans.   Formerly known as Guaranteed Student Loans (GSL), these are federally subsidized, low-interest loans to students who demonstrate financial need. In 1988–89, a student could borrow from $2,625 to $4,000 per year as an undergraduate, with a five-year maximum of $17,250. Graduate students could borrow up to $7,500 per year to a total of $54,750 (including undergraduate loans).

Students start repaying the loans six months after leaving school and begin at an interest rate of 8 percent, rising to 10 percent in the fifth year. There is also a 5 percent loan origination fee, and states may charge insurance premiums.

Supplemental Loans for Students and Parent Loans for Students. Supplemental Loans for Students (SLS) and Parent Loans for Students (PLUS) are federally sponsored loans to help middle-class families who might not qualify for other aid. These loans are not subsidized by the government. They are offered at a variable rate of interest, which in 1989 was not to exceed 12 percent. In 1989, these provided up to $4,000 a year, whether taken out by the student or the parent. Repayment typically begins within 60 days after the loan is received.

State Government Programs

Your state education department can describe aid programs available for residents. These can be significant.

Schools and Colleges Themselves

In addition to administering federal financial aid programs, schools and colleges offer their own grants, scholarships, loans, and fellowships. Amounts available vary widely, from nominal awards to full tuition.

Often, more expensive schools will have extensive grant and scholarship programs in order to ensure a diverse student body. In addition, scholarships may be available for exceptional scholars and outstanding athletes as well as for those who excel in areas such as music, debating, drama, or dance. Scholarship funds are often specifically restricted to students with a special background, talent, or academic interest.

Special Aid Programs.   Special aid programs vary widely. Some schools offer a tuition discount or rebate when more than one family member attends. At one school, children of alumni get a 10 percent discount. Other schools give scholarships to match state regent awards or to reward members of the National Honor Society.

Another school will pay the loan origination fee for a Guaranteed Student Loan. Sometimes students over a certain age are given a tuition break. Clearly, it pays to explore the options thoroughly. Talk to the college placement counselor at your child's high school and to the financial aid office of any colleges you're seriously considering.

National Merit Scholarships

Merit Scholarships are the largest, most prestigious, and most competitive of the private undergraduate awards. An independent nonprofit organization, the Merit Scholarship Corporation, awards about six thousand scholarships each year, basing the awards on test scores, and academic and extracurricular achievement.

Merit Scholarships may be either a renewable annual award, ranging from $250 to $2,000, or a one-time award of $2,000. In addition, many large corporations sponsor Merit Scholarships for their employees' children with renewable annual awards ranging from $500 to $8,000.

To compete for a Merit Scholarship, students take the Preliminary Scholastic Aptitude Test/National Merit Scholarship Qualifying Test (PSAT/NMSQT) in the fall of their junior year in high school. Need is not considered in selecting Merit winners, but it is a factor in determining the size of the stipend for renewable awards.

Private Sources

Although federal and state governments and financial institutions are the major sources of student assistance (with schools and colleges not far behind), some diligent digging can turn up a community group, business, church, labor union, professional society, or foundation that offers a financial aid program. You should know, however, that most private scholarships, grants, and loans are not very large, eligibility criteria are often quite specific, and there may be substantial competition for the awards. Organizations that provide aid include the following (some give awards only to those with some tie to the organization):

- *Community groups:* Organizations such as the Rotary, Elks, American Legion, 4H Club, PTA, and Chamber of Commerce often make scholarship awards.

- *Employers:* Large employers often have scholarship programs for employees and/or employees' children. Some also offer assistance to students majoring in fields related to the company's activities or to those who come from a town where a major plant is located.

- *Professional and trade associations:* Some associations sponsor awards based on a specific field of study or career plans.

- *Unions:* Many unions sponsor scholarships for members and their children.
- *Religious groups:* Most denominations sponsor student aid awards, and not all are for those who intend a religious vocation.

Check with your financial aid or school counselor's office or your local public library for more information.

Aid for Veterans and Veterans' Families

Veterans may qualify for U.S. Veterans' Administration educational benefits or for state benefits, as may spouses or children of veterans who died or were totally disabled in the service. For more information, contact your local U.S. Veterans' Administration office and your state department of veterans' affairs.

Programs for Teacher Training

Both the federal government and state governments have special aid programs for students who plan to become teachers. The federally funded Congressional Teacher Scholarship Program provides scholarships of up to $5,000 annually for four years, starting in the sophomore year of college. After graduation, the recipient must teach two years at any level from preschool through high school for each year a scholarship was received.

APPLYING FOR AID

Do Some Research

When the time approaches for college applications, you'll want to do research on the current options.

A reference librarian can help you find the best current books. Many are published annually, so you should check *Books in Print*, an annual guide available at the reference desk of most libraries, to make sure you have the most recent edition.

One excellent source is *Don't Miss Out: The Ambitious Student's Guide to Financial Aid*, by Robert and Anna Leider. Copies are available for $4 from Octameron Associates, P.O. Box 3437, Alexandria, VA 22302.

The College Board offers a free publication, *Meeting College Costs*, that can help students estimate the amount of financial aid for which they may be eligible. For copies, write to the College Scholarship Service, The College Board, 2099 Gateway Place, Suite 480, San Jose, CA 95110.

To learn more about federal financial aid programs, send for a free government brochure, "The Student Guide: Five Federal Financial Aid Programs," available by writing to Federal Student Aid Programs, Dept. CY-88, Pueblo, CO 81009-0012.

Ask Schools for Their Aid Information

At the same time you start gathering information on colleges to attend, gather information on the types of aid they offer. This information can be a factor in selecting where to apply.

Even though the cost of two schools may be similar and both have the same information about your resources, the aid packages they offer you may differ significantly. For one thing, the required family contribution calculated by a needs-assessment service may be either increased or decreased by a college's financial aid officer. In addition, schools may have different amounts of aid available to meet their students' need and may have different policies regarding how that aid is to be allotted. Some schools may not have the resources to help all those whose applications show need; others may require that each student pay a certain base amount toward the need shown by the analysis service. Some schools set a ceiling on the total amount of aid any student can receive. Further, schools may estimate required summer earnings differently. Some will increase the earnings contribution required as the student advances through college; others will not.

The way financial aid packages are structured can vary significantly, too. As we have seen, there are self-help aid (loans and work-study) and gift aid (scholarships and grants). Although two schools may offer the same amount of aid, one may offer a package with a greater proportion of gift aid, while the other may require more from the student in the form of work and loans.

Watch Your Calendar

The processes involved in getting admitted to college and in applying for financial aid are separate, and both have many deadlines. Be aware of them. Each school sets its own deadlines, and missing one may jeopardize the chances of getting aid. The earlier you do the research and complete your financial aid applications, the better your chances.

Tests used for college admission come first, in the fall of the junior year of high school. Tests for National Merit Scholarships are also taken at this time.

You'll generally wait until January or February to complete applications for financial aid. That allows the student and the family to complete tax returns for the prior year.

Financial aid procedures and applications differ significantly from school to school. It's likely that you'll have to complete more than one aid application. However, use the same personal financial data on each application, and save all records used to prepare your applications.

Answer all the questions on an aid application, and include all the supporting data requested. If information is incomplete, the application is delayed, and the student may not get the assistance. Getting the application in early is important.

Once the Student Is in School

For each academic year, the student must update financial aid applications and supporting documents to maintain eligibility. To continue to qualify for financial aid, the student generally must be making satisfactory progress toward a degree.

Educational costs are likely to increase each year, as tuition costs recently have been rising roughly twice as fast as inflation. At the same time, your family financial situation may change from one year to the next. The aid package will be adjusted annually to take into account any significant developments.

Many schools have special scholarships and awards for academic achievement that are open only to enrolled students. Other schools may discount tuition for students who maintain high grades. Keep a sharp lookout for these programs.

And when you've done all that, you can sit back and contemplate another event you've been planning carefully for—retirement. That's our next subject.

Chapter Nine

Planning for Retirement

The earlier you start planning for retirement, the better. Even if it's 20 or 30 years away, there are things you'll want to do now.

- Get at least a rough idea of the amount of money you'll need once you've retired; that requires you to think about the kind of life you'll want to lead then.

- Make a rough estimate of the amount of money you can expect from Social Security and pension and other retirement plans at work; that tells you if there's a shortfall (there probably is) and how much you'll need to make up from savings, investments, and other sources.

- Get started with a specific plan to build, through savings and investments, the amount you've determined you'll need; give yourself the benefit of time to accumulate money and to compound your interest on it. Don't do what many people do: postpone developing a plan until after you've taken care of college tuition for the kids. You may find you simply don't have enough years left before retirement to save the amount you'll need.

No matter how many years off your retirement is, one good technique is to imagine that you will retire at the end of this month. That forces you to do some hard thinking about future needs. And it's always easier to save when you have a clear picture of the purpose of your saving (or the dire consequences if you *don't* save).

You may protest: how can anyone plan so far ahead? How can I imagine my life 20 or 30 years in the future?

Things won't be as different, and you won't be as different, as you might think.

Even in our mobile society, a significant percentage of the people who retire this year will do so in the house where they lived 25 years ago. Most will stay right where they are for the rest of their lives.

Barring physical impairment—which, statistically, is unlikely by age 65—you won't be a fundamentally different person at retirement age than you are now. Your likes and dislikes, what you enjoy doing in your free time, the level of your luxury needs: these are probably fairly well fixed. You can project them to the future with some confidence.

Retirement planning is so important, and yet so easy to postpone, that we encourage you to engage in a little brainstorming to help determine what you should be doing now, in terms of money decisions, career choices, and perhaps lifestyle adjustments, to prepare for it.

A BRAINSTORMING EXERCISE ON RETIREMENT

We'll use the technique we employed in Chapter 5. On a pad of paper write: "Things I'll Want in Retirement." As you did earlier, put down whatever comes to mind. Don't censor or try to organize your thoughts.

Couples should do the exercise at the same time, but separately. One may well have a very different vision from the other's.

Then, as you did before, number the items, linking those that seem to duplicate each other. Divide by 3 to get your number of "votes," then check off that many as representing the things that are most important to you. Rank-order those, if you like.

When you're done, examine the results. What picture emerges?

Do you find yourself thinking of a retirement community in the sun, with housekeeping and meal services, where you spend your days golfing, fishing, and playing tennis? Or are you assuming that you'll stay in the home you have now, still very active, perhaps pursuing a second career?

Whatever your vision of your future, consider the actions you need to take now if that vision is to become a reality. Ask yourself questions such as these:

- How much income will it take to provide what I want?
- How much can I expect from a pension?
- What will Social Security provide?
- How much do I need to save between now and then? How will I go about it?

• What other things should I be doing now to lay the foundation for the life I will want later?

Here are some examples of where this kind of exploration can lead.

• A woman has been climbing the corporate ladder by changing companies frequently. When she stops to consider the need to accumulate pension funds, she realizes she has never stayed at a company long enough to become sufficiently "vested" in a pension plan. As things stand now, she is not guaranteed a comfortable monthly income when she retires. She resolves to reexamine this aspect of her career planning.

• A man decides to combine his vacations with retirement planning and investments. He decides to spend summers scouting potential places to retire 20 years hence, shop for property here and there, and maybe make a little money selling properties he doesn't want.

• A woman thinks she might like doing interior design work in retirement. She volunteers at work to serve on the committee that will be handling the planning of the new offices. She also signs up for some night courses.

• A man thinking ahead to becoming a consultant decides to make a point of having lunch with the consultants his company uses, to learn more about what's involved.

PREDICT AND MANAGE YOUR RETIREMENT NEEDS

Let's look at a hypothetical situation and rough out an approach to developing financial goals for retirement planning. After seeing how the analysis is done, you can adapt the process to your own situation.

Forgetting inflation for the time being (we'll come back to it), consider how many dollars a month it would take for you to live the way you want if you were to retire at the end of this month. The idea is to see how close you would come to your goal based on your present course, taking into account Social Security and pension-plan benefits. If there's a shortfall, either you need to scale down your expectations, or you should begin strengthening your savings and investment plans.

A Case Study

For the purposes of this case study, we'll suppose that you are 40 years old, self-supporting, and earning $45,000 per year. Having explored your vision of retirement, you've come to some provisional conclusions.

You think you'll probably like to stay where you are when you retire, close to friends and family. Country club retirement isn't really your style, and, besides, it would cost a lot more.

You expect to explore some second-career possibilities, both because you want to stay busy and because you'd like to add to your income.

You'll also want time and money to be able to travel a bit. You presume that by age 65 most of your big bills will be behind you—the kids' college tuition taken care of, the mortgage on your house paid up. Having roughed out some calculations, you estimate that you'll be able to do pretty well if your regular income is two thirds of your current level of pay.

On that basis, and deferring the issue of inflation, you're shooting for $30,000 a year. What will you need to produce that?

First, what will your Social Security benefits be? Projecting those benefits involves a complicated formula, to say nothing of the many variables, both fiscal and political, that affect what may happen in the future. You'll want to consult expert advice before counting on a specific amount.

Still, you can estimate what you would receive by asking your local Social Security office to give you the form "Request for Statement of Earnings." You can fill that out, send it in, and get a current estimate of your retirement benefit. This is a good thing to do every few years to detect any errors. (If you changed jobs, do they show the new payments?) Also, checking up keeps you current with any disability, death, and cost-of-living changes.

For the purpose of this exercise, we'll use an estimate of the annual benefit that would go to a worker retiring at age 65 who has made the maximum contribution to Social Security in each year of employment. Social Security payments are deducted from the first so many dollars you earn each year ($48,000 in 1989); "maximum contribution" means you made at least that much and paid the Social Security tax on it each year. As of 1989, such a worker's annual pension would be about $10,000. (To give you a feel for amounts based on lesser pay, the annual benefit for someone who has contributed only half of the maximum each year would be roughly $8,500.) So, thus far you have $10,000 in Social Security income toward your goal of $30,000.

Next, what will you get from your employer pension? That depends on many factors, as we discuss a little later in this chapter. For now, let's assume that you continue in your current employment. You may question whether you'll still be where you are now when you retire, but it's a good idea to check out what your pension would be in that case. You can use that as a basis for your deliberations, as well as for comparisons if you do contemplate changing jobs.

For this exercise, let's use a typical formula. Multiply your years of service by the average of your salary for the past five years. Take

1 percent of that as your annual pension benefit. So, if you've already been with your current employer for 10 years, and will be there for another 25 (assuming retirement at age 65), then you will end up with 35 years of service. If you're earning $45,000, let's suppose that the average of the past five years comes to $43,000. (Remember, we're ignoring raises and other increases for the time being.) Multiplying that by 35 years yields $1,505,000 (whee!); taking 1 percent of that (thud) gives you an annual pension income of $15,050.

So, your total projected income from Social Security and your company pension comes to $25,050.00.

To meet your target of $30,000, that leaves you about $5,000 in annual income to obtain from savings, investments, or other sources. Continuing to postpone the subject of inflation, let's consider what you would need to do to be able to generate that $5,000 in income at age 65.

To produce $5,000 in annual income at a return of 8 percent, you'll need $65,000 in capital. To have $65,000 when you retire in 25 years, you need to sock away $2,600 a year. (We're not including interest yet; in a few paragraphs, we'll cover that in our adjustment for inflation.)

Incidentally, you could also think in terms of an annuity under which you'd be paid a certain amount each year until you die. That involves actuarial (how long you're likely to live) and other considerations that we won't go into here. It would typically cost you less, because you use your money up, in contrast to the invested-capital approach we're imagining here, whereby you or your heirs still have the $65,000.

Before we go further, we finally have to confront the inflation issue. Maybe *your* brain can handle inflated numbers easily, but for many people, reality seeps out the edges of a picture that is painted either with yesterday's deflated numbers or tomorrow's inflated ones. Can you really visualize your grandfather's five-cent hamburger or believe that the house where you were born cost $15,000? And can you believe that the house you're in *now* may someday sell for a million dollars?

To keep things simple, we'll presume that your income between now and retirement will at least keep up with inflation and that your investments will grow at least as fast as inflation. For the purposes of this exercise, we can decide that Social Security will keep up with inflation as well. We will assume that your benefit payments at age 65 will be worth as much then as the estimated benefit of $10,000 is now. (Is that a reasonable assumption? You'd think so, for political reasons, despite some fiscal issues.) We can also assume that your salary and therefore your company pension will rise at least as much as inflation.

If we assume that inflation will affect both the income and outgo sides of your financial planning in roughly the same way, we can equalize them by using percentages in this way: the $2,600 you would need to put away each year to make up the shortfall in retirement income represents about 5.8 percent of your gross income of $45,000. If you keep that percentage constant as your income rises, you will increase the dollar amount you put into savings. It's $2,600 this year, but if your income rises 10 percent next year to $49,500, the 5.8 percent means you put away $2,871. By the time income has doubled to $90,000, you're socking away $5,220 a year. If income and inflation rise at the same rate, the amount you're saving will keep you even.

You may feel that 5.8 percent is a big chunk of pre-tax income, and it is. But this example is simply meant to suggest a process you can use in determining what your own dollar figure and percentage would be. In reality, we have been very conservative. Many pensions are more generous than the 1 percent figure we used. The constant-dollar assumption should prove to be conservative, too. After all, you hope that your income rises significantly faster than inflation. And you hope your savings and investments produce a return greater than inflation.

And remember that (as of this writing) as much as one half of your Social Security benefit is nontaxable and the portion that is taxable will be taxed according to your tax bracket in retirement, which presumably will be a lower one than you occupy now. Finally, we've not made any provision for earned income after retirement.

At the same time, you have to ask whether income will continue to keep pace with inflation *after* you reach 65. There may be cost-of-living adjustments in Social Security, and perhaps your pension will be indexed to inflation (though not many are).

As you can see, there are lots of complexities—and we've barely scratched the surface. The purpose of our example is to illustrate a process for examining your own situation and coming up with a rough idea of where you stand. When you get down to making the hard decisions, you should seek professional advice.

Once you have a rough idea of the amount of money you'll need to accumulate for the retirement life you envision, you'll need to start thinking about specific ways of getting it. We've already discussed savings and investment strategies in previous chapters, so here we'll look at pensions and savings plans designed specifically for retirement.

COMPANY PENSIONS

As you chart your career path, consider employer pension plans as an important variable. Not all companies have them, and among those that do, there are big differences in the way pensions are calculated and therefore in the amount of money you're actually paid. In addition, some pensions are reduced by your Social Security receipts: on the plus side, some include medical benefits, and some provide cost-of-living escalators.

There are lots of other differences as well. Pension plans vary in early-retirement provisions. They also vary as to *vesting*, or how long you have to be in the program before you can collect on it or carry it with you if you leave the company.

The Employment Retirement Income Security Act of 1974 (ERISA), amended by the Retirement Equity Act of 1984, lays out rules that must be followed by pension plans (though an employer is not required to have a plan). As of January 1, 1988, ERISA regulations allow a company with a plan either to provide full vesting after five years of continuous service or to provide it on a graduated scale—for example, 20 percent vesting after two years, adding 20 percent each year to full vesting after seven years. The exact vesting schedule will vary according to plan rules.

ERISA regulations also require employers to supply employees with a full description each year of their pension benefits. Review it and see where you stand for planning purposes. If you're changing jobs, compare pension plans in deciding which employer you choose.

Employer Retirement Plans

The plan we described in our case study, with pension payments calculated on the basis of a formula incorporating income level and years worked, is an example of a widely used system. It's in a category called *defined benefit* or *target benefit contribution plans.*

The federal government has rules about the use of these plans, designed to protect the employee. Also, these plans are insured by a federal agency, the Pension Guarantee Credit Corporation.

The employer determines what the plan will be, and that can vary company to company. Employers decide when they establish the plan what portion you receive if you retire early. Your plan may allow you to voluntarily contribute a certain percentage of your salary. If so, it is possible that these contributions will not be considered part of your income for tax purposes.

There are several varieties of defined contribution plans. Let's look at them briefly.

Salary Reduction or 401(k) Plans.   In this type of plan, you choose to make nontaxable contributions to the plan, and your salary is reduced by the amount of your contribution. Often the employer will match a portion of the contribution. You don't pay tax on the contributed amounts until you receive them in the form of pension payments.

If you make contributions that do not reduce your taxable wages, these are called after-tax contributions. Since you've already paid taxes on this income, after-tax contributions are recovered tax-free on a pro-rated basis when you receive your distributions after retiring.

If you are in one of these plans, under the Tax Reform Act of 1986 your participation may affect the deductibility of Individual Retirement Account (IRA) contributions. But the 401(k) achieves much the same effect for you as the IRA, which we'll discuss later.

Money-Purchase Pension Plans.   In these plans your employer sets aside an amount for you based on a predetermined percentage of your compensation each year.

Stock-Bonus Plans.   In these plans, your employer buys stock in your company for you. The stock usually is held in trust until you retire, when you can receive your shares or sell them at their fair market value.

Profit-Sharing Plans.   In these plans, the employer's contribution depends on the company's profits. The employer decides the size of the contribution each year, figured as a percentage of compensation for each eligible employee.

Participatory Savings Plans

In participatory savings plans, you direct a portion of your pay to a long-range saving plan into which the employer makes a contribution matching yours in whole or in part. Some of these plans give you the option of putting your money in fixed income bonds, common stocks, or a money fund. This is very much like a small family of mutual funds, where the investments are professionally managed at no cost to you (the employer pays those expenses). As such, however, the funds are subject to market fluctuations.

Tax-Sheltered Annuities (TSAs)

A TSA can be one of the most flexible and advantageous arrangements for retirement planning. To be eligible, you must be an employee of a public school system or a tax-exempt organization operated exclusively for educational, religious, charitable, or scientific purposes. Insurance companies and financial planning firms sell TSAs.

Each year you can contribute up to 20 percent (more in some cases) of the amount of your income that is subject to tax to a TSA. Taxes on contributions (subject to certain limitations) and their earnings are deferred until you start drawing retirement benefits.

SAVING FOR RETIREMENT
OUTSIDE COMPANY PLANS

The federal government has deliberately created a number of programs offering tax benefits designed to encourage us to save our own money for retirement. The Tax Reform Act of 1986 has reduced the application of these for people already covered by company plans. But they continue to be important for people who are not covered or who are self-employed.

Individual Retirement Accounts (IRAs)

IRA investments can take any one of a number of forms: certificates of deposit, mutual funds, bonds, limited partnerships —most of the vehicles described in Chapter 7. Talk to your investment adviser about the options you have.

Anyone whose earned income is at least $2,000 can put up to $2,000 a year in an IRA plan, plus $250 for a non-working spouse. Tax on the earnings is deferred until you take the money out.

The amount you put into your IRA may or may not be tax deductible. The rules concerning the tax deductibility of IRA contributions changed as a result of the Tax Reform Act of 1986. The key point under the new rules is whether you are covered by an employer's pension plan.

If you (or your spouse, if you're married and file jointly) are *not* eligible to participate in an employer-sponsored retirement plan at any time during a tax year, you're allowed a deduction for your IRA contribution on your federal tax return. Employer-sponsored plans include qualified pension plans, including the 401(k) plans mentioned earlier; profit-sharing or stock-bonus plans; qualified annuities; SEPs; and certain other retirement plans. Check with your employer to determine whether you're considered an active participant.

If you (or your spouse, if you're married and file jointly) *are* eligible to participate in an employer-sponsored retirement plan, your eligibility for a full or partial federal tax deduction for your IRA contribution depends on your filing status with the IRS and on the amount of your adjusted gross income for that tax year.

State tax rules regarding deductibility of IRA contributions may differ from the federal rules. Consult your tax adviser for more information on your eligibility for these deductions.

If you make withdrawals from an IRA before age 59½, generally you must pay income tax *plus* a 10 percent nondeductible federal tax penalty (and a state tax penalty), unless the withdrawal is made because of death or disability.

You can withdraw funds tax-free from your IRA once every 12 months if you deposit them in another IRA within 60 days after receipt. This is known as a *rollover*. You can also roll over distributions you receive from a qualified retirement plan, subject to certain restrictions. If you don't receive any funds, but instead authorize your IRA custodian to handle the transfer, you may transfer funds as often as you like tax-free.

You must begin withdrawals from your IRA by April 1 of the year following the year you reach 70½, or you face penalty taxes. You don't need to take it all out—just a portion described by a formula based on life expectancy. The government intends that you draw it all out eventually and pay tax on it.

Simplified Employee Pension (SEP) Plan

If you own a business or are self-employed, you can contribute up to 15 percent of your annual earned income, or $30,000, whichever is less, to an IRA under a SEP plan. Even if you're not self-employed, your employer can make contributions to a SEP plan on your behalf.

The employer may choose a SEP plan that allows employees to make pre-tax contributions to a SEP-IRA through deductions from paychecks. These contributions are limited to $7,000 per year. They are not included in earned income for federal tax purposes.

If *you* have employees, by the way, you must contribute the same percentage of their compensation to SEP-IRAs for their benefit as you do for your own; these contributions are a business expense, which makes them a tax deduction for the business. You may change or eliminate contributions, year by year.

Except for contribution limits, all the rules applying to IRAs also apply to IRAs under a SEP plan. Eligibility to participate in a SEP means that you are an active participant in a company-sponsored retirement plan for the purpose of determining the deductibility of your regular IRA contributions.

Keogh Plan

In a Keogh plan, contributions and the interest they earn are tax-deferred. When you own a business and begin a Keogh plan for yourself, you must include in the plan any employees who meet certain requirements. If you're the owner and sole employee, you can choose from a range of investments similar to those available for an IRA.

In a Keogh organized as a defined contribution plan, the overall federal limit on annual contributions is 25 percent of annual compensation or $30,000, whichever is less. You can deduct contributions of up to 15 percent of annual compensation for federal income tax purposes. When calculating the contribution limit or the deductible amount, the compensation of the self-employed participant (such as an owner or partner) is defined as his or her earned income reduced by deductible contributions made to the Keogh or other qualified plan.

If you're self-employed, you also can make voluntary contributions according to the provision of the Keogh plan. Your employees can do the same. Usually, voluntary contributions are limited to 10 percent of compensation (earned income, if you're self-employed).

Eligibility to participate in a Keogh means that you are an active participant in a company-sponsored retirement plan for purposes of determining the deductibility of your regular IRA contributions.

Do all these options and legalities leave you feeling bewildered? If so, you're not alone. Fortunately, there's plenty of help around. As we've noted, you can get an estimate of your Social Security benefits simply by requesting it. Your employer will furnish you with a projection of your pension benefits. Financial and tax advisers can help you negotiate the thicket of regulations and tax provisions governing IRAs and other forms of voluntary retirement saving.

In short, you can get the information you need. The part that no one else can do for you is determining what will be important to you when you retire—and having the foresight and determination to start your planning now.

Chapter Ten

Buying and Selling a Home

Buying a home, especially your first one, can be frightening—almost paralyzing, when you realize how much of your future happiness can be riding on your decision.

For most people, a home is the biggest dollar commitment they will ever make. It dominates their entire budget and financial plan for years into the future.

Buying a home is a decision that can shape careers and personal lives to a profound extent, especially for families with children. You're not just getting a place to eat and sleep; you're getting a lifestyle.

Still, in a typical year, millions of people gather up the gumption and the money to take that plunge for the first time, beginning the process of fixing up, selling, and buying again (a bigger house, a house in a better neighborhood)—an average of seven times before settling down for good. It's the American Way, a kind of slow-motion nomadic style, driven in no small part by tax policy.

If all those people can do it, so can you.

DECIDING TO BUY A HOME

In this chapter, we'll describe factors to help you select the home that best meets your needs at a cost that makes sense in light of your income and personal priorities. Later in the chapter, we'll discuss selling homes, and in the next chapter we'll look at home improvements. But for now, we're talking to you as a buyer.

So, why do you want to buy a home?

If you're like most other people, the fiscal-financial reason is to get the tax advantage that comes with being able to take deductions for your mortgage interest, property taxes, and certain other expenses. Moreover, under the Tax Reform Act of 1986, about the only way to get a deduction for the consumer interest you pay for other purposes is to borrow on the equity in a home through home equity loans and lines of credit. So that's another good reason to get a home, and then build up some equity in it.

Another financial reason for first-time buyers is simply to get a foothold on the property-value escalator: you may feel that if you don't buy soon, prices will rise beyond your capability ever to meet them.

A third reason is that, over the years, owning residential property has been—for most people—one of the best ways to outpace inflation.

If you are contemplating this step, the sensible sequence is this:

1. Look at your income and the cash amount you can spend on a home.
2. Learn about financing and decide what type of loan fits your cash and income, and how to get the best interest rate.
3. Set your goals: What do you want this home to do for you? What should you look for?
4. Go house hunting.

That's the sensible sequence, but if you're like most people, you'll probably start with number 4, do number 3 as you go, then try to make number 2 and number 1 fit the great place you find on the edge of a park.

We'll deal with the process in the sensible sequence, however, and tell you as we go why it's better.

DECIDE WHAT YOU CAN SPEND

Before you start shopping, get a firm fix on the amount you can afford to pay. Otherwise, you may become enamored of a place you can't afford. You'll suffer disappointment and wasted time, or worse, push yourself into a financial bind.

Unfortunately, it's very difficult for you to answer in advance, by yourself, the biggest question in your mind: how much house can I get with the amount of money I have?

You can get a very rough idea by taking your annual income and multiplying it by 2.5 or 3. For example, suppose your household income is $45,000. That suggests you can afford a house in the range of $112,000 to $135,000. For the sake of this discussion, let's say you settle on $126,000 as your limit.

Now that is very rough, and when you get to a lender, you may find you can't go this high. Or maybe you can go much higher. It depends on so many things that lenders have to use computers to answer the question. But our rough formula gives you a place to start.

How about your down payment? For a $126,000 house, you'll need between $12,600 and $25,200 as down payment (10–20 percent), plus $3,000 to $5,000 for "closing costs."

If it appears that your money—both continuing income and cash up front—does not match the market yet, maybe you'll have to save a little longer, and get that income up. But if your money is close to what you need, you're ready for the next step.

Look more closely at what you can afford. To do that, borrow a formula from people who make mortgage loans. They say that, generally, your monthly housing expenses—including your loan payment, property taxes, insurance, and homeowner's dues—shouldn't exceed 30 percent of your gross monthly income. In addition, these costs, plus all your other consumer debt payments, shouldn't be more than 38 percent of your gross monthly income.

For our example of a $45,000 annual income, that's $1,425 per month for housing and consumer debts, with no more than $300 of that total going to non-housing debts—car, credit card payments, and so forth.

If you've developed a budget and income statement as described in Chapter 1, all you need to do now is pull them out to see where you stand.

Otherwise, you'll need to do some figuring. Take your income after taxes and other deductions and the income of anyone else participating in the purchase. Use an average figure if income varies month to month.

Then list your monthly expenses for non-housing items—food, clothing, emergency savings, debt payments, and so on—and subtract them from your monthly income.

What's left is the amount you have available for home ownership: mortgage payments, taxes, maintenance, and utilities.

SHOP FOR FINANCING

This next part is hard, and boring, but it's crucial. You can't know what your money will buy until you check out interest rates, down payment requirements, and other financing factors that can change week to week.

Since these costs vary from lender to lender, it pays to shop. And it's a lot easier to shop coldly, before you have a real house in mind. Once you're under the pressure of getting a specific loan quickly for a house you or your partner has fallen in love with, you can make an unfortunate decision.

You won't be able to get the actual loan, however, until you've identified a specific property. At that point, you may find you can assume an existing loan on a specific house. But before you start your search, you'll be wise to know what your financing options and costs are.

This advance effort can also help you bargain better. If you have a letter from the lending institution spelling out your loan eligibility, it can help you negotiate the price of the specific house you ultimately select. Deals are typically made on the basis of the buyer being able to obtain financing, and everything is put on hold until that issue is clarified. If you can give assurances up front that financing won't be a problem, the seller may take your offer over a higher one from someone whose qualifications are still in question.

Talk to several lenders about your eligibility for a loan, the maximum amount you can reasonably expect, the term (length) of their current loans, the interest rates, the monthly payments for different loan amounts, loan fees, and the repayment periods.

Home loans (mortgages) are available from many sources, including banks, savings and loan associations, credit unions, insurance companies, and mortgage companies. Most lenders offer fully amortizing loans in which you repay the principal (the amount borrowed) and the interest over a specified period of time. At first, most of the payment goes toward the interest. As you continue to make payments, an increasing part goes to pay off the principal and a decreasing part to the interest. As you pay off the principal, you build up your *equity*— the current value of your home minus what you owe on it.

Some lenders also offer home loans that are not fully amortizing; that is, the monthly payment is not enough to pay off the loan over the specified term. In some cases, the final payment, often called a *balloon payment*, can be greater than or equal to the original amount borrowed. In that case you'll probably have to refinance your home to pay off the loan.

LOAN PROGRAMS

Conventional and Government-Insured Loans

The chief types of loans are (1) *conventional* loans, which simply involve you and your lender, and (2) loans the federal government insures, after setting specific rules: FHA-insured and VA-guaranteed loans.

Conventional Loans.   In a conventional loan, neither you nor the lender gets involved with the government agencies most involved with mortgages, the Federal Housing Administration (FHA) and the Veterans Administration (VA). A conventional loan can be more flexible than government-insured loans, with different variations in arrangements governing interest rates and higher totals (FHA and VA loans each have upper limits). Also, conventional loans often can be processed more quickly.

FHA-Insured Loans.   Depending on circumstances, you may do better with an "FHA," a loan approved by the Federal Housing Administration. The lender can be the same one that offered you a conventional loan. The FHA insures the lender—not you—against loss. Generally, you pay the premium for the insurance, but you can negotiate this charge with the seller.

An FHA loan generally involves a lower down payment and interest rate and, in some cases, a longer repayment period than a conventional loan. To compensate for the lower interest rate, lenders usually charge a substantial one-time fee—called *points*—for FHA loans. Each point is 1 percent of the loan amount. The number of points charged depends on market conditions. You can negotiate who pays the points with the seller of the home; often points are split between buyer and seller.

VA-Guaranteed Loans.   If you're a qualified veteran, the widow or widower of a qualified veteran who died of a service-related cause, or an eligible member of the Armed Forces, you may apply for loans from any lender approved by the Veterans Administration (VA). The VA guarantees to repay part of the loan if you don't repay as agreed.

Unlike FHA insurance, you don't pay for this guarantee. However, at the time of settlement, you pay a fee based on the value of the loan.

Down payment requirements and maximum loan amounts depend on the lender, the price of the home, and the VA's estimate of the home's value. The interest rate and repayment period usually are the same as for most fixed rate FHA loans, and the lender typically charges points that the seller of the home must pay along with other loan-related fees.

There are a great variety of home loan arrangements, created to meet changing interest-rate and other conditions. Furthermore, new arrangements continue to appear as lenders compete for your business. Today you have more choices than ever before.

A key consideration, of course—involving many thousands of dollars—is the interest rate.

Types of Loan Arrangements

Interest rates vary from one type of loan to another, and the rates offered on new loans change often to reflect what's going on in credit markets generally.

The rates of some mortgages are fixed for the life of the loan. These are called *fixed rate loans*. Until recently they were the only kind readily available. In the last decade, however, another form of home loan became widely used: the *adjustable rate mortgage* (ARM). As the name implies, interest rates on these loans are not fixed. Usually they start lower than those for fixed rate loans, but subsequently they rise or fall with overall interest rates over the years.

Home loans also differ in the length of their terms: 30-year and 15-year loans are the most common.

Because of the variety and complexity of the home loan market, you should check with several lenders to find out what loan programs they offer at the time you're in the market. What follows should help get you started.

Fixed Rate Loans

With a fixed rate loan, the interest rate and monthly payments remain the same for the term of the loan (usually 30 years).

Some lenders may offer fixed rate home loans with shorter repayment periods (usually three to five years) that aren't fully amortizing; that is, your monthly payments aren't enough to pay them off. Your monthly payments are calculated as if you were paying the loan over 30 years, which keeps them low. But your final payment must pay off the entire principal balance and any unpaid interest. For some, those loans are the only way to get payments low enough to afford. But such people will have to get more money later, or refinance the loan.

You may wish to explore a 15-year fixed rate loan to help lower the amount of interest you'll pay over the life of the loan. Lenders sometimes offer 15-year loans at a lower interest rate than longer-term fixed rate loans. These are less attractive from a tax standpoint, however, because there is less interest to deduct.

Adjustable Rate Mortgages (ARMs)

When inflation went into double digits some years back, a different financing device became popular: the adjustable rate mortgage (ARM). The lender can increase or decrease the interest rate on these loans at specified intervals to keep pace with changing market conditions. The frequency of the interest rate changes and the limit, if any, on the amount of each change are set by the lender and must be specified in your loan documents and disclosure.

Lenders determine changes in the interest rate based on movements in an interest rate index that is independent of their control, such as the rates paid on U.S. Treasury securities. All lenders must tell you which index they will use; banks must give you a ten-year history of the index. Consider how often and by how much the index has changed in the past to get an idea of how the interest rate on your loan can change.

Many adjustable rate loans feature limits, or caps, on the amount the interest rate can change. There are two types of caps: periodic and overall interest rate caps.

A *periodic interest rate cap* limits the amount your interest rate can change at each review period. A 2-percentage-point periodic rate cap, for example, limits increases or decreases in your interest rate to two percentage points at each review period. A periodic interest rate cap may be offered separately or together with an overall interest rate cap.

If the interest rate is adjusted, the amount of your monthly payment may change accordingly. Some lenders, however, offer adjustable rate loans on which monthly payments may be fixed for specified periods of time, or on which payment adjustments may be limited, regardless of a change in the index. In this case, the allocation of your monthly payment to interest and principal will change. If the rate increases, more of the payment goes to the interest and less to the principal; the opposite occurs if the rate decreases.

When payment adjustments are limited, it's possible for increases in the index to cause your interest rate to rise to the point that your monthly payment covers only part of the accumulating interest. In this circumstance the amount of interest not covered is added to your loan balance, a process called *negative amortization*.

The lender may set predetermined limits on negative amortization. If at some point the lender determines that the amount of negative amortization is about to exceed the specified limit, the lender may increase the amount of your payment sooner than originally scheduled. Lenders will notify you in advance of any change in your payments.

Before you sign an ARM agreement, make sure you understand from your lender the maximum you could end up paying each month, the maximum total for the loan, and the factors that would make the difference.

For more detailed information on adjustable rate mortgages, ask your lender for the *Consumer Handbook on Adjustable Rate Mortgages*, a publication prepared by the Federal Home Loan Bank Board and Federal Reserve Board.

COMPARE LOAN TERMS

Before you select a loan, it's critical that you compare the following loan terms for similar types of loans.

Down Payment and Loan Fees

The required down payment and loan fees vary with the lender and the type of loan. It's possible to get a loan with no down payment through VA, for instance. With most loans, the down payment will be 10 to 20 percent of the amount of the loan.

Fees can include *origination cost*, more commonly known as *points*, and private mortgage insurance (PMI) you purchase to protect the lender against nonpayment. Those can be important cost factors in your choice of loan and lender.

Interest Rate

The interest rate determines the cost of borrowing the money and usually is a percentage of the loan amount. Even a small variation in the interest rate can add up to thousands of dollars in the total cost of the loan.

The lender is required to tell you the annual percentage rate (APR). This is the cost of the loan per year, including interest and additional finance charges, such as loan origination and certain closing fees. The APR expresses these charges as a percentage.

With an adjustable rate loan, the lender will tell you the APR (based on the initial interest rate and the fully indexed rate for your loan), the maximum amount the interest rate can change at each interval, and any limit on interest rate increases over the life of the loan. The lender also will tell you what index will be used to determine your interest rate changes. In addition, the lender may give you an example of how your monthly payments could change if your interest rate increases to the maximum amount allowed.

Repayment Period

With a fixed rate loan, the longer the repayment period, the higher the total cost of the loan. A shorter repayment period, however, generally means a larger monthly payment. With an adjustable rate loan, the total cost and the monthly payment are affected by interest rate changes as well as by the repayment period.

Prepayment

A lender may reserve the right to charge a fee, called a *prepayment premium*, if you pay back all or part of your loan before it matures. Your promissory note (loan contract) usually will contain a clause describing under what conditions you must pay this premium. If the promissory note isn't specific, ask what these conditions are.

INVESTIGATE OTHER TYPES OF FINANCING

Instead of, or in addition to, getting a new loan from a lender, you may be able to obtain financing for a home in other ways.

Assumptions

If the seller's own loan is "assumable," you may be able to take it over. You simply pay the seller the difference between the amount still owed on the loan and the purchase price. Then you take over payments where the seller left off. Assumable loans used to be very common, before interest rates rose suddenly. Now, federal law permits lenders to make most loans nonassumable. To find out whether you can assume the seller's loan, check with the seller's lender.

An assumption can be a good arrangement if you can take over the loan at a lower-than-current interest rate. Some lenders, however, may require you to assume the loan at the current rate.

You may need more financing to make up the difference between the purchase price and the sum of your down payment and the amount assumed. The seller often may carry a loan—that is, grant you credit—for a short time, usually three to five years. Depending on the amount you finance and the credit terms, you could have a large balloon payment.

If you're thinking about having the seller carry a loan, consider whether you'll be able to meet the credit terms and make any balloon payment when it comes due. You'll also need to determine whether refinancing will be available, and, if not, whether the seller will extend the term of the financing agreement.

As an alternative to assuming the seller's loan, you might negotiate with the seller's lender to give you a loan for the difference between the purchase price of the home and the down payment. In many cases, you can obtain an interest rate that's between the rate on the seller's original loan and the current rate.

Buy Downs

Buy downs involve money advanced, often by a seller or builder, to subsidize (reduce) the buyer's monthly payments. With a buy-down arrangement, either you, the builder, or the seller pays the lending institution an amount to lower the interest rate on your loan.

If you're dealing directly with the lender, you may be able to pay higher up-front fees in exchange for a lower interest rate and smaller payments over the life of the loan. If you're dealing with the seller or builder, the lower interest rate usually is in effect for a specified period of time—typically, one to five years. After this period ends, you pay the interest rate the lender was charging at the time you took out the loan. This is known as a *temporary buy down*.

Equity Sharing

Equity sharing involves arranging for other investors to pay part of the loan, the down payment, or closing costs in exchange for part of the equity in your home. Often, a parent will be the investor, gaining tax benefits while helping a son or daughter purchase a first home. In addition, many real estate agents, and some state and local government agencies, offer this kind of financing arrangement, sometimes called a *shared-appreciation* program.

Variations

In addition to all these financing alternatives, the seller may offer a variety of other arrangements. When considering any type of loan, be sure to get professional legal, tax, and real estate advice.

Once you have mastered all these financing options and have an idea what kind of loan will work for you, and how big it will be, then you can start thinking about specific houses.

DESCRIBE YOUR GOALS

If you take some time to lay out your goals thoughtfully, *before* you're out making the rounds with a real estate agent, you will increase the efficiency of your search. You can tell the agent precisely what you want, and the agent can key immediately to homes that fit that description.

Further, you can evaluate each house against specific criteria. You'll find it easier to make the final selection—and you'll be happier with your choice.

Ask yourself what you want your home to do for you, now and in the future. (Couples need to do this together.) Be very honest with yourself about the things that are most important to you. Try to suspend judgment about whether you *ought* to feel the way you do.

For some people, for instance, the most important aspect of a home is the way it will advance their careers or social aspirations. If you feel that makes you out to be a snob, ask yourself: Do you have any intention of changing? If not, you're better off making decisions that reflect the way you really feel.

You may be willing to pay a high premium for an impressive home, or one that's in a prestigious neighborhood, and you may be prepared to skimp on other things to free up money for this purpose.

Even so, you may find that you will have to settle for less space, perhaps a condominium or townhouse rather than a detached house. The point is, the choice is one only you can make.

Most likely, though, determining your goal involves considering a number of factors. To begin with, consider couple/family needs:

- Work/school/shopping convenience
- Schools, playground, playmates
- Space needs—now, future
- Privacy

Consider lifestyle:

- Are you very gregarious? Would you like a neighborhood where people drop in for coffee or have block parties?
- Are you recreation-minded? Do you want a community with a good pool, tennis courts, golf course?

Consider features and amenities:

- Want a pool? Jacuzzi? Sun room?
- Workshop?
- Heated garage?

And then there are things you *don't* want. You might compile your very own "Avoid at All Costs" list:

- Big yard to take care of
- Noise
- Nosy neighbors who drop in for coffee and expect you to come to their block parties

Spend some time determining which characteristics are very important to you, which ones are less so, and which ones don't really matter to you at all—no matter how big a deal the real estate agent tries to make of them.

The person who does the windows may feel that the home simply must have windows that tilt in for easy cleaning. Someone else may require a den with a fireplace—that or nothing.

It's not relevant whether something *"should"* be important to you. If it is, and you understand why it is, then it's important, and it belongs on your list of criteria.

For couples, being open and explicit about your idiosyncrasies avoids "hidden agenda" conflicts that can otherwise arise. Those are the conflicts in which the partners present "good" reasons for the way they feel about a potential purchase, while the real reasons lurk beneath the surface.

But how do you actually *do* all this? How do you lay out and prioritize your deeply felt attitudes about something so complex as a home?

One technique is the one presented in previous chapters: brainstorm lists of (1) Things I Most Want in a Home and (2) Things I Most Want to Avoid in a Home. Quickly write down everything that comes to mind in each category. Collect them without evaluating or organizing them in any way, scribbling down the trivial and the profound without hesitation.

Count up the number of items on the list. Divide that number by 3. You had 33 items? OK, go back and circle the 11 that are *most* important to you. Now circle the 4 that are the most important of those. Doing this forces you to make some choices about what's really important to you.

Couples can develop these lists together or separately. In any case, they'll want to go over their lists together, noting the items they both consider important, discussing and trying to understand those they feel differently about.

Two tips:

- Develop the lists over a period of time, as new thoughts occur to you. Review them now and then, adding new items that occur to you.

- Phrases should contain some detail: "No pink in kitchens" is better than just "Nix on pink" or "No pastels." Writing out a phrase encourages you to think through what you really mean (maybe pink is OK in the nursery).

SHOPPING FOR A HOME

Once you've surfaced all your attitudes and emotional requirements, you'll be much better prepared to deal with the reality of finding a home that suits you. Here are some basic decisions and points of comparison to guide your home shopping.

What Type of Home?

The analysis of your personal needs will help you make an important decision:

- Do you need, or very much want, a detached house?

- Would you prefer, or be equally happy in, a townhouse?

- Or might you be interested in a condominium (a townhouse or, more likely, an apartment), where you own the space within your walls and share the grounds and the rest of the property with the other owners?

- Or perhaps your needs and wants could be met by a cooperative apartment, where you own a share in the total structure and grounds.

Price may make this decision for you. "Condo" apartments are usually cheapest, then townhouses, and then detached houses. On the other hand, you may feel so strongly about space and privacy that you'll put up with other things—a long commute, for instance—for a detached house with a large yard.

Where to Look?

On the basis of the criteria you've established, you know the kind of area you want: whether it's near work or something else important to you, whether or not it needs to be in a higher- priced neighborhood.

Drive around the area you're considering, noting the neighborhoods that appeal to you. Then call a real estate agent and lay out your needs as completely as possible.

You can shop on your own, but since the agent's fee is paid by the seller, it doesn't cost you anything directly to take advantage of the agent's services. Sometimes you can buy direct from the owner, and the owner may give you part of the 6 percent fee that would otherwise go to the agent. But restricting yourself to houses you can buy directly limits your choices severely.

You may find a new development that you can buy into by going directly to the builder, bypassing the agent. (Many builders, though, list with agents to handle the selling chores for them.) There can be many advantages to this: you'll probably be able to make a number of choices—carpets, tile, fixtures, appliances—to personalize the home while it's still under construction. Also, the price and value of the home often—but by no means necessarily—rise faster in a new development. But there are disadvantages, too: living in a construction area, starting your own lawn and shrubbery, screwing in all the hooks and brackets, and doing the other "breaking in" tasks that someone else already has done in an existing home.

As you get closer to a decision, ask city officials, local business-people, and your prospective neighbors about the following points.

Public Services.   How close is the fire station? Where is the nearest hospital? Is reliable public transportation available? Are good schools nearby? Can your children safely and easily walk to school or take transportation to get to school?

Public Safety.   Get crime statistics from the local police. Ask for a report or map indicating the crime rates for various areas. A Community Watch program is a good indicator not only of safety but also of community spirit.

Environmental Conditions.   City or county planning officials can tell you about such problems as flooding, erosion, smog, fire hazards, and earthquake faults that are present in the area.

Zoning.   Contact the city or county planning department about plans for your area. Are there plans to widen the streets or add new buildings nearby? Is the lovely cul-de-sac permanent, or do they plan to run a street through at the end? Who owns those nice woods? You'll be tempted to rely on the real estate agent for answers to questions like these, but you'll feel more confident about the answers if you do this research yourself.

Taxes.   Ask the local tax assessor about assessments—charges for local public improvements such as paving, street lighting, and public transit. Have they been rising sharply, and are they likely to continue doing so?

Property taxes can be a large item and can vary importantly from area to area, school district to school district. Early on, ask questions to determine what factors influence these rates in the areas where you'll be shopping.

Houses in a school district that's financing a big building program can carry a much larger percentage property tax than similar ones not far away in another district. By the same token, one district may benefit heavily from the taxes paid by a factory within its borders, and houses in that district will enjoy relatively lower taxes.

While the marketplace tends to reflect these disadvantages and advantages in the current selling price, they will not reflect future changes so accurately. In selecting areas to shop, you'll want to determine whether taxes may be a factor in your future costs (and the resale value of your property). Ask good questions about the future course of those tax rates: Is there reason to think the district will need additional schools or other public facilities? Any reason to think that factory may close? Also, find out about any local homeowner's tax exemptions or other tax credits you may be entitled to receive.

CLOSING IN ON THE DECISION

Once you get a specific house in your sights, you need to pin things down in more detail.

Inspect the Home

Inspecting the home means, among other things, scrutinizing it closely for hidden problems. It can be a wise investment to hire a housing inspector, who will provide a detailed, written evaluation of the home's condition. Fees typically range from $100 to $200. Before hiring an inspector, make sure he or she is licensed and bonded. Find out whether the inspector's written evaluation is guaranteed and, if so, for how long.

You also should have a licensed pest control inspector check the home, whether or not the lender requires such an inspection. The buyer normally pays for the cost of the inspection, while the seller usually pays the cost of any work resulting from the inspection.

In some areas where radon gas is a problem, you can ask for an inspection to determine the level that occurs, if any. Check with local health department authorities.

Investigate Warranties

The seller may provide a home protection contract, or home warranty. If not, you can purchase one from a home protection company. A typical warranty on a newly built home is good for a term from one to ten years and covers the home's structure, its major systems (plumbing, heating, and electrical), and any appliances sold with it. On an existing home, the warranty generally covers the major systems and appliances for one year.

Get Detailed Costs

To clarify monthly homeowner costs, get specific information about property taxes, insurance costs, and utility expenses.

On a house you're seriously considering, ask to see the tax receipts for the last couple of years. Note the tax amounts, the assessment of the property, and how assessments and tax rates have changed.

Ask the owner what the cost has been for property insurance. The cost of insuring a home varies with the home's age, type of construction, and location. As a general estimate, the annual insurance premium is one third to one half of 1 percent of the home's price. Lenders usually require you to carry enough insurance to cover the loan amount, but you may consider getting more, based on the cost of replacing your home.

Repairs and utility costs vary with the home's age, size, design, and condition. A professional housing inspector can give you a detailed report on the condition of a specific home and estimate the costs of major and minor repairs. That report can include an estimate of the life left in the appliances. Ask the owner, builder, or utility company for the highest and lowest monthly utility costs to get a range.

Use the data you've collected to see what your monthly operating costs will be in that home, and add those to your mortgage payments. Are your overall housing costs still within your guidelines?

If so, it's time to square away your up-front cash needs.

Down Payment

The usual down payment required by lenders is 20 percent of the home's total cost, but as we've discussed, the actual amount depends on the type of loan, your lender's policy, and current economic conditions. FHA and VA loans accept lower down payments.

Typically, for down payments of less than 20 percent, the lender will require you to purchase private mortgage insurance (PMI), which protects the lender against loss if you don't pay as agreed. The cost of the insurance is typically 1 percent of the mortgage amount minus the down payment.

Set down the figure that you'll need, based on the financing plan and the cost of the house. For a house costing $150,000, you'd need $15,000 for a 10 percent down payment. Since you're paying less than 20 percent down, you'll also need to pay the PMI, which would come to $1,350. To the total figure, you'll need to add the closing costs and possibly the cost of credit insurance to arrive at the amount of up-front cash required.

Closing Costs

Closing costs are fees for services, including those performed by the lender, escrow agent, and title company. They can range from several hundred to several thousand dollars. Federal law requires the lender to send you an estimate of the closing costs within three business days after you've applied for the loan. Although local custom usually determines who—you or the seller—pays for which costs, you may be able to negotiate some of the fees.

For a full explanation of various closing fees, read the booklet on settlement costs prepared by the U.S. Department of Housing and Urban Development (HUD). It's available free from lenders and HUD offices.

MAKING THE PURCHASE

OK, you've picked out the house, the monthly costs are within your range, you've got financing tentatively lined up, and you have enough cash at hand to cut a deal. You're ready to make an offer.

Make an Offer

By now, you've looked around, and you've read the listings to find out what people have paid for comparable housing in the same area. So you have a pretty good idea of what the market is. In some localities, the real estate agent may be able to give you an even better idea by calling up a computer listing of comparable homes, with asking prices and the prices at which they were actually sold.

Remember that the listing agent represents the seller, not you. But you can ask questions about the marketplace—for instance, whether or not houses have been selling at close to the asking price, how fast they've been selling, and so forth. Then decide on an offer.

Typically, the first offer is less than the buyer is willing to pay. The seller will probably assume that's the case. You should be prepared for some negotiating.

The Purchase Contract

When you decide what price to offer, you or your agent will draw up a purchase contract stating the sale terms and submit the offer to the seller or the seller's agent. The seller either accepts it as is or makes changes and sends it back to you. The contract goes back and forth as many times as necessary to reach an agreement.

Sign the final contract only when you are satisfied. Make sure it covers all the sale conditions you want included. Here are some points you may wish to cover:

- Who pays the "points."
- The conditions under which the contract may be canceled without penalty—for instance, if you can't get the financing you want, if you're unable to sell your current residence, or if the home doesn't pass professional inspection.
- The closing costs you'll pay and those the seller will pay.
- An itemized list describing furnishings, appliances, and other personal property the sale includes and excludes.
- The date on which you'll check the home's condition before the sale is final.
- The date you take possession of the home.

Because a home purchase is a major financial transaction, consider having the assistance of a legal and tax adviser. Professional help is especially important if the transaction is more complex than usual, or if there are aspects about it you don't understand.

The Deposit

At the time you sign the contract, you'll be asked for a deposit, sometimes referred to as "earnest money." The amount can range from hundreds to thousands of dollars, depending on what you're willing to give and what the seller is willing to accept.

The deposit usually is applied to the down payment or to your share of the closing costs. The contract should specify whether the seller will have the right to keep part or all of the deposit if the sale falls through. This may depend on the reason why the sale wasn't completed.

Escrow

In many states, but not all, once you and the seller have signed a purchase agreement, the next step is *escrow*. This is a procedure in which your deposit and other pertinent documents are placed in the keeping of a neutral third party, called the *escrow agent*. You and the seller must agree on the agent, who may be from a title insurance company, an escrow company, or the lender's escrow department. Where escrow is not followed, an attorney typically serves as the third party.

Escrow can begin before or after you've arranged financing. You and the seller sign a set of escrow instructions listing the conditions (including financing) that must be met before the sale is finalized. When the conditions are met, the escrow agent distributes the money and documents according to the escrow instructions.

Formally Applying for a Loan

With the deal agreed upon, make an appointment with a lending officer to apply formally for a loan. Take along a personal financial statement and a copy of the purchase contract. To save time, also bring a list showing the account numbers and addresses for all your creditors. If you're self-employed, take your federal income tax returns and profit-and-loss statements for the past two or three years.

The lender will ask you to fill out an application in which you state your current financial status, list the loan amount and terms you want, and briefly describe the property. Based on the verification of this information—plus a credit report from a credit reporting agency and the lender's appraisal of the home—the lender decides whether or not to grant the loan. Some lenders allow reduced credit documentation if your down payment is 25 percent or greater.

Credit Insurance

Depending on what insurance policies you already have, when you take out your loan you might consider getting a credit life and disability insurance policy to pay off your loan if you die, or to make payments for you if you're disabled. You can arrange for a policy yourself, or some lenders can do it for you. Be sure to compare various policies for their amount of coverage and cost.

Closing the Deal

Closing—also called *settlement*—is the final step. In states where the escrow procedure is followed, before the sale is made final you must deposit in escrow all of the down payment and your closing costs. You will be asked to sign the loan documents, then your lender will forward the loan proceeds to the escrow agent.

At the close of escrow, the agent will record the grant deed and give your deposit and loan funds to the seller. After the recording, you'll receive the grant deed by mail in about 30 days.

Where escrow is not followed, checks are exchanged around the table and the deal is closed once all conditions are met.

HOW TO SELL YOUR HOME

The process of selling a home is in many ways the mirror image of the process of buying one. You'll probably want to work through a real estate agent again. You can handle the sale yourself, in hopes of pocketing all or part of the 6 percent commission. If you think you already have a buyer at hand, you should obviously try that first. But a knowledgeable agent understands the selling process and can guide you through it. The agent will handle advertising, show the home, and help with negotiations and paperwork.

Interview several agents about their experience selling homes. During the interviews, ask each agent what your home should sell for and how each one would go about marketing it. Ask for names of several former clients and contact them for their opinions, or ask a friend or relative to refer you to an agent with whom they've had a successful relationship.

Remember that agents' fees are not set by law, so they can be negotiated. The most common fee arrangement is the percentage commission, generally about 6 percent of the home's selling price.

Listings

You can list your home with an agent in various ways, depending on the agent:

- *Exclusive right to sell:* This is the usual type of listing. Only your agent may sell your home during a specified period of time. If you or anyone else finds a buyer, the agent still gets a fee. However, if your home is listed in the *Multiple Listing Book*, any agent who is covered by the service—in addition to your agent—can sell your home. The agent who finds a buyer shares the fee with the listing agent.

- *Exclusive agency listing:* Under this less common type of listing, yours is the only agent who can sell your home within a specified time—but if you find a buyer yourself, the agent doesn't get a fee.
- *Open listing:* Your home may be listed with more than one agent, and you pay whichever agent finds a buyer. If you find a buyer yourself, you don't pay a fee.

Before you sign a listing contract, ask these questions:

- Is the fee arrangement clear?
- How long will the listing be in effect?
- How do you renew or cancel?

Improve "Curb Appeal"

Obviously, you want to entice buyers, and one way to do that is to make your home look as attractive as possible. Consider your home's exterior appearance: would you stop for a closer look? Also evaluate your home's interior from the buyer's perspective. Make improvements that are necessary or that enhance salability, but don't overdo it. You probably won't recover the cost of major improvements when you sell. Your real estate agent can advise you on whether the improvements you're considering are likely to return their cost.

Prepare a Data Sheet

Taking the time to write down specific information on a data sheet will help you set an asking price, interest buyers, and negotiate a selling price. Include the home's age and size (number and dimensions of rooms and approximate overall square footage), the size of the lot, major improvements and repairs, type of heating system, estimated taxes, utility costs, zoning restrictions, availability of public transportation, and nearby facilities such as schools and shops. Also describe the type of ownership: Is your home a single- or multiple-family residence, a condominium, or a planned unit development (PUD)?

Advertise

If you're using a real estate agent, he or she will take care of advertising. If you're selling on your own, place ads in the local newspapers (weekend editions usually generate a greater response). Put a "For Sale" sign in front of your home if municipal ordinances permit, and ask your friends to be alert for potential buyers.

Set an Asking Price

Setting an asking price takes thought. Underprice, and you'll sacrifice money; overprice, and you could scare away buyers.

To find out what your home is worth, check prices of comparable homes in your area. Get an estimate of your home's value from your real estate agent. You may also be able to get listings of sales in your area from title insurance companies, either free or for a small fee.

Once you've established a fair market value, you may decide to price your home 3 to 5 percent above that figure to allow room for negotiations. If you're trying to sell your home quickly, you may want to lower the price. Make sure to determine the minimum price you'll accept, below which you won't negotiate.

If your present lender requires a prepayment premium (a charge for paying off your loan early before it matures), consider adding that to your price.

How to Show the Home

If you're using an agent, you should stay out of the way when the agent shows the home. The agent knows what to say, and what not to say. Also, a potential buyer may hesitate to ask a pivotal question for fear of offending you.

If you're showing it yourself, first hand out a copy of your data sheet. Try to start and end the tour with strong points, and let buyers take their time looking.

If your home is a condominium or in a planned unit development (PUD), state law typically requires that you also show prospective buyers copies of any homeowners' association rules governing your property.

Disclosure Statement

Some states (California, for instance) require you to fill out a statement in which you must make certain disclosures to buyers about the condition of your property. You may be required to disclose defects or malfunctions of your home's basic systems and components. In addition, you may be required to describe any circumstances about the property that may pose a problem to buyers, such as termites, neighborhood noise, drainage problems, or property shared with adjoining land owners.

Under such laws, even if you're selling your home "as is"—which means that you won't pay to repair any problems—you must inform the buyer of any defects you're aware of in order to protect yourself from legal problems after the sale. You can get a copy of the required disclosure statement from your real estate agent.

Arranging Financing

The buyer usually arranges the financing to purchase a home, but, depending on your timetable and the housing market, you may have to help out. Consider these possibilities.

Assumptions.   The buyer may be able to assume (take over) your present loan at a below-market interest rate. (Below-market loans may be subject to special tax treatment. Consult your tax adviser for more information.) Since federal law permits lenders to make most loans nonassumable, you'll need to ask your lender whether the buyer can assume your loan and interest rate. Find out what conditions your lender would set and whether you're liable for repaying the loan if the buyer defaults.

Buy Downs.   You or the buyer may be able to pay the lending institution an amount to buy down (lower) the interest rate on the buyer's loan for a specified period, typically one to five years. Lower initial monthly payments may help the buyer qualify for the loan.

Acting as Lender.   If you're willing to wait for payment, you could act as the buyer's lender and provide seller financing. The advantages are that you may find a buyer more easily and may receive higher interest from the loan than from other types of investments. You and the buyer can negotiate on the interest rate, repayment period (usually three to ten years), and all other loan terms. The main disadvantage is the risk that the buyer won't pay you as agreed, and you could end up with the hassle and cost of a lawsuit.

There are other financing arrangements you may want to consider. If you've almost paid off your loan, or if you own your home outright, you might give the buyer a loan secured by a first deed of trust on your house. The buyer borrows from you the difference between the purchase price of the house and the down payment, making monthly payments to you at an agreed-upon interest rate.

If the buyer is assuming your loan or taking out a new one, he or she may need additional financing for the down payment. You might take back (provide the buyer with) a loan secured by a second deed of trust. If the home is sold later to meet the buyer's credit obligations under the first deed of trust, you'll be paid only after the holder of any prior deed is paid.

Because the lender's risk is greater, a loan secured by a second deed of trust usually has a higher interest rate than one secured by a first. Before you consider this arrangement, check with the buyer's lender; some lenders don't permit second loans.

Your lender or a qualified real estate agent can explain seller financing and other types of loan arrangements. Be sure to consult an attorney specializing in real estate law before you make any agreements.

Completing the Sale

Negotiations.   A real estate agent will handle direct negotiations for you. If you're involved in the financing, you also may want your attorney present. In general, you and the buyer negotiate—in writing—the price and terms of the buyer's offer until both of you agree or one of you stops the negotiations.

Points.   If the buyer arranges for a loan insured by the Federal Housing Administration (FHA) or guaranteed by the Veterans Administration (VA), you may be asked to pay all or part of a loan fee, usually called *points*. This is a one-time fee charged by lenders to compensate for the lower interest rate on these loans. FHA points are negotiable between you and the seller; VA points are paid by the seller. One-time loan fees charged on conventional mortgages also may be referred to as points.

The Purchase Contract.   Your real estate agent can help you draw up the purchase contract, which states the price and all other terms of the sale.

According to law, no agreement for the sale of real estate can be enforced unless it's in writing. Although your agent or attorney can assist you with this contract, you should understand it thoroughly. Look over the contract carefully to make sure it covers all the sale conditions you want included.

Earlier in the chapter, we described these conditions from the viewpoint of the buyer. Here they are again, with you as the seller in mind:

- The closing costs you'll pay and those the buyer will pay
- The date the buyer will qualify for his or her loan
- An itemized list describing furnishings, appliances, and other personal property the sale includes and excludes

- The date on which the buyer will make a final inspection before the sale is finalized
- The date the buyer will take possession of the home

If you're selling on your own, you can buy sample purchase contract forms at a stationery store or copy them from books on selling homes. Remember that a sample contract may not contain all the necessary provisions. Before you sign any contract, it's a good idea to check with a real estate attorney.

The Deposit.   As we described in discussing the purchase of a house, the buyer makes a deposit—earnest money—when you and the buyer sign the agreement. The amount can be whatever you and the buyer agree on, but the larger the deposit, the greater your assurance the buyer will complete the deal. The contract should specify whether you or the buyer will have the right to keep part or all of the deposit if the sale falls through. This may depend on why the sale wasn't completed.

Once the purchase agreement is signed, the final process is the same as we described for buying a house. When all sale conditions are met, the money and documents are exchanged to complete the sale.

Tax Considerations.   When you sell your home, you may have to pay federal and state income taxes on any gain (profit) you make. If your home qualifies as your principal residence, federal income tax on the gain will be deferred if you purchase or build—and occupy—another home within two years of the sale. The new home must qualify as your principal residence and cost more than the adjusted sale price of your old home. You also may be eligible for a once-in-a-lifetime exclusion from federal and state income taxes, depending on the tax law provisions at the time.

Seller-financing arrangements may affect how your profit is taxed. Because the tax consequences can be complex, consult your tax adviser or attorney. For more information on tax considerations, read Publication 523, "Tax Information on Selling or Buying Your Home," which you can obtain from the Internal Revenue Service.

Buying or selling a home is the biggest transaction most of us will ever be involved in, so it pays—both financially and in peace of mind—to have a command of the basics. In the next chapter, we look at another potentially big-ticket transaction: home improvements.

Chapter Eleven

Planning Home Improvements

Making changes in the house where you live can be a preferable alternative to moving; you can keep what you like about your home while adding or rearranging space to make it match your needs.

In this chapter, we'll discuss the things you need to consider. Many of them apply to making major repairs as well as improvements.

BEFORE YOU BEGIN HOME IMPROVEMENTS

Like just about every other topic in this book, home improvements, if they're done wisely, take careful planning. Let's look at what you need to find out about, and what decisions you need to make, before you plunge into a home improvement project.

Check Out Restrictions and Effects

If you're contemplating a major change in your home, you'll want to consider immediately whether there are legal restrictions and whether the change will affect your property taxes. That doesn't usually apply to repairs, but it probably does apply to the addition of a family room or a bathroom.

Check out the project you have in mind with your local tax assessor and the local building department. Your tax assessor can advise you about the tax consequences, and the local building department can tell you whether approvals are needed and how to go about getting them. You may need a *zoning variance*—permission for a project that wouldn't be allowed otherwise.

There also may be restrictions imposed by your homeowners' association or by the agreement with your condominium or planned unit development (PUD). Check your own mortgage loan agreement, too, to see whether it places any restrictions on you.

Ask the agent who holds your homeowner's policy what effect, if any, the change will have on your insurance. Also think about the effect of the change on your home's resale value, and discuss the matter with your real estate agent. You may assume that you'll get the cost of a swimming pool back when you resell, for example, but that's not necessarily true: a prospective owner may not want one.

Don't over-improve in relation to the value of other houses in your neighborhood. If you'd have to price your home above the general range to recover the cost of an elaborate remodeling job, you might have difficulty selling the home later on.

Deciding Who Will Do the Work

You can tackle the job yourself, or you can call in professionals to help with detailed planning and construction. For an idea of what's involved, consider these factors:

- While being the "owner-builder" can save you money on certain projects, be careful that you don't overestimate your skills or underestimate the time a project will take.
- If you decide to do some of the work and hire licensed subcontractors only for the rest, you might be required to provide worker's compensation insurance. Find out by contacting your insurance agent.
- As the owner-builder, you'll be responsible for scheduling work assignments and supervising construction—time-consuming tasks that are sometimes better left to a professional.
- If you require financing for your project, your lender will carefully consider your qualifications for the job before approving your loan.

So, if the project would take more skill or time than you have, look for professionals to do the work.

Drawing the Plans

You can get a good idea of what you'd like by making your own rough sketches. To prepare the final plans and specifications, you'll need a draftsperson, building designer, architect, or contractor. Besides preparing the finished drawings, a draftsperson or building designer also may coordinate engineering surveys and apply for building permits and zoning variances. Or an architect can take over the entire project, including reviewing the work for you.

Many contracting and remodeling firms will prepare plans and specifications as part of their estimating service. If you later decide to hire the firm to do the work, the cost of the plans may be deducted from the job price.

Getting Estimates

When you have decided what you want done and how much you can spend, you're ready for estimates of the project's cost. Get at least three estimates in writing. Make sure the estimates cover identical plans and specifications so you can compare prices accurately.

Ask for a detailed description of materials. It's a good idea, for example, to ask that specific grades of lumber or even brand names and model numbers of appliances be included in the estimate.

Read each estimate carefully. Don't sign anything unless you completely understand the document and agree to all its terms. Any bid or estimate you sign may become the contract. Scrutinize any bid that is substantially lower than the others to make sure the contractor hasn't made a mistake or left out part of the work.

WORKING WITH A CONTRACTOR

You'll want to choose your contractor with care, of course; in addition, there are a number of things you should know about working with one.

Look for a contractor with an established reputation in your community. If your project calls for only one type of job (plumbing, for instance), you can look for a contractor licensed in that specialty. For work that requires a combination of skills, such as kitchen remodeling, you'll probably need a licensed general building contractor.

Your best sources of referrals are friends and neighbors, local builders' and contractors' associations, and your architect or interior designer, if you've hired one. You also may want to contact your local Better Business Bureau, Chamber of Commerce, and any public or private consumer complaint agencies to find out whether a contractor you're considering has a good record.

For any major project, ask the contractors on your list for the following information:

- How long the contractor has been in business.
- The names and addresses of homeowners for whom the contractor has worked in the past year. Contact these clients to find out

whether the work was satisfactory and whether the job was completed on time and within budget. If possible, arrange to see the work yourself.

• References from suppliers, subcontractors, and business associations.

• The coverage of the contractor's general liability and worker's compensation insurance. Make sure you and your property are adequately protected against any property damage or accidents that could occur as a result of the construction.

Understanding Liens

If the contractor fails to pay subcontractors, suppliers, and others involved in your project, you could be exposed to significant financial risk. In many states, contractors, subcontractors, and others who furnish labor and materials for your home improvement project can file a claim against your home if they're not paid. This claim, known as a *mechanic's lien*, means that your property could be sold and the proceeds used to pay off what's owed.

Paying your contractor in full won't guarantee a lien-free project. If the contractor doesn't pay the others involved, they still can file a mechanic's lien against your home. As a result, you might end up paying a bill twice to avoid a claim on your property.

Be wary of signing a contract that establishes your home as security for repayment of a home improvement loan. If you don't make payments as agreed, the creditor may sell your property to pay your debt.

"Preliminary Notice."   After work begins on your project, you might receive *preliminary notices* from subcontractors and material suppliers. These notices don't indicate that a lien has been filed against your property, but they do alert you that the subcontractors or suppliers may have lien rights if they're not paid.

Unconditional Lien Releases.   Require your contractor to furnish you with an unconditional lien release from any person or firm that sends you a preliminary notice. This release is a formal document acknowledging that the subcontractor or supplier has been paid and the mechanic's lien rights waived. While in most cases this release will protect you, make sure you document that the supplier or subcontractor actually was paid.

Ways to Avoid Trouble

While most contractors are honest and competent professionals, some are not. The most common complaints against contractors concern inaccurate estimates, unfinished projects, and shoddy workmanship. But in some cases, homeowners who refuse to pay for poor work or faulty products are threatened with mechanic's liens.

Selecting your contractor carefully, following the guidelines suggested earlier, should help you avoid home improvement fraud. Here are a few additional tips:

- Don't let door-to-door salespeople pressure you into buying their materials or services.
- Be wary of a person who promises extremely low prices or offers bargains on materials that "just happen to be in the truck."
- Avoid any contractor who offers to use your home as a model and promises you a commission or kickback for any customers you refer. In some states, it's illegal for a contractor to make such an offer.

Write a Good Contract

A clearly worded contract, spelling out all the conditions on which you and your contractor have agreed, is your best assurance that the work will be done to your satisfaction. These are the points you'll want your contract to include:

- The name, address, and license number of the contractor, and the name and registration number of any salesperson who solicited or negotiated the contract.
- The approximate dates when the work will begin and be substantially complete.
- A description of the work to be done and the materials to be used. The description can include blueprints and specifications lists.
- Specific warranties promised by the contractor.
- Specification of who is responsible for cleaning up after the work is complete.
- The total price of the job, together with a breakdown of all the costs for materials, labor, and so on.
- A schedule of the payments and the amount of each payment.
- Specification of who is responsible for obtaining lien releases.
- A special "Notice to Owner," which explains the state's lien laws and your rights and responsibilities as a homeowner.
- A notice stating that you have the right to require the contractor to obtain a performance bond. (We discuss bonding momentarily.)
- Any additional terms needed to specify exactly what you expect.

You also might want to include a clause that lets you retain a percentage (ordinarily 10 percent) of each payment or of the total job until all the terms of the contract have been met and the lien period has expired.

After the contract is drawn, make sure you understand and agree to all the terms. Don't mistakenly sign an estimate that could become a contract or any document that has blank spaces. If you have any concerns about the contract, consult an attorney before signing. If you're borrowing funds for the project, make sure your lender agrees with the payment schedule.

Once you've signed the contract, get a copy for yourself. After the contract is signed, you and your contractor may decide on changes in specifications, materials, or equipment. Make sure these revisions and any price changes are added to the contract, and keep a signed copy.

Right to Cancel

If you sign a home improvement contract for $25 or more *in your home*, you have the right to cancel it—the right of *rescission*—within three business days of signing. Furthermore, any time you sign a credit contract or loan for personal, family, or household purposes that involves a lien against your home—regardless of the amount of the contract or where you sign it—federal law gives you the right to cancel the contract or loan within three business days of signing.

Contractors and creditors must notify you of the three-day cancellation period when you sign a contract. If you decide to cancel, call the contractor or creditor, and follow up with a written notice within the three business days. Use registered mail so that you'll have a record of the date.

Bonding

Consider asking your contractor to obtain a payment and completion bond, especially for costly projects. (Your lender may require it.) The bond protects you from the contractor's failure to pay suppliers or subcontractors or to complete the work. Usually the contractor buys the bond, which typically covers the full amount of the contract, and adds the bonding fee to the price of the job.

Controlling the Funds

Instead of you or your lender making payments on a large or complicated project, you can hire a licensed funding control company to handle the payments. You or the lender gives the money to the funding control company, which in turn pays the contractor, subcontractors, and material suppliers upon receipt of proper invoices and unconditional lien releases.

Look for a funding control company, specializing in construction, that will determine whether the estimate is realistic and inspect the work as it progresses. Funding control companies usually charge a small percentage of the contract price for their services. Ask your lender for names of approved funding control companies in your area.

Keep a Job File

As a protective measure, keep a file of all papers related to your project. Include the signed contract and any change orders, plans and specifications, bills and invoices, payment receipts, lien releases, and all correspondence with your contractor.

In addition, keep a list of subcontractors who work on your project. Note which part of the work each one does and the time taken to complete the job. Also keep a record of deliveries made by suppliers, including the name of the supplier, the date of the delivery, and a description of the material supplied. If you keep good records, you can check lien releases from subcontractors and suppliers against your list and verify who has been paid.

Notice of Completion

For further protection, you or someone acting on your behalf (such as the general contractor) can file a "Notice of Completion" with your county recorder. This statement, which verifies that the project has been completed to your satisfaction, should be filed within ten days after the job is finished.

Once the notice is recorded, subcontractors, laborers, and suppliers have 30 days in which to file any lien; the general contractor has 60 days. If you don't submit a completion notice, the filing period for liens is extended to 90 days.

How to Handle Problems

If you're not satisfied with the work performed, talk with your contractor first. If the contractor refuses to correct the problem, you can file a complaint with your local contractors' license board or your local building department. You also may want to consult an attorney.

BORROWING MONEY

If the cost of your project puts you in the market for a loan, it's best to start your shopping early and determine what terms are available before you sign a contract.

As we discussed in Chapter 4, you can compare different lenders' costs by looking at their annual percentage rate (APR) and finance charge. The APR states the cost of your loan per year, expressed as a percentage. It includes interest and can include certain other charges, such as loan fees or insurance. Find out what's included in the APR you're quoted.

With a fixed rate loan, the APR remains the same for the entire term. With an adjustable or variable rate loan, the APR can increase or decrease at specified intervals.

The finance charge is the total dollar amount you pay for the loan. It includes interest and also may include other charges, such as a loan fee.

Find out about any additional costs, such as appraisal and title report fees.

Before approving a loan for your project, the lender will evaluate your creditworthiness and may require you to submit a personal financial statement. If you're self-employed, you'll be asked to provide profit-and-loss statements for the past few years. If you have income other than wages, you may be required to provide income tax returns.

Personal Loans

You're granted a personal loan on the basis of your good credit history and your ability and willingness to repay. This type of loan may be suitable if you need only a few thousand dollars and can repay the loan in a fairly short time, such as one to four years. The lender may require you to secure the loan with collateral, such as a savings account.

Most institutional lenders—such as banks, savings and loan associations (S&Ls), credit unions, finance companies, and insurance companies—make personal loans. Credit unions lend to members only; life insurance companies lend to those who hold policies with sufficient cash value.

Home Improvement Loans

In general, home improvement loans offer larger loan amounts, longer repayment periods, and sometimes lower interest rates than personal loans. The institutional lenders just mentioned (except life insurance companies) and stock brokerage firms may offer these loans.

When you apply for a home improvement loan, you'll probably be asked to bring copies of the contractor's estimate or contract and any building permits needed for the job.

Home Equity Loans

If you need money for home improvement and other major expenses, you might consider securing a loan with the equity in your home. Your equity is the current value of your home, minus what you owe on it. Under the Tax Reform Act of 1986, the interest you pay on a home equity loan can be tax-deductible, which is not true of a home improvement loan.

A home equity loan usually has longer repayment periods than a home improvement loan. Stretching out the repayment period can lower your monthly payments, but it increases the *total* cost of the loan. The amount you can borrow depends on the lender's policy and appraisal of the property's value, the amount of your equity, and your creditworthiness.

Banks, S&Ls, credit unions, finance companies, and stock brokerages can make home equity loans. Terms and requirements vary, but in all cases, you secure the equity loan with a deed of trust, pledging your house.

Home Equity Credit Line

Some banks, S&Ls, and stock brokerage firms will grant you a revolving line of credit for as much as 75 percent of the equity you have in your home. The big advantage is flexibility: once you establish your credit line, you write your own loans by check and pay interest only on the amount you borrow. Fees generally are lower than for a home equity loan, but the interest rate may be higher.

It's important to remember that you pledge your house as security for your credit spending under this arrangement. If you overspend and fall behind on your payments, you risk losing your home.

Refinancing

With the equity in your home, you can refinance—that is, take out a new home loan based on your home's increased value. Then you can pay off existing loans and use the surplus for home improvements.

You may be charged a prepayment premium for paying off your present loan ahead of time and other fees for such services as processing the new loan, title insurance, and property appraisal. In addition, the new loan will be made at current interest rates. If current rates are higher than the rate on your present loan, you could wind up paying significantly more in interest over the life of the loan. Remember, however, that this interest can be tax-deductible.

Contractor Financing

Some contractors offer financing by arrangement with lending institutions. You negotiate the rates and terms of the credit contract with the contractor, who usually assigns (sells) the contract to a third party, generally a lender such as a bank or other financial institution. Once the contract is assigned, you make payments to that third party.

Financing of Rural Homes

The federal Farmers Home Administration (FmHA) makes home improvement loans directly to eligible farmers and other residents of designated rural areas. For further information, contact your state office of the Farmers Home Administration, or write to the Farmers Home Administration, 14th Street and Independence, S.W., Washington, DC 20250.

Fixing Up an Older Home

You may be able to obtain a low-interest loan for the purchase and renovation of an older home through one of several federal, state, or local government programs. Generally, your eligibility depends on your income and the home's location.

To find out more about these programs, you can contact the U.S. Department of Housing and Urban Development (HUD), listed in the white pages of your telephone directory under "United States Government." You can also contact your local community development office or planning department.

If your house has an important history or is an example of a classic architectural style, you may qualify for a grant or an exemption on your federal tax return that will cover part of your renovation expense. For more information, contact the National Trust of Historic Preservation, Washington, DC.

TAX CONSIDERATIONS

If you sell your home for more than it cost, you may have to pay income tax on some or all of the gain (profit) you make. However, the cost of any major improvements you've made affects the calculation of that gain and may benefit you at tax time as well. Keep accurate records of all improvements; they can add up to a substantial sum in a few years and save you tax dollars after you sell.

For detailed information on how to figure your gain, obtain Publication 523, "Tax Information on Selling or Buying Your Home," from your nearest Internal Revenue Service office, or call (800) 424-1040 to request a copy.

You may also want to consult your attorney or tax adviser to help you with these calculations.

Chapter Twelve

How to Get Information and Advice

You don't have to go it alone in money matters, and the complexities are such that you probably shouldn't try. Happily, there are plenty of people available to help you, some for free, others for a share of the action you generate, still others for a specific fee.

We're talking here about accountants, bankers, financial planners, insurance brokers, lawyers, real estate brokers and stockbrokers, plus those in government and nonprofit offices.

It can make all the difference in the world if you know how to make good use of people who really know their business, but many people have trouble doing this. They feel intimidated by experts and fear they'll be taken advantage of. Further, they find it difficult to assert their own financial interests effectively and hesitate to press a question or request.

It's important to make certain that you are not persuaded to do something that's against your better judgment, or to take action you don't fully understand. And that means finding ways to deal with experts comfortably and with confidence.

Toward that end, we have asked for help from psychological consultants at Psychotherapy Associates of Collegeville, Pennsylvania—on the subject of asserting yourself. They developed a mini-quiz you can take to get a feel for your tendencies, and they offer advice on how to use what you learn from it in your dealings with financial experts.

Even if you're already familiar with some of the literature on assertiveness or don't usually have a problem asserting your interests effectively, recognize that dealing with financial matters can be different.

Money can cast a special spell. (And it's not all imaginary: the arcane language of finance and the imposing architecture of banks and stock exchanges were undoubtedly intended, in part, to sharpen the division between people who have money and understand it and the rest of us.)

Still, if you want to skip the quiz, turn to the section "What This All Means" (p. 197). If you want to bypass the assertiveness discussion entirely, proceed to "Dealing with Experts" (p. 200).

MINI-QUIZ: ASSESSING ASSERTIVENESS

Instructions: The questions in the following quiz are straightforward. Their purpose is simply to help you learn something about yourself. There are no "right" or "wrong" answers, and there are no trick questions.

Please take out a ruled pad. Create three columns. Label the first column "Yes," the second "Maybe/Sometimes," and the third "No." Number 22 lines down the left margin.

After reading each question, put a check mark in the column that reflects your answer to that question.

1. I find it hard to say no to requests people make of me.
2. I am reluctant to interrupt and terminate a telephone solicitation that comes at a bad time.
3. I generally second-guess my opinion when it is challenged.
4. When I'm asked for my opinion, I try to guess what the other person wants to hear.
5. I usually don't protest when someone cuts in front of me in line.
6. If someone asked to borrow a new book I hadn't read yet, I'd probably lend it.
7. If I discover I've been mischarged, I'm reluctant to correct the error.
8. When there is something wrong with my food in a restaurant, I usually don't complain to the server.
9. If a salesperson has spent a lot of time with me, I find it hard not to buy something.
10. I feel that people frequently take advantage of me.
11. I often worry about hurting other people's feelings, even at the expense of my own.
12. I don't like to open conversations at a party.
13. I put off making calls to business establishments.

14. I would rather apply for a job in writing than by phone.
15. I sometimes keep unwanted merchandise rather than return it.
16. I hesitate to ask questions, for fear of sounding stupid.
17. I don't like to negotiate prices with salespeople.
18. If people are talking during a movie, I'm reluctant to ask them to stop.
19. I'm reluctant to interrupt and ask questions when I don't understand.
20. I often wish afterwards that I had spoken up.
21. I tend to accept the opinions of experts, even when I disagree.
22. I've bought clothing that didn't suit my tastes because the salesperson said it looked good.

Scoring: To score your answers, add up the check marks from the "Yes" column and record this number. Then add up the checks in the "Maybe/Sometimes" column, and record that number. Multiply the number in the "Yes" column by 2, and add the result to the number in the "Maybe/Sometimes" column to get your score. ("No" answers are zero.) Here's how to interpret your score:

0–5: Highly assertive

6–19: Moderately assertive

20 or over: Nonassertive

If you scored in the nonassertive range, or above the center of the moderate range (above 13, say), then you tend to be somewhat passive, which is the case with the majority of people. Most of us have at least some difficulty asserting ourselves.

If you scored in the highly assertive range, or close to it, you're probably effectively assertive, which is good, as we discuss in a moment. If you scored zero, though, you may lean toward being aggressive rather than effectively assertive, which is *not* good.

WHAT THIS ALL MEANS

With the other personality characteristics we discuss in this book, we usually encourage you simply to recognize the way you are and act accordingly. But this is different.

It has been pretty well established that assertiveness is a good thing to have. Moreover, unlike some personal characteristics, assertiveness is something psychologists say we can change and control. It's merely a matter of learning some new skills and practicing them until we're good at it. They also tell us that it's a skill we can use, or not, depending on the situation; we can deal with our pastor differently, if we choose, from the way we deal with a telephone solicitor.

To understand assertiveness better, let's get some terms down. Think of a spectrum where "passive" is at one end, "aggressive" is at the other, and "assertive" is in the middle.

Psychologists describe "passive behavior" as acting in a way that enables your rights to be violated by another—for example, not resisting when someone takes advantage of you, being afraid to make a request, being afraid to say no.

They describe "assertive behavior" as standing up for your rights in a way that does not violate the rights of others.

And they describe "aggressive behavior" as standing up for your rights in a way that *does* violate the rights of others.

No one is all one or the other, in all situations. But in most situations, being assertive—without aggressiveness—is the most effective way to be.

When we're in the passive mode, we're saying "I must be nice to people or they won't like me." We find ourselves agreeing to something we don't really want to do, or we hesitate to press a request. When we have an opinion different from others', we keep it to ourselves—or even pretend to agree when we don't.

Our culture teaches us to act this way. But most of us don't like ourselves much when we do this, and we don't get what we want and need from other people.

When we're aggressive, we're saying "I'm tough to show that I'm better than other people." We get loud, demanding, push other people around, strive to win in a way that makes it clear that someone lost. This kind of behavior sometimes gets results, but it's hard work and it alienates others, which means that no one is going to want to make things any easier for us.

But when we're assertive, we're saying "I have a right to try to get what I want, and I'd like to work with you to get it." We're not trying to win approval, but neither are we trying to win a battle. Assertive behavior generally feels better, and we're far more likely to get what we want than when we are either passive or aggressive.

For the purposes of this book, the best thing about the assertive mode is that it allows us to operate comfortably in an area where we aren't expert. It helps us to relax and accept a degree of dependence on others, even with something as vital to us as our money, while at the same time asserting our wants and needs.

By contrast, in the passive mode, we may be so concerned with not offending our stockbroker that we end up buying something really dumb. In the aggressive mode, we may be so concerned with proving we're tougher than our stockbroker that we end up buying something really dumb.

Psychologists say that to become assertive, many of us have to start by freeing ourselves from attitudes created by our upbringing. For instance, here are some of the things you may have been taught:

• It's selfish to put your own needs first.

Comment: You have the right to take care of your needs, as long as you don't hurt someone else in the process. Moreover, financial professionals assume, from the minute you walk in the door, that you're looking out for Number One. They're happy to help you do that, especially since that helps them take care of their own Number One. We'll talk in a minute about ways to make both of you happy.

• If you're not "nice," people won't like you.

Comment: It's your choice whose approval or affection you seek. You have the right not to worry about others' approval. In particular, consider some self-psyching before going in to sit down with an attorney or accountant. Tell yourself: "I'm here for help. I'm paying for it. I don't really care whether he likes me. I don't care whether he thinks I'm smart. I don't care whether he approves of me. I just want good advice, and I'll concentrate on that."

• You aren't supposed to react emotionally, to be against something just because you don't like it; you have to have good reasons for your preferences and choices.

Comment: You don't have to justify your emotions to other people. If an investment doesn't feel good to you, then it doesn't (and most stockbrokers will respect that). If a house doesn't appeal to you, the real estate agent may press for a reason, saying it would help her in selecting other candidates for you. You can decide whether to try to analyze your feelings or to say "That's just how I feel about it."

• You shouldn't disagree with people.

Comment: You have the right to disagree and to say so. With experts, you may tend to defer to their superior, specialized knowledge, but that doesn't mean taking things on faith or not challenging things you don't understand. You have the right to require experts to convince you in language you understand. You may find yourself saying, "That may well be good general policy, but I'm not sure it applies to my situation, because . . ." And you might be right.

• When someone gives you advice, you should accept it, because the other person knows better than you do.

Comment: You have the right to question advice and the right to ignore it. Even if you're sorry later you'll have made your own decision. You won't have done something you felt forced to do by interpersonal pressure.

DEALING WITH EXPERTS:
EMPATHY, CANDOR, AND ACCOMMODATION

Our psychologist consultants offer these three elements to guide us in developing effective assertive relationships with the people involved in our financial life: empathy, candor, and accommodation.

Start with empathy, or the ability to take the other person's perspective and identify with his or her situation. In particular, understand the experts' stake in doing business with you, and the pressures on them. For instance:

- Your banker wants to help, but one way or another, what she does for you has to benefit the bank.

- Your stockbroker and real estate agent live on commissions. They're not in business *just* to serve your needs: *they* need to make a sale.

It may seem strange to stress that *you* need to cultivate empathy toward experts; after all, you're the one who wants help. But you need to understand how they operate so that you can work within their limitations. And letting them know you understand will help you establish good faith on both sides.

That's not to say that you must subordinate your needs to theirs. Tell yourself: "It's not my responsibility to protect her against me; if I ask for too much, push too hard, make an unreasonable request, she'll let me know. That's her problem, not mine."

The second element of a successful relationship with experts is candor. Spell out your needs clearly, and be open about conflicts between your interests and theirs. Tell your real estate agent: "Look, I know you don't like to spend time with someone who's still just looking, but I have to start somewhere."

Third, pursue accommodating action. In other words, assume the responsibility for proposing a course of action that meets your needs while taking theirs into account. Thus, you might say to your real estate agent, "I'm not in a terrible rush; I'll let you suggest the times that are easiest for you, as long as we can get it done by the first of the month." Or if a session with your stockbroker or banker isn't going where you want it to go, intervene. Press your needs. If he says he doesn't know the answer to one of your questions, you can say, "It's very important to me; is there someone we could call to find out?"

Let's apply these principles to some dealings with experts and specialists. We'll start with bankers, since almost everyone needs a bank. Much of what is said about how to work with bankers, including what their motivations are and how to make the relationship work, can be extended to apply to other experts and specialists—stockbrokers, accountants, attorneys, real estate agents, insurance brokers, financial planners.

WORKING WITH BANKERS

In this section, we'll use "banker" for convenience. The person you're working with can be at a savings and loan, or at your credit union—wherever you do your banking.

Let's take an empathy reading for this relationship: what's in it for your banker?

Your banker is judged by the amount of business he or she generates—numbers of accounts, interest income, loans made, credit cards sold. Your banker wants to do business with you and is willing to invest time with you toward that end. The banker knows that people just starting out are future candidates for car loans, house loans, CDs, and investments. And the level of their accounts will rise as their income and assets grow.

Many banks are attempting to fortify the relationship by making it beneficial to you to bunch your business with them and keep it there. As an incentive, many offer lower fees or better interest rates for those who give them all their business.

Getting Started

If you're just starting out, go see the person responsible for accounts and explain exactly what your situation is. Make your best estimate as to the balance you expect to be able to maintain, the number of checks you expect to write. The account representative will tell you the best way to meet your needs at that bank. The bank is looking for a happy customer who will be there over the long haul.

Ask about the bank's other services, for future reference. Ask why it would be in your interest to do all your banking there. Give the bank every chance to make its case to you, and apply the principles we've described: press questions until you get an answer you understand, and test the answers against your own needs. For example, maybe you want to ask the bank to compare its services and charges with those of competitors; you have a right to do that. It can be a good way to understand your options better, and you may discover that a competitor *would* be better for you.

Applying for a Loan

If you're thinking of a major purchase and need a loan, you may be intimidated by the feeling that you're a supplicant asking institutions to give you some of their money. A little assertiveness psyching may be helpful here. If banks don't lend money, they don't *make* money; they want you as much as you want them. If you have the required income and the necessary credit rating (evidence that you pay bills on time), you're in. Whether you get a loan is *not* based on your charm or the deference you show your banker, or how "nice" you are to the loan officer.

It's true that in marginal cases, the loan officer exercises personal judgment, so let's look at some of the empathy factors that operate here. When bankers approve a loan that doesn't meet the usual guidelines, they're sticking out their necks. And others are watching. Such loans are posted and reviewed routinely. A banker can lose his or her job if too many of these "exceptions" turn sour.

What does that tell you? First, bankers won't run a risk simply because they *like* you. So why *would* a banker run such a risk? Bankers know they have to keep generating new business. They have to consider whether you represent a future prospect who will otherwise go to a competitor. Bankers who take no risks at all eventually go broke. So bankers look at your character and economic potential: despite your limited assets now, are you the kind of person who will take this debt seriously and pay it off (and be appreciative, bringing more business to the bank in future years)?

When to Apply.   You may feel you need to wait until you're close to a decision before you should bother the bank's loan officers. Not so. A substantial loan is serious money, and that makes you a serious interest to them. They're happy to meet with you early and willing to educate you, in hopes that you'll end up taking the loan from them.

As we noted in the chapter on home buying, it also can help you in the buying process, and strengthen you in the negotiating process to *know* that you qualify for a loan of a certain amount. (And knowing the upward limit of the amount you can borrow can keep you from overspending.)

Start with your own bank and make an appointment. The people at the bank will be more helpful because you're a customer. Your own bank may offer you a lower rate than it would a non-customer if you agree to have your loan payment transferred automatically from a deposit account there. (Or, if you call on another bank, say that you want to do all your banking at one place—assuming that's true—and that you'd move your accounts if you got your loan here. You're attractive in both roles, as a customer your bank wants to keep and as a new customer another bank would like to gain. Make you feel important?)

Explain that you're just starting the loan process and want to know what your choices are. Lay out your finances with candor, and be prepared with any details.

Ask how the bank's rates and fees compare with those of other banks around. The loan officer will know and will probably give you reasons why, all things considered, you'd be better off with his or her bank when it comes time to get the loan. Listen to those reasons; they can be important. Later, if you've shopped around and find another institution with better rates, come back and give your bank a chance to match them. Don't worry that the people at the bank will take offense because you shopped around; they'll welcome a second shot at the loan. And even if they don't make that sale, they'll want to hold on to your other business.

Some loan officers can offer you extra services that can be very valuable. If you're looking for a residence, a loan officer may have advice about where to look, factors to consider, changes to investigate. Where there is something approximating the country banker of old, you may get a lead on a specific property, the best real estate company, a reasonable lawyer, a cheap title company. That kind of local expertise is a lot harder to find these days, and banks may have rules against their people making even informal endorsements. But where the equivalent of the country banker exists, they can provide very helpful, informed, and objective advice.

In the case of business loans, getting to the banker early is particularly important. When your idea is still a gleam, ask to see a loan officer and describe your intentions. Bankers very much want to be on the ground floor of plans such as these. They can give you advice on accumulating capital, building a line of credit, and testing your assumptions.

The happy fact is that they want you to succeed and will work hard with you so you do. They know that many of their most profitable accounts started exactly that way, and for most bankers, getting businesses started is the most satisfying part of the business they're in.

But don't expect business bankers to be equity investors in your deal. They want you, or others, to provide the bulk of the initial investment.

WORKING WITH STOCKBROKERS

Stockbrokers operate in many of the same ways bankers do. They want to create a relationship that will grow over time, and they will invest some time to make it work.

Stockbrokers have a much narrower base of income than bankers do, however, and it's necessary to understand that and other limitations on what they can do for you.

One broker was very forthright when presented with some complicated questions about financial planning. "Look," he said, "I don't want to pretend that I'm something that I'm not. I'm not a financial planner. I sell stocks. That's what I do, and I don't make money unless I sell something. But I would like to be in this with you for the long haul, and I can spend some time now in hopes that the time will come when we can do business together."

His view of the stockbroker relationship appears to be fairly typical. A broker can't afford to spend a lot of time with you unless it generates sales commissions, sooner or later. The ethical broker will not push you to trade when you don't want to, nor will an ethical broker try to steer you to securities that pay the highest broker commissions. Still, successful brokers never lose sight of their own bottom line, and it's good for you to remember that so you understand their reactions.

You might find yourself discussing your investment strategies with your stockbroker and wondering why he seems impatient with your clever plans for stashing some money in the high-rate certificates of deposit your bank just offered. You might misinterpret this lack of enthusiasm as meaning the CDs aren't smart investments. Actually, his wandering attention could be due to nothing more mysterious than the fact that he isn't going to make money off CDs you buy from your bank. If you take your money out of the funds he's managing for you and put them into CDs, you've reduced his commissions and you've made yourself less important to him. Fair enough.

WORKING WITH REAL ESTATE AGENTS

As you deal with real estate agents, it's important to remind yourself where your interests are synonymous with theirs, and where they aren't.

If you're selling a house, the agent works for you and has the responsibility of seeing that you get as much for your property as possible. As discussed in Chapter 10, the fee and arrangements have been spelled out in writing at the outset.

If it's a multiple listing, as most are these days, you'll probably deal with several agents representing other real estate firms as well as your "own" agent. You may find yourself thinking of those others as representing the buyers they bring in, but they aren't. They are paid by the seller—you—if their deal goes through. (They get a share of the fee that was set at the beginning.)

If you are *buying* a home, you may get the feeling—since the agent is being so helpful—that the agent is working for you. But don't forget that the agent is paid by the seller and is trying to get the price that seller seeks. Not only is that the agent's commitment to the seller, but the agent has a financial stake in a high price, since the commission is a percentage of the purchase price.

These differences are blurred, however, by the fact that what the real estate agent wants most is simply to complete a sale, as quickly and easily as possible. The agent will work hard to get both parties together, and good agents are excellent facilitators, suggesting creative ways to resolve conflict. Theoretically, they should always be pushing for the highest price, but if there's a difference of, say, $3,000 in the asking and offering prices, the difference to the agent in a multiple-listing arrangement may be only $60. The agent might willingly sacrifice that $60 to get the deal settled and done.

Another factor that encourages the agent to help people agree—to work on both sides of the table—is the fact that the agent would like to do business later with either or both of you. If at all possible, the agent wants to leave everyone happy. Most depend heavily on referrals; they hope you are pleased enough to send others to them and that you'll remember their name when that opportunity arises. They also know from statistics that you're likely be back in the house-selling, house-buying mode every seven years.

For the same reason, real estate people have many good business reasons for keeping a relationship alive after the completion of the sale. If you liked them, why not encourage that? After all, you went through an important experience together. You may find them a knowledgeable source of useful information and advice: a good contractor for a roof job, a suggestion on how to get a zoning change, thoughts about refinancing, estimates on trends in property values.

USING FEE-BASED ADVISERS

Of course, you can pay for advice and assistance directly. Attorneys and accountants typically operate on the basis of specific fees and charges related to the amount of work they do for you. That can make it easier for you to be clear about motivations: they are working for you, rather than taking their income from the size and nature of the transaction. This can give you better control over the relationship. You can make specific requests and estimate what the corresponding services will cost.

Many people, however, feel uncomfortable asking explanations about technical matters. They fear their questions will be interpreted as questioning the expert's competence, or they simply don't want to reveal their own ignorance.

Worse, they may hesitate to ask hard questions about fees and charges. Surrounded by the leather and oiled wood of an attorney's office, they may feel it's hardly the place for haggling over a few dollars.

If you have any of these reactions, some assertiveness psyching can help. Before you sit down with a prospective accountant or lawyer, remind yourself: "It's my money. I'm paying for help here. I want to make sure I get what I need, and I don't want to pay any more for it than I have to."

With these thoughts in mind, ask your prospective advisers to describe exactly how their fees operate. Do they charge a certain amount per hour? Is that amount only for the hours they spend with you in the room? How much is the charge for other hours of work they spend on your affairs? If someone more senior, or more junior, gets involved, what happens to the hourly rate? How about the cost of advice given over the telephone?

Ask them to give you a feel for what some specific tasks are likely to cost. The cost of preparing a will or a tax return can vary, but an attorney or accountant can give you a pretty good idea of what to expect and what factors drive up the cost.

Remember: these transactions and relationships may be new to you, but they aren't new to the professionals you're working with. They have been asked all these questions many times before. You're not being rude or putting anyone on the spot. If they're any good, they'll quickly put you at ease, encouraging you to ask questions. They want your trust, and you want to be able to give it. If you have the slightest suspicion that they would overcharge you on fees, you surely don't want to use them for decisions involving thousands of your dollars.

Many lawyers, financial planners, accountants, tax advisers, and other professionals have arrangements under which introductory consultations of 30 minutes or an hour are available at $25 or $50, or sometimes even free. These are opportunities to get acquainted and to find out what services would cost. You might get some specific advice, but you would probably do better to concentrate on using these first meetings as a shopping expedition.

Even if there isn't that kind of low-cost introduction, it can be useful for you to buy a short session specifically to check out costs and your compatibility with someone you're thinking of using.

If you feel that your prospective advisers' fees are simply more than you can afford, say so. Costs can be negotiable in terms of the amount of time you require, what you're willing to do yourself, and the level of expertise needed. Sometimes someone starting out will have a lower rate for people whose business they feel will grow.

MEETING WHILE THE METER'S RUNNING

This section presents some general guidelines for making the most of experts. The method it describes applies especially to attorneys and accountants (where the meter is ticking off dollars every minute you're using their services).

Do Your Homework

Before you talk to expert advisers, read some relevant literature and collect questions. Keying questions to literature from the expert's organization ("On page 3, you talk about . . .") can speed things up.

Think through your specific questions in advance; you might even rehearse them out loud. See how many of your questions you can answer yourself, saving the tough ones for the face-to-face meeting.

Prepare an Agenda

It's your money, so you want to make sure you get what you want out of any meetings or telephone conversations. Plan in advance to determine specifically what you want. Set the sequence of topics or questions. You'll probably want to start with the most important and work down to the least. Present a copy of the agenda to the person you're meeting, or send it in advance, and get a reaction. If the expert suggests a more useful arrangement, so much the better. Either way, you'll save time and money while ensuring that you come away from the meeting with the information you need.

Use the "Desired Outcomes" Method

People who make a living designing and running meetings have developed a method you can adapt to your one-on-one sessions. It's a four-part process that is easy to use and that works the very first time. Here's how to use it.

Before setting up a date to see someone, take a pad of paper and write these headings, each on a separate sheet:

1. Desired Outcomes
2. Preparation
3. Take-along
4. Action Recap

To illustrate how you'll use these sheets, let's say you're about to start house shopping, and you feel you should probably sit down with your banker. Before you make an appointment or drop in at the bank, prepare the four sheets.

Take out your Desired Outcomes sheet. Ask yourself, what do I want from this meeting with my banker? Jot down things as they come to mind, uncritically:

Desired Outcomes

Find out about loan rates.

Ask about qualifying.

Check on closing costs.

Are points deductible on income taxes?

Does that include everything? You think so? OK, now pick out the item on the list that's most important, and put a 1 beside it. If you get nothing else from the meeting, you want to be sure to get this. Then put a 2 beside the next most important, and so on.

Having a little problem? The list doesn't really get at what you're after? And what is *that*?

"Well, what I'd *really* like is for the banker to tell me I qualify for however much money I need and that he'll get me the best terms and best rates in town."

That's better. Let's rethink the meeting and see how close we can come to your (real) desired outcomes. Would the following be a realistic expectation?

"The banker tells me realistically how big a loan I can expect to get and what it would cost me." All right, then, rework the list. "Ask about qualifying" becomes

1. Determine how big a loan I can get.

"Find out about loan rates" becomes

2. What are his interest rates?

3. How do they compare?

4. What terms would be best for me?

"Check on closing costs" becomes

5. What would be my total costs?

"Are points deductible on income taxes?" You decide this one is your lowest priority; you'll ask only if there's an opening or everything else gets covered.

6. Are points deductible on income taxes?

You've converted a tentative, unfocused information-gathering meeting to an action-decision meeting with clear objectives. Thinking this way about desired outcomes will help with your "preparation" and "take-along" lists as well.

Now take out your Preparation sheet. Look at each desired outcome and ask what you need to do in advance to make sure the meeting can achieve its purpose, and note those things on your Preparation sheet. For instance, for

1. Determine how big a loan I can get.

You realize you'd better decide how much you *want* to borrow. On your Preparation sheet, you write:

1. Review budget.

You'll probably add some other items as well, such as "Check out tuition cost increases," "See whether Bill expects to repay his loan on time," "Think about when to replace the car," "Review stocks and CDs."

Let's look at your next three desired outcomes:

2. What are his interest rates?
3. How do they compare?
4. What terms would be best for me?

For these, you decide that your preparation should include:

1. Read up on current rates (real estate section?).
2. Call several other institutions.

And so on.

Next, do your Take-along sheet on the same basis. Here you list everything you want to be sure to bring to the meeting (or have at hand, in the case of a phone call). Once again, work from your desired outcomes. Thus, for:

1. Determine how big a loan I can get.

You might write:

1. Updated financial statement.

And that suggests another item to add to your Preparation list: "Update personal financial statement."

Other take-alongs for your first desired outcome:

1. A copy of last year's tax return?
2. Some payroll stubs to verify income?

At this point you *may* find yourself breaking into a cold sweat: "Oh boy, I'm not sure I really want to go this far this fast." And that's OK, because you've discovered that you haven't really made up your mind yet. You've been so wrapped up in the details that you've postponed deciding whether you *want* to buy a house right now. Maybe your real desired outcome is simply to determine how much money you could borrow if need be, so you'll know what your options are. In that case, it can be a quicker, easier meeting; maybe a phone call to the loan officer is all that's necessary. You've saved yourself some time and anxiety, and you've saved the banker's time as well.

If you do want to proceed, though, the final sheet, Action Recap, comes into play. That's where you'll take notes at the meeting on decisions made and actions to be taken, including who is to perform them by what date.

Now you're ready for a productive, focused session with your banker. Obviously, the advantages of that are even greater when you're meeting with an adviser whose time costs you money.

One extra refinement can be very useful: Convert your Desired Outcomes list into an agenda to guide the meeting and to ensure that time doesn't run out before your needs do:

Agenda

(Preliminary Remarks)

1. Determine how big a loan I can get.
2. What are the interest rates?
3. How do they compare?
4. What terms would be best for me?
5. What would be my total costs?
6. Are points deductible on income taxes?

As we've discussed above, it's good to provide the agenda in advance to the person you're going to see, maybe with a few words to make sure it's clear what you want.

At the Meeting

Use Your Agenda.   Pull out your agenda. Have a copy for each person there (tip: go a few minutes early and ask the secretary to make copies you need). Use the preliminary remarks at the beginning of the meeting to restate exactly what you're after, going down the items one by one, to make sure the purposes are clear.

Then ask the other person(s) if that approach is OK, standing ready to make any suggested amendments. If suggested changes *don't* work for you, persist. For example, suppose the banker says, "We can skip the rates question; I have a sheet that lists those that I can mail you." You may want to respond, "Fine, that will give me the details. But I would still appreciate it if we took a few minutes for you to explain them to me in person, so I'll be sure I understand how they work."

Watch the Clock.   If you've bought an hour of your accountant's or your attorney's time, it's in your interest to get as much accomplished in those 60 minutes as possible. Your attorney will probably get a chuckle out of your tale about hacking your way out of the woods on the 13th hole, but at $120 an hour, he's a pretty expensive audience.

Be Clear as You Go.   A word of caution about your use of the homework reading you did in advance: You may feel you should skip over anything that was covered on paper, to save time when the meter is running. In principle, that's good, but you may find yourself thinking "I don't really understand this, but I can catch up on it when I get back home." Tilt. Unless you're sure it's trivial, stop and get the point clarified. In general, be clear about the resolution of each item on your agenda before moving on.

Don't Worry about Appearing Dumb.   You may be tempted to show off the shiny new specialized nomenclature you just learned, so you inject some of these terms deftly into the conversation, with a knowing toss of the head. But if you don't really know what the words mean, you can create one of several unhappy situations:

- The expert assumes you're much more knowledgeable than you are, answers you at that high level of sophistication, and leaves you baffled. (Who among us is so secure as to say, "Er, I'm sure that was a fascinating discussion of new opportunities with arbitrage, but to tell the truth, even though I used the word, I don't have the foggiest notion what arbitrage *is*.")

- More likely, the expert suspects that you're in a little over your head, but won't know how far. As a result, the expert is so careful not to offend you that the conversation won't go as smoothly as it should.

- The expert decides you're faking it and determines to get this over with as quickly as possible.

Far better to do what many smart journalists do when they conduct interviews with experts: pop a humility pill, say that you don't know much at all about the subject, then ask naive questions.

Describe in plain language the problem that you're trying to solve, then listen carefully. When you don't fully understand what you're being told, say so. Help the expert along: "The part I don't quite get is . . ."

To make sure you understand, play back what you're told in your own words: "So you're telling me that sometimes what they call a three-year adjustable rate mortgage really isn't, and that it can go up every year after the three years are up? Is that right? And how will I recognize one of those?"

Take Notes.   You'll need them to make sure you don't forget key facts or the actions you or others are supposed to take. Record your notes and reminders of follow-up actions on your Action Recap sheet.

Working efficiently with experts is the way to deal with all the technical and specialized information and procedures you need to handle your affairs without giving up control over the essentials: your own needs, wants, and goals. Those are the things only *you* can be expert about. In our last chapter, we suggest ways of further developing that uniquely personal expertise.

Chapter Thirteen

Matching Your Money Plan to Your Psychological Needs

Throughout this book, we have talked about how our money decisions are shaped by emotional forces. We have made the point that if you ignore your emotional needs, it can be difficult to make decisions that will be satisfying over time.

For the most part, we've encouraged you to make your money decisions match the way you are. In this final chapter, however, we suggest that you step back and look to see whether some of these forces interfere not only with the management of your financial affairs but with obtaining full satisfaction in life. If so, you may want to consider changing the way you are.

And how can you do that? For the answer, we've called upon the expertise of the psychological consultants mentioned earlier, Psychotherapy Associates of Collegeville, Pennsylvania. They have developed two brief tests you can take to identify your tendencies. They've also provided suggestions for what you may want to do, based on the results.

Our psychologists point out that getting the most from your money requires more than coldly applying rational rules and pragmatic principles. It demands some understanding of yourself—what money means to you symbolically and psychologically, not just materially.

The fact is that money meets a host of needs—rational and nonrational—and the complex of needs is unique to each individual. Often we work to maximize our financial position less out of a straightforward desire to provide for our physical requirements than out of a yearning for psychological gratifications.

And for that reason, there are often times when our emotional money agenda conflicts with our "cognitive" money agenda—the one based on what we know and believe. We may be perplexed at times when we find ourselves resisting a course of action that seems entirely reasonable and financially sound. These occasions are triggered by conflicts between our emotional and our rational needs.

If we make the effort to uncover and understand the hidden emotional factors that shape our spending and saving behavior, then we can consciously decide what we want to do about them. Some people will decide to make changes in their lifestyle or the ways they handle money, based on new insights into their inner workings. Other people, once they understand themselves better, may simply relax and accept their individual preferences.

Either way, the first step is to determine your own predispositions so you can decide on any adjustments you feel are desirable. After you develop a clearer picture of how your personality shapes your attitudes about money, you may be in a better position to squeeze every ounce of satisfaction out of your money. And you'll recognize why the approach that works so well for your neighbor might make you richer but less happy.

This self-understanding can also be invaluable to couples. When people are unaware of their emotional needs, they cannot openly articulate them. Instead, they frequently find themselves making up illogical rationalizations. Their frustrated partners don't understand the actual reasons behind the choice and often are exasperated by the pseudo-explanations that are offered.

Knowing about your emotionally grounded preferences can help prevent you from playing defensive games that disguise and distort your real motivation for preferring one money decision over another. You'll find it easier to communicate your reasons for favoring a money decision that isn't necessarily defensible from a purely practical standpoint. And your partner will be better able to understand why a logical investment strategy might make you sick with worry. Accurate self-knowledge, when it's shared, can make compromise easier. You'll both have a better feeling for which accommodations would be especially painful and which ones wouldn't hurt a bit.

SYMBOLIC FUNCTIONS OF MONEY

Some people see money simply as a way of buying the things they need. For them, purchasing decisions are straightforward: what product does the best job for the least money? With any surplus, their tendency is to do the "rational" thing and save. They store up money to purchase something they want. Or they store it for a future requirement, including needs they have not yet identified.

For these people, managing money is a straightforward, almost mathematical task requiring effort, discipline, denial, and patience. Everything in its time, or do without.

Economists wish we were all so rational in our money decisions, because that would make their predictions a lot more accurate. Advertising executives thank heaven we're not.

For most of us, money means a lot more than its face value or what material goods it can be exchanged for. It has symbolic functions, too, which means that it can come to stand for deep inner issues and conflicts. This symbolic meaning of money can give rise to anxiety and irrational behavior.

While many factors come into play as we make day-to-day and long-term decisions about how to use our money, some of the most influential issues cluster around two dominant concerns: security and status. Although these two broad areas of concern influence almost everyone's financial behavior to some degree, for some people the effect can be so severe as to seriously limit their satisfaction and financial effectiveness. In this chapter we'll explore these two sources of motivation in detail.

SECURITY CONCERNS

Many people see money chiefly in terms of its ability to offer protection from future need, as a bulwark against uncertainty. This orientation may reflect conflicts about dependency and provide a way of circumventing anxiety about someday having to depend upon others.

The following quiz will help you identify the role security motivation plays in your attitudes toward money. For couples, an especially revealing exercise is to take the quiz a second time before comparing results, with the partners each responding as they imagine their partner would respond. Then compare the predicted responses with the ones your partner actually made. Discussing your shared and contrasting responses can be a way of enhancing mutual understanding and accommodation.

A Self-Quiz on Money and Security Needs

The following quiz isn't one of those mind-probing things that says if you like rectangles more than triangles, and orange better than blue, then you should put your money in five-year Treasury bills. The questions are straightforward. There are no "right" or "wrong" answers or trick questions. We've made the quiz as easy to take and to score as possible.

Instructions: Please take out a ruled pad. Create three columns. Label the first "Yes," the second "Maybe/Sometimes," and the third "No." Number 15 lines down the left margin of your paper. For each of the following questions, put a check mark in the column that reflects your answer.

1. I wouldn't like my income to be heavily dependent on commissions or something else that I couldn't predict in advance.

2. I often worry about serious economic difficulties and whether I could survive.

3. One of my biggest fears is that there will be another bad depression.

4. I'm nagged by thoughts about not being able to meet unforeseeable expenses.

5. If my income were suddenly to drop by 30 percent, I would panic and not know what to do.

6. I don't understand personal financial matters and am frightened by the prospect of having to deal with them on my own.

7. I have a savings plan that should meet my future financial needs, but I still worry a lot about having enough money in the future.

8. To tell the truth, I can't imagine ever having enough in savings that I would feel I could relax about the future.

9. It's hard for me to imagine ever having enough money to buy all the things I want.

10. My long-term savings plans don't assume that relatives would be able to help out, if worse came to worst.

11. One of my biggest fears is becoming a financial burden to my children or my parents.

12. My parents had a tough time when they first started out; I want to make sure I don't go through the same thing.

13. I have never had to worry about money; the thought of ever being in that position is very scary to me.

14. I have had to pinch pennies quite a bit in my life and as a consequence have determined never to get in that situation again.

15. I know from experience that it would be very difficult for me to get along with less money.

Scoring: Add up the check marks from the "Yes" column, and record this number. Then add up the checks in the "Maybe/Sometimes" column. Multiply the number in the "Yes" column by 2 and add that to the number in the "Maybe/Sometimes" column. That's your score. ("No" answers count zero.) Here's how you rank on need for security when it comes to money:

20 or over: High

6–19: Moderate

0–5: Low

If you scored in the low range, you may still want to skim what follows to help understand people you live and work with. Or you can skip to the section "Money as Proof of Success."

If you scored in the moderate or high ranges, you're among the majority of people, based on this sampling of your attitudes. You relate to money in a way that is frequently shaped by issues related to concerns about security.

Money translates into emotional security for most people, and it is—rationally—a good instrument for protecting yourself against bad things that can happen. Your concern becomes a problem, however, if it is so strong that you simply can't feel safe, if you're preoccupied with thoughts of doom, loss, and deprivation. This kind of attitude can create an insatiable need. It comes from the false belief that you can eliminate fear with money if you simply have enough of it.

If you scored in the high range or close to it (say, above 13), you may be so concerned with security that your feelings conflict with the full enjoyment of your money, reduce your opportunities to make more of it, and interfere with good financial decisions. A tendency to respond in this way can also create conflict in a marriage and problems between parents and children. For instance:

- Excessive concern with security creates hoarding behavior that makes it difficult to enjoy money and possessions. Vacations come hard; so do "luxuries."

- Purchasing decisions are more difficult: you may underspend on a residence, then be sorry when the house turns out to be inadequate to the family's needs.

- Investing choices are limited or unnecessarily painful; you're so concerned with safety that you don't get the return you need.

- Budgeting creates excessive anxiety. You're likely to set unreachable goals and feel perpetually frustrated that you can't stay within the limits you impose on yourself.

Let's look at the characteristics of people with excessive security needs. Then we'll discuss some remedies.

People who score high on security concerns share three main characteristics. First, they tend to wrestle with a lot of fear. They are deeply concerned about having enough money to meet their needs. Their fear often involves a combination of pessimism, superstitious behavior, and powerlessness. They assume that bad things will happen to them and have little confidence in their ability to control their own fate.

Second, those with excessive security concerns often display counterdependency, a tendency to fight against being dependent on others. They feel threatened by the prospect of admitting their need for others and respond by trying to achieve an unrealistic level of financial independence. Indeed, such people are doubly afraid of money emergencies because, in addition to worrying about deprivation itself, they worry about having to ask for help.

The fear of confronting their reliance on others often leads counterdependent people to have distorted views of relationships. They may minimize the benefits they receive from others while exaggerating the benefits others receive from them. Moreover, they're afraid to make their needs known, in part because they assume others feel as they do and would look down on them if they knew how they felt. It's therefore safer for them to avoid that disclosure. They can't feel comfortable asking for help.

Third, people with excessive security needs may find that their anxiety is boundless; nothing they can do is enough to alleviate it. As a result of this vague and limitless anxiety, it's extremely difficult to make rational financial choices.

Do you recognize a little of yourself in this description? If so, read on. We'll look at each characteristic of people who are excessively high in need for security and suggest some possible remedies.

Fear

Fears about financial security often are linked with a pessimistic perspective, superstitious behavior, and perceptions of powerlessness. Let's examine each of these.

Pessimism. "Pessimism" can be nothing more than your view of the world as being made up of half-empty glasses, simply your way of assessing potential happenings. It becomes a problem when it fosters a strong and persistent anxiety—a generalized fear concerning money matters that is not tied to any specific events or probable events.

The possible origins of this dysfunctional attitude include childhood stress. Perhaps you have memories of financial problems your parents faced when you were a child. Whatever you saw your parents experiencing, you saw through the helpless eyes of a child. There was nothing you could do. The people you depended upon in your own helplessness seemed helpless themselves. Further, as a child, you had no sense of future, no concept that there was time for things to work out. Quite possibly you overreacted, perceiving a much more serious problem, and greater fear and helplessness on your parents' part, than was real. Since you could not visualize a remedy, you might have felt overwhelmed.

Such an experience would not have to be severe to leave its mark on you in the form of an emotional residue that clouds your judgment as an adult and generates anxiety as you go about making your day-to-day money decisions.

What are some remedies? To begin with, reexamine anxieties in light of your present adult capabilities and see whether there aren't some you may now recognize are unrealistic. Accept that while your fears were an understandable reaction when you were a child, that experience has little to do with you and your life today. You are no longer helpless or wholly dependent on someone else, and there is a future in which you can deal with problems.

Perhaps you have a "Gloomy Gus" personality, a tendency to look on the dark side of life that is too deeply embedded in your personality to root out. If so, there are some simple 'thought-stopping' maneuvers you can use to alleviate the symptoms and reduce the level of your anxiety.

This strategy involves making conscious choices about how you will think, then making a contract with yourself to redirect counterproductive thinking. It gives you more control over negative thoughts.

Let's say you have determined that a portion of your portfolio must be in common stocks to give you the growth you need to retire properly. And let's say that this is a well-researched, deliberate plan; you know, intellectually, that it makes sense for you. But you worry about another stock market crash so persistently that you have a serious problem sticking to the plan. In this case, when you catch yourself worrying, think: "Wait a minute. I have a good broker, and he's watching things. I don't need to. So I will make it a point to worry about this only on Wednesday mornings. I'll think about it then, and I'll call my broker, if need be. But if it pops into my mind, I will push it back and tell myself: this can wait until Wednesday."

Superstitious Behavior.   To what extent do you believe that snapping your fingers is what keeps the tigers away—that if you ever stop worrying about financial disasters, they'll surely happen? You may have inadvertently learned to worry continuously because time and again, imagining bad outcomes has been followed by relief. Your worst fears have *not* materialized (luckily), but unwittingly you've set things up so that you've been rewarded for worrying. So you keep doing it.

This kind of behavior is "superstitious" in the sense that there's no real connection between your worrying and the absence of disaster;

you'd be exactly as well off if you *didn't* worry constantly. However, being obsessive about disasters can create the *illusion* of control. Maybe you feel that if you don't worry, you'll get lax and spend too much. Or that if you don't keep invoking the specter of gloom, your *partner* will get lax. Mentally steeling yourself for the worst assures you that you won't be caught unprepared, but this benefit comes at a very high price. Your mind is filled with gloom and doom.

Remedies? Try using the thought-stopping technique. Tell yourself "Sally, stop. You're playing voodoo again! Do you really think your worrying will keep property values from falling?"

If the thought-stopping technique works for you, you'll have developed a powerful capability for dealing with your world. You can't control the stock market, but you *can* learn to control your reaction to it.

It may help to examine the reasons why you worry. Chances are you'll see they are unrealistic and can be replaced with substitute thoughts that are more productive. For instance, do you worry because you feel your discipline would falter if the force of anxiety weren't behind it? If so, try to replace your general anxiety with specifics: spell out explicit number goals and targets, and measure yourself against those.

Powerlessness.   Many people have such strong doubts about their ability to deal with financial problems that could arise in the future that they have difficulty enjoying the money they have. Either they never had reason to develop the necessary skills, or they underestimate the ones they have.

Lack of experience in making or managing money can magnify fears of loss. You're not sure where it came from or what it took to get it, and you can easily imagine it all disappearing. This is a common problem with non-working spouses, especially those who have never held a paying job.

It can also be an issue with individuals who have been well-off from childhood on, who have never learned to deal with money matters and have no experience of privation. Because of their good fortune, they have never learned how to deal with financial problems and can easily fall prey to an exaggerated belief that having a lot of money is essential to happiness.

The remedy? Solving this problem is relatively straightforward. If you feel powerless when it comes to finances, what you need is clear information about money matters that empowers you to take a more active role in financial decision making. The preceding chapters should help. Greater knowledge, then practice, will strengthen your coping skills and help you dissipate this anxiety.

Counterdependency

People with intense security concerns are likely to resist dependence on others to a degree that creates difficulty. If you feel you don't dare call upon children, parents, relatives, or friends—if, in fact, you feel a need to dramatize to them that you will never need their help—you greatly increase the amount of money you feel compelled to save.

When you consider worst-case scenarios, it can be paralyzing to contemplate an accident or medical circumstance that would put you in the position of total physical dependency. If you feel you must somehow provide enough money that you would never need to call upon family or friends, you have set a very challenging task for yourself. By the same token, you may have a severe aversion to the idea of accepting help, if it came to that. If you refuse categorically to investigate those possibilities, you unnecessarily limit your choices.

The remedy? Our psychologist consultants say it's important to take a fresh look at our love of independence. Independence is among our highest national values. But for you, in your personal life, it may not always be a strength or a legitimate source of pride.

Total independence is simply a myth. None of us functions in a social vacuum, and few thrive without social contact and support. The cultural ideal of self-sufficiency makes it hard for some people to accept the simple reality: we are all necessarily dependent on others. Interdependence is the basis of human communities. Reciprocal dependence characterizes most mutually beneficial relationships. It allows us to empower each other.

Try asking: "To what defect in my personality do I attribute my fear of being dependent?" Does that recast the issue a little bit?

It may help to confront a hypothetical financial situation of dependence. If you're worried about being a burden to your children, for example, imagine the circumstances under which this might occur. You can try to estimate exactly how much, or how little, money you might need from them, in light of other resources available to you. It can make it easier to have a finite number in mind rather than the generalized image of being a "financial burden."

Then you can ask some other questions:

- Would it be unreasonable of you, considering all you've done over the years, to request help, if it's really needed?
- How would *you* feel if the situation were reversed? Doesn't it feel good to be in a position to help loved ones?
- How would you feel if your children badly needed help, but didn't trust you enough to ask for it and instead put themselves through terrible trials?

The fact is, most people take deep satisfaction in helping someone they care about and will accept considerable sacrifice to do so. *You* feel that way, don't you? So why assume others are less gracious or less generous than you are?

Boundlessness

We use the term "boundlessness" to describe a third condition common with people who are high in the need for security—namely, that premonitions of financial ruin are so ill-defined that it's impossible for them to set aside a precise sum of money to allay their fears. That kind of limitless anxiety about having enough money inhibits thoughtful problem solving.

If you have this kind of anxiety, you become preoccupied with the idea that money won't be there when you need it, without fully understanding why you feel that way. You're never satisfied that the amount of money you have is adequate, and so you have an unfulfillable demand for money.

Psychologists say that it can help if you confront your fears and the vagueness of your concerns by using the systematic exercise on planning we discussed in Chapter 5. Ask yourself, what are the specific things you're worried about? What could cause them to happen? In particular, what's the *worst* thing that can happen? List your answers:

Spouse dies or leaves

Lose job

Serious medical problem

Economic disaster

Then you can go through a problem-solving exercise. For each item, ask, how likely is this to happen? What steps could you take to prevent it happening? How much money will it take to deal with it, if it does happen? What resources will be available to you? List them:

Insurance

Savings

Help from government/public

Help from family and friends

To combat the vagueness of your fears, it helps if you push yourself to quantify in every way possible: actual dollars in lost income, actual loans and debts outstanding, dollars potentially available. (What exactly would insurance pay? How much assistance might be available from family?)

Is there a shortfall? Then what can you do now to reduce the bad effects?

Increase my marketable skills

Get more involved in the household finances to develop my knowledge and confidence

Make a will

Buy appropriate insurance

Establish a specific "disaster fund"

What accommodations could you make, if you had to? ("Let's see, if there's a money problem, we'd have to revise college plans for the kids, but they could still go to a community college. Come to think of it, they'd probably qualify for financial aid.")

In short, try to visualize possible outcomes and options in as much detail as you can. This kind of picture-drawing can convert an aching generalized anxiety into a specific fear, with specific boundaries. That's a lot easier to handle.

MONEY AS PROOF OF SUCCESS: STATUS CONCERNS

In addition to its security symbolism, money can have a powerful influence as a symbol of our success in living and our worth as persons. What we are able to accumulate in bank accounts and possessions can confirm our sense of accomplishment and productivity. We can come to see money as providing tangible validation of the worth of our work and the value of our time and talents.

In short, we may use money as a way of keeping score in life and come to want frequent, clear, and meaningful reminders that we're "winners."

There is strong social support for the concept that money and possessions are a measure of your worth as a person. Our social system rewards people who produce results, and money is the reward. In that sense, money is society's way of communicating its valuation of us. The Nobel Peace Prize is cash.

So what's bad about all that? We'll answer that question in a moment. First, take the following short quiz to get a view of your attitudes toward money as a measure of success and personal worth. As before, there are no right or wrong answers, no trick questions. Just answer candidly so that you can use the quiz for your own guidance.

A Short Quiz on Money and Success

Instructions: Please take out a ruled pad. Create three columns. Label the first one "Yes," the second "Maybe/Sometimes," and the third "No." Number 13 lines down the left margin. For each of the following questions, put a check mark in the column that reflects your answer.

1. You have a choice between a famous imported sports car that stretches your budget and one that costs less and performs equally well, but has far less prestige. Do you choose to buy the famous import?

2. Even after you had enough to meet your family's basic needs, would you continue to sacrifice time with the family to make more money?

3. You have a new outfit from a big-name designer. Someone compliments you on it and asks if it came from Jones, a good store, but one that does not carry big-name designers. Would you let the inquirer know it's a designer label?

4. Do you tend to purchase prestige brands of products?

5. Would you be reluctant to have visitors to your home notice that you use generic products?

6. You have been the highest-paid person in your section. Now your boss tells you that a new person has been transferred into your section at a higher pay level than yours, but only because of the person's seniority within the company. Your boss reassures you that you're still considered the section's most valuable employee. Would you disbelieve your boss and feel that the company doesn't really consider you the most valuable if it doesn't pay you accordingly?

7. Do you make a strong effort to know the salaries of your friends and associates?

8. If you made more money than your colleagues, would you want them to know?

9. Does it bother you if you discover that a friend or neighbor is making a lot more money than you?

10. Would you dislike a job where pay was strictly a function of job classification rather than individual performance?

11. If you find you're making less than someone you feel deserves less than you, does your self-esteem suffer?

12. When completing an anonymous survey, do you ever overstate your income?

13. Have you established salary goals for yourself to attain at specific age levels?

Scoring: Add up the check marks from the "Yes" column, and record this number. Then add up the checks in the "Maybe/Sometimes" column. Multiply the number in the "Yes" column by 2 and add the result to the number in the "Maybe/Sometimes" column. That's your score. ("No" answers count zero.) On the basis of this small sampling of your concern with money as a measure of your worth, here's how you rank:

20 or over: High

6–19: Moderate

0–5: Low

If you scored in the low range, you can read on as a matter of interest—or you can go about your business; you've finished the book.

If you scored high or moderately high, what does that mean? Is that bad? If so, why? And what should you do about it?

We're concerned here with an excessive preoccupation with the numerically rare—with being on the top, Number One, having the most—and with the pursuit of money and possessions as a means of gaining the approval of others. People who have this tendency to excess never feel they're quite OK, quite good enough. To the extent that you fit this description, you define "success" in comparative, competitive terms to an excessive degree. You need to feel you've won.

Psychologists say that these tendencies can operate at two levels: private and public. The private, internal level has to do with having status in your own eyes. Here, money is a primary measure in your own self-evaluation. You find it hard to feel good about yourself unless you've made enough money.

The public, external level has to do with having status in the eyes of others. Here, financial success is equated with social success. This level embraces the need to display worth to impress and get approval from others—spending conspicuously, needing status products to display, making sure others know how well you're doing. You find it hard to feel adequate around others unless you've made enough money—and they know about it.

People who have this tendency are characterized also by boundlessness, the anxiety that goes along with shooting at a perpetually moving target. You don't know how much "enough" money is. You constantly reevaluate your own salary in terms of what others are making, usually to your consternation. You are never content that your display of wealth is as impressive to others as it should be.

The reason these tendencies are "bad" is that they don't work very well. Pursuing the numerically rare—striving to be the highest-paid person at work, to make more money than any of your siblings, to have the biggest house in the neighborhood—is a game that, by definition, has many more losers than winners. It's trite but true: there is only so much room at the top. So, setting that kind of goal sets you up for failure.

Furthermore, pursuing the approval of others through money can be self-defeating. You make money and accumulate possessions so you can display your success. You display your success to win the respect and approval of others. But what you're more likely to get is their enmity: they don't like you because they feel threatened by your success.

What are the sources of these tendencies? And what can you do about them?

Psychologists believe that much of the need we're describing can stem from childhood and the models provided by parents, particularly if money was used for reward and punishment. Perhaps you grew up in a home where receiving a regular allowance or fun money depended upon your behaving well (or at least that's the way you saw it). If you did your chores, watched your manners, and kept your clothes reasonably clean, you pleased your parents and so got the money for the movie or other pleasure that was important to you. Good report cards probably earned you money, too. If you behaved badly and displeased your parents, the money was withheld. (Skip the allowance. No money for ice cream.) Chances are, teachers, neighbors, and peers operated by similar rules and reinforced what you were learning at home.

This pattern isn't that uncommon, of course, and millions come through it unscathed. But it sets up two emotional propositions that are badly flawed and that can present formidable adjustment problems in adult life:

1. Money is the sole measure of achievement and worth and is a more or less inevitable reward for performance.

2. Money represents love and approval.

Let's look at each of these in turn.

Money as the Sole Measure of Achievement and Worth

As a child, it's easy to develop the concept that you will indeed get money if you do things right: behave properly, work hard, persevere. The child doesn't understand that good performance may not be properly rewarded, that circumstances can interfere. And the child doesn't understand that one kind of good work is rewarded more than another kind.

The danger is that you carry into adulthood the belief that these rewards come inevitably to good boys and girls, and if they don't come to you, there's something wrong with you. If you don't question these oversimplifications, you may question instead the worth of your performance, the value of the work you do, the limitations of the financial success you have achieved, even your basic worth as a person. You can be dissatisfied with a job that doesn't pay sufficiently well and blind to how well you're doing it. Because you rate yourself in financial terms, you enjoy yourself less.

The remedy? Our psychologists say you should recognize that it's within your power to change your ways of identifying rewards and evaluating performance and self-worth. In short, you can create a better way of keeping score.

Further, now, more than ever, society facilitates your redefining of success. Not too many years ago, most people accepted with little question an arrangement under which most of their lifestyle decisions were dictated by one factor: their jobs. They lived according to where their employer was, then moved to another location if the company sent them there.

Then things began to change. More and more people began to think of where they lived in terms of the schools, the climate, access to recreation, safety, and commuting times. More and more of them decided they would try to fit their jobs to their broader needs instead of the other way around.

Then the media joined in, and quality-of-life measurements appeared that rated cities, countries, companies, and careers in these terms. Of course, these scales typically include pay scales, employment opportunities, cost of living, and other factors relating to employment and finance. But these are set in the context of all the things that affect the joy of living.

In a similar way, you can broaden the context of your personal self-appraisal structure and examine it critically: "What are my priorities? Why is *this* one so important? Does it really help me feel more satisfied, happier? I felt great when I got that raise, but how long did that feeling last? How soon before I was already worrying about the next one? I'm ahead of my goal; I'm making more now than I expected to be making at this age. But why don't I feel good about it? I felt *bad* enough when I was *behind* my goal!"

Once more, our psychologist consultants suggest that you approach this self-examination systematically, as a problem-solving exercise. Step back and think about all the things in the past two years that have made you feel good. Generate as wide-ranging a list as you can: Trout fishing? Playing the harp? Running the marathon?

Do any interesting patterns emerge? How many items on the list have to do with income, purchases, possessions?

Next, gather your top five, then the second five (or however many), and construct a new scorekeeping system. Income and possessions will be there, of course, but maybe the new list will have a little more texture to it, a dash more of you as a person; and probably it will yield more satisfaction if you act on it.

Try measuring yourself against the new list and see whether you can develop some new score keeping that works better from now on.

Money as Signifying Love and Approval

A tendency to relate money to love and approval is a serious possible outcome of the conventional childhood. It sows the seeds of a difficulty many people have as adults in dealing with money.

This tendency can be created when a child mistakes parental rejection of temporary misbehavior for rejection of his or her whole person. It can easily happen. When children misbehave, parents often respond impulsively and out of anger. Reprimands can be global and timeless instead of specific and tied to the occasion: "You're a *bad girl!*" The parents' response can imply total rejection of the child. Nonverbal expressions of disgust and rage confirm the child's fear that her parents wish she would disappear.

It's understandable why children conclude from these episodes that they are less lovable. Enough repetitions of such apparent hostility and rejection can convince a child that he or she is unworthy as a person.

When financial punishment is incorporated within such anger, children associate denial of money with withdrawal of love and a rejection of self. Further, monetary punishments often are imposed in an atmosphere of anger and threat: you left Dad's saw out to rust in the rain, and the storm *really* broke: anger, no dessert, no allowance money! And that withheld allowance is tangible proof of the loss of parental love.

It works the other way, too: extra money signifies that the child is still loved and presumably OK. However, this state of affairs is tenuous; make a mistake tomorrow, and goodbye, allowance.

The remedy? If you think factors like these could have been at work in your own life, then it may help to recognize and analyze them. Whatever impression you received in childhood about the connection between money and self-worth, you're an adult now, and you can reexamine it.

From an adult perspective—especially if you are a parent yourself—you can appreciate the complexities of love and approval, and work to discard the notion that money could express those things. There may be issues of parental affection that you still need to resolve, but at least you can disentangle them from money issues.

In your dealings with others, it can be helpful to realize that trying to obtain social acceptance by "scoring" financially usually backfires. People may admire your accomplishments, but they may not like being around you very much. Since one reason for knocking yourself out in the first place was to win the approval and love of others, that's self-defeating.

If you need a greater sense of belonging and being connected with others, it can help to identify specific ways that you are flaunting financial success and driving others away. Then stop doing it.

Simultaneously, consider diverting some of the energy you've spent so lavishly in attempting to attain conspicuous success and apply it instead to building satisfying relationships. We've encouraged you to plan financial steps; now you may want to put tasks relating to specific personal relationships on your "to do" lists. You may find, too, that investing yourself in cooperative community pursuits leaves you feeling a lot richer than some of the other uses of your time.

CLOSING COMMENTS

If you work through the exercises in this chapter and they don't seem to help, recognize that your needs run deep, and habits are difficult to change. Sometimes your actions are going to be counterproductive, but spare yourself the additional pain of self-condemnation. You have lots of company. Keep at it.

But we hope instead that you have discovered some useful ways to begin dealing with forces that can interfere with making satisfying decisions. Then you can proceed with the happy task of getting the most of everything from your money.

Index

A

Acceleration clause, 79
Accountants, use of, 205–206
Achievement, money as measure of, 226–227
Adjustable rate mortgages (ARMs), 166–167
Advanced placement courses, 140
Advertising home for sale, 180–181
Advice. *See* Information and advice
Age and credit, 65
Annual interest rate, 110
Annual percentage rate (APR), 168
  for home improvements, 192
Annuities, 131–132
  TSAs, 156
Anxiety and security, 222–223
Approval, money and, 228–229
Architects, plans by, 186–187
ARMs, 166–167
Assertiveness, 197–199
  assessment quiz, 196–197
  loans, applying for, 202
Assumption of mortgages, 182
ATMs, 24, 29–30
  regular checking accounts using, 38
  restrictive endorsements for deposits through, 46
  rights and responsibilities of, 31–32
  special considerations for, 31–32
Attorneys, use of, 205–206

Automated teller machines. *See* ATMs
Automatic transfers. *See* Electronic fund transfers (EFT)

B

Back-end load mutual funds, 130
Balancing checkbooks, 50–58
  worksheet for, 56
Balloon payments, 62
  on assumable mortgages, 169
  on fixed–rate mortgages, 164
Bank credit cards, 28
Bankruptcy, 83–88
  Chapter 7, 83–84
  Chapter 11, 85
  Chapter 13, 84
Banks and bank accounts, 23–36.
    See also Checks and checking accounts; Deposits, Money market accounts; Savings accounts,
  automatic transfers, 24, 33
  budget management and, 14–15
  depositing money, 45–47
  electronic banking, 28–34
  home banking, 33
  loans from banks, 27–28
  menu of services, 27–28
  new ways of, 24–25
  services menu, 27–28, 111
  shopping for services, 25–26
  working with bankers, 201–203
Bank statements, 51–52
  sample of, 53

understanding of, 52–55
Blank endorsements, 45
Blocking credit, 79
Bonds and notes
    corporate bonds and notes, 126
    municipal bonds and notes, 126
    zero coupon bonds, 126–127
Boundlessness and security,
    222–223
Brainstorming exercise
    on retirement, 150–151
    on serious worries, 98–106
    on wants and needs, 90–97
Brokerage houses, 112
Brokers, 204–205. *See also* Stockbro-
    kers
    real estate agents,
Budgets, 1–22
    adjustment of plan, 21
    bank accounts and, 14–15
    cash box budgeting, 16
    credit and management of, 60
    credit cards and, 15
    deficits in, 21–22
    insurance, provisions for, 106
    making budgets work, 13–19
    new budget writing, 10–13
    reconciling budgets, 19–22
    set-aside accounting record,
        16–19
    steps in writing, 3–13
Builders. *See* Contractors
Buy downs, 169–170, 182
Buying a home. *See* Home-buying

C
California financial aid programs,
    142
Cancellation of home improvement
    contracts, 190
Capital risk, 122
Cash box budgeting, 16
Cash flow tracking, 16–19
Cashier's checks, 35
Cashing checks, 43–45
Casual budgets, 2
Certificates of deposit (CDs), 28,
    110, 112–113
    additional deposits, 113
    early withdrawal penalties, 113
    fees for, 128–129
    for high involvement invest-
        ment style, 135
    investing in, 124–125

Chapter 11 bankruptcy, 85
Chapter 13 bankruptcy, 84
Chapter 7 bankruptcy, 83–84
Charge accounts. *See* Credit cards
Check guarantee cards, 43–44
Checkbook register, 51–52
Checks and checking accounts,
    37–58. *See also* Endorsements
    automatic transfers, 24, 33
    balancing checkbook, 50–58
    budget management and,
        14–15
    cashing checks, 43–45
    with credit unions, 23
    depositing money in, 45–47
    endorsing checks, 44–45
    establishing credit with, 67
    face of check, 40–43
    forged checks, 48
    free checking accounts, 39–40
    interest-bearing checking
        accounts, 27, 39–40, 114
    lost checks and checking
        accounts, 47
    money market checking ac-
        counts, 27
    NOW accounts, 27
    overdrafts, 49
    regular checking accounts, 27, 38
    rejected checks, 49
    with savings and loan associa-
        tions, 23
    stolen checks, 47
    stop payments, 48
    summary on bank statement,
        53–54
    super NOW accounts, 27
    telephone assistance with, 40
    tips for handling, 49–50
    updating records, 58
    writing checking accounts,
        40–43
Christmas Club accounts, 114
Closing of home sale, 179.
    costs, 176
Clothing, set-aside accounting
    record for, 19
Cognitive money agenda, 214
Collection of debts, laws on, 81
College education, 137–148
    applying for financial aid,
        146–148
    cost-cutting possibilities, 140–141
    deadlines for financial aid,
        147–148

decision making re, 138–140
financial aid for, 141–148
planning for, 97
prestige schools, 138–139
private sources of financial aid,
    145–146
requesting information on aid,
    146–147
schools, financial aid from, 144
sources of financial aid,
    142–146
types of financial aid, 142–146
updating financial aid applica-
    tions, 148
College work-study programs
    (CWS), 142–143
College-Level Examination
    Program (CLEP), 140
Comakers, 67
Commissions. *See* Fees
Community groups, college aid
    from, 145
Community Watch programs, 174
Completion bonds, 190
Completion notice, 191
Compound interest method, 110
Computers, home banking, 24–25,
    33
Condominiums, 172–173
Consolidation loans, 78
Consumer Credit Counselors
    (CCC), 81–83
    address of, 82
*Consumer Handbook on Adjustable
    Rate Mortgages*, 167
Contingency income, 4
Contract for home improvements,
    189–190
Contractors
    financing by, 193–194
    for home improvements,
        186, 187–191
Convenience cards, 28
Conventional mortgages, 164–165
Corner market of check, 42
Corporate stocks. *See* Stocks
Cosigners, 67
Counterdependency, 221–222
Court actions by creditors, 80–81
Credit, 59–87. *See also* Credit cards;
    Debts; Home equity credit
    additional charges, 79
    denial of, 70–71
    establishing credit, 64–71
    extension by creditor, 77–78

first time credit, 66–67
    forms of, 61–64
    help with, 81–83
    management of, 73–76
    moving and, 70
    overextension on, 76
    personal credit identity, 69–70
    setting limits on, 74
    shopping for, 71–73
    sources of, 64
    tracking, costs, 74–75
    uses of, 59–61
Credit cards, 61
    bank credit cards, 28
    budget management and, 15
    as check cashing identification,
        43–44
    fees of, 72
    finance charges, 72
    limits on, 72
    merchants accepting, 73
    overdraft protection with, 49
    secured credit cards, 67
    small accounts opening of,
        66–67
    special features of, 72–73
Credit counselors, 82–83
Credit insurance on mortgage,
    178–179
Credit record
    bankruptcy, rebuilding after, 85
    contents of, 68–69
    denial of credit and, 70–71
Credit register, 75
Credit repair clinics, 83
Credit unions
    savings accounts through, 111
    share-draft accounts, 23
Creditors rights and limitations,
    79–81
Custodial and informal trust
    accounts, 115

D
Daily balance on bank statement, 55
Damage control, 101
Data sheet for home-selling, 180
Death
    financial planning in case of,
        102–104
    spouse, credit on death of, 70
Debit cards, 24, 31–32
    rights and responsibilities of,
        31–32

special considerations for, 31–32
Debt consolidators, 82–83
Debts. *See also* Credit; Loans; Mortgages
  collection laws, 81
  credit and debt record, 65–66
  danger signals, 76
  extension by creditor, 77–78
  listing of, 76–77
  management of, 82
Default judgments, 81
Deficits, in budget, 21–22
Defined benefit plans, 155
Denial of credit, 70–71
Deposit on house, seller's perspective, 184
Deposits, 45–47
  bank statement listing, 54–55
  less cash deposits, 57
  records of, 51–52
Deposit slips, 45–46
Deregulation of banking, 23
Desired outcomes method for expert advice, 207–210
Diagnostic budgets, 3
Disclosure for home-selling, 181–182
Discount brokers, 128
Diversification of investments, 124
Divorced persons, credit of, 69–70
Domestic money orders, 34
Don't Miss Out: The Ambitious Student's Guide to Financial Aid (Leider & Leider), 146
Down payments, 67
  for homes, 176
  for mortgages, 168
Driver's license for check cashing, 43

E
Early warning, 101
Early withdrawal penalties for CDs, 113
Earnest money, 178
Education. *See* College education
Electronic banking, 28–34
Electronic Fund Transfer Act, Regulation E, 31–32
Electronic fund transfers (EFT), 24, 33
  balancing checkbook and, 56–57
  bank statement showing, 51–52

Employee identification badges, 43
Employment
  college scholarship programs of, 145
  investments through employer, 133
  loss of, 101–102
Employment Retirement Income Security Act (ERISA), 155
Endorsements on checks, 44–45
  restrictive endorsements, 46
Environmental conditions and home-buying, 174
Environmental scanning, 101
Equal Credit Opportunity Act, 64
  denial of credit and, 70–71
  personal credit identity and, 69–70
Equity, 164
  sharing, 170
ERISA, 155
Escrow, 178
Establishing credit, 64–71
Exclusive agency listing, 180
Exclusive right to sell, 179–180
Expenses
  credit and, 65
  fixed expenses, 21–22
  past spending description, 6–10
  of savings account, 109–110
  worksheet for, 8–10
Expert advice. *See* Information and advice

F
Face of check, 41–43
Fair Credit Reporting Act, 68, 70–71
Farmers Home Administration (FmHA), 194
Fears about security, 218–220
Federal agency issues, 125–126
Federal college education financial aid, 142–144
Federal Deposit Insurance Corporation (FDIC), 26
Federal Savings and Loan Insurance Corporation (FSLIC), 26
Fees
  for CDs, 128–129
  for credit card, 72
  for home inspections, 175
  for IRAs, 128–129
  mortgage fees, 168

for mutual funds, 130–131
stockbroker fees, 128–129
for U.S. Treasury bills, 128
FHA-insured loans, 165
problems with, 87
Finance charges, 72
Finance companies, 112
Financial planning, 89–106
wants and needs lists, 90–97
working with financial
planners, 205–206
Fingerprints, for check cashing, 43
Fire, action list for, 105
Fixed annuities, 131–132
Fixed income securities, 125–127
Fixed rate loans, 166
Foreclosure
on mortgage, 86–87
selling home to prevent, 87
Forged checks, 48
401(k) plans, 155–156
Free checking accounts, 39–40

G
Garnishment, 80
Ginnie Mae issues, 126
Goal-directed budgets, 3
Government National Mortgage
Association, certificates by, 126
Grants for college education from
federal government, 142–143
Guaranteed student loans (GSL),
144
Guarantors, 67

H
Hidden expenses, 11–12
High involvement investment style,
135
Home banking, 24–25, 33
Home equity credit, 62–64, 193
checklist for comparison shopping, 63–64
Home equity loans, 192–193
Home improvements, 185–194
borrowing money for, 191–194
cancellation rights, 190
completion bond requirements,
190
contractors , 186, 187
contract requirements, 189–190
estimates for, 187
job files, 191
loans, 192

older homes, financing for, 194
plans for, 186–187
preliminary notices by subcontractors, 188
restrictions on, 185–186
rural homes, financing for, 194
taxes on, 194
Home loans. See Mortgages
Home protection contracts, 175
Home-buying, 161–184. See also
Mortgages
assumption of loans, 169
buy downs, 169–170
closing of, 176, 179
costs, clarification of, 175–176
decision to buy home, 161–162
deposit, making the, 178
down payment requirements, 176
earnest money, 178
equity sharing, 170
escrow, 178
financing options, 163–164
goals for, 170–172
inspection of home, 175
offer, making of, 177
purchase contract, 177
settlement, 179
shopping for home, 172–174
spending limits, decision on,
162–163
Home-selling, 179–184
asking price, setting of, 181
completing the sale, 183–184
curb appeal and, 180
data sheet for, 180
disclosure statements, 181–182
financing arrangements, 182–183
listings, types of, 179–180
negotiations, 183
purchase contract, 183–184
seller-financing, 182–183
showing a home, 181
HUD, mortgage taken over by, 87

I
Identification, for check cashing,
43–44
Improvements. See Home improvements
Income
credit and, 65
credit management and, 73–74
determination of, 4–6
estimating projected income, 4–6

investing for, 120, 134
worksheet for, 5–6
Independence and money, 221–222
Independent students, 141–142
Individual accounts, 69
Individual retirement accounts. *See*
    IRAs
Inexperience with money, 220
Inflation
    credit and, 60
    home-buying and, 162
    real estate investment and,
        132–133
    retirement planning and,
        153–154
    risk and, 122
Informal trust accounts, 115
Information and advice, 195–211
    bankers, working with,
        201–203
    dealing with experts, 200
    desired outcomes method for
        expert advice, 207–210
    fee-based advisers, use of,
        205–206
    meeting with experts, 210–211
    note-taking at meetings, 211
    planning for time with advisers,
        206–211
    real estate agents, working
        with, 204–205
    stockbrokers, working with,
        203–204
Installment credit, 61–62
Installment loans, 27
Insurance. *See also* Life insurance
    determinations regarding,
        106
    loans against, 64
    property insurance, 175
Interest-bearing checking accounts,
    27, 39–40, 114
Interest rates. *See also* Mortgages
    for home equity credit, 62
    risk, 122
    on savings accounts, 110
International money orders, 34
Investments, 119–135. *See also*
        Risks; Stocks
    annuities, 131–132
    diversification of, 124
    employer investment programs,
        133
    for income, 134

life-changes, investing for, 120
life insurance as, 132
limited partnerships, 131
liquidity of, 124
mutual funds, 129–131
places for, 124–127
real estate as, 132–133
return on, 122–123
reviewing goals and styles,
    133–135
savings compared to, 115–117
style of investing, 120–122
IRAs, 28, 116–117. *See also* SEP IRAs
    retirement savings through,
        157–158
    service charges for, 128–129
Issue managers, 100–101

J
Job files for home improvements,
    191
Jobs. *See* Employment
Joint accounts, 69–70
Judicial foreclosure of mortgage, 86

K
Keogh plans, 116–117
    retirement savings through,
        158–159

L
Legal liability action list, 105
Less cash deposits, 57
Liability insurance, 106
Liens by contractors, 188
Life insurance
    employment, policies through,
        102
    as investment, 132
    determinations regarding, 106
Limited partnerships, 131
Lines of credit, 28
    home equity lines of credit, 193
    overdraft protection with, 49
Liquidity
    of investments, 124
    of savings accounts, 109
Living wills, 104
Load on mutual fund, 130
Loan companies, savings accounts
    through, 112
Loans. *See also* Home equity credit;
        Mortgages
    applying for loan, 201–203

automatic fund transfers to pay, 33
from banks, 27–28
consolidation loans, 78
for home improvements, 192
government-guaranteed student
    loans, 143–144
refinancing, 78
revisions, 78
Long-range planning budgets, 3
Lost checks, 47
Love, money signifying, 228–229
Low involvement investment style,
    134–135

M
Magnetic code of check, 43
Matching fund investment plans,
    116
Mechanic's lien, 188
Meeting College Costs, 146
Military
    college tuition plans and,
        140–141
    ID cards, 43
    veterans, scholarships for, 146
Minors, custodial trust accounts for,
    115
Money market accounts, 40,
    113–114
    automatic transfers, 24
    checking accounts, 27
    investing in, 124–125
Money orders
    domestic, 34
    international, 34
Money-purchase pension plans, 156
Moody's, 126
Mortgages. *See also* FHA-insured
    loans
    adjustable rate mortgages
        (ARMs), 166–167
    annual percentage rate (APR),
        168
    assumption of, 169, 182
    comparing terms of, 167–168
    credit insurance on, 178–179
    fees, 168
    fixed rate loans, 166
    formally applying for, 178
    prepayment premiums, 168
    problems with, 86–87
    repayment period, 168
    selling home to prevent foreclo-
        sure, 87

shopping for, 164
types of interest rates, 165–167
VA-guaranteed loans, 165
Moving, credit records when, 70
Multiple Listing Book, 180
Municipal bonds and notes, 126
Mutual funds, 129–131
    companies, 112
    fees for, 130–131

N
National credit cards, 73
National Direct Student Loans
    (NDSL), 142–143
National Foundation for Consumer
    Credit, Inc., 82
National Merit Scholarships, 145
    deadlines for taking, 147
Negative amortization, 167
Net income. *See* Income
No load funds, 130
Notes. *See* Bonds and notes
NOW accounts, 27

O
Odd lots, 128
Offer on home, 177
Oil and gas limited partnerships,
    131
Older homes, financing for improv-
    ing, 194
Open listing, 180
Ordinary life insurance, 132
Origination cost, 168
Overdrafts, 49

P
Parent loans for students (PLUS),
    143–144
Parents, planning for disability of,
    104
Participatory savings plans, 156
Passbook savings accounts, 112
Passports, 43
Pell Grants, 142–143
Pensions. *See* Retirement
Periodic interest rate cap, 167
Perkins Loans, 142–143
Personal credit identity, 69–70
Personal identification number
    (PIN), 30–31
Personal loans, 192
Pessimism, 218–219
Pest control inspections, 175

Picture-taking devices for check cashing, 43
PIN, 30–31
Point of sale (POS) cards, 24, 31
Points, 168, 183
POS cards, 24, 31
Postdated checks, 41
Powerlessness and money, 220
Power of sale, foreclosure under, 86–87
Preauthorized transfers, 24, 33
Prepayment premiums, 168
Preservation of capital, 124
Private mortgage insurance (PMI), 168, 176
Proactive issue management, 101
Problem-solver budgets, 3
Professional associations, scholarships from, 145
Profit-sharing plans, 156
Projected income estimation, 4–6
Property insurance, 175
Property taxes, 174
Prospectus of mutual funds, 129–130
Psychological needs, 213–229
Psychotherapy Associates of Collegeville, Pennsylvania, 213
Public services and home-buying, 173
Purchase contract, seller's perspective, 184

Q
Quiz
    assertiveness assessment quiz, 196–197
    on security needs and money, 215–218
    on success and money, 223–226

R
Real estate. See also Home-buying; Home-selling
    as investment, 132–133
Real estate agents, working with, 204–205
Reconciling budgets, 19–22
    running reconciliation, 20
Refinancing, 78
    for home improvements, 193
Regular checking accounts, 27, 38
Regular savings accounts, 112
Rejected checks, 49

Religious groups, scholarships from, 146
Remodelling. See Home improvements
Repossession right of creditor, 80
Rescission of home improvement contract, 190
Restrictive endorsements, 46
Retirement, 149–159
    brainstorming exercise on, 150–151
    case study for, 151–154
    company pensions, 154–156
    IRAs, savings through, 157–158
    loans against savings plan, 64
Return
    on investments, 122–123
    on savings accounts, 110
Revisions of loans, 78
Revolving charge accounts. See Credit cards
Risks, 121–122
    style, review of, 134–135
    types of investment risk, 122–124
Rollovers, 158
ROTC, 140–141
Round lots, 128
Running reconciliation of budget, 20
Rural homes, financing of, 194

S
Safety considerations and home-buying, 174
Salary reduction plans, 155–156
Savings accounts, 40, 107–117. See also Christmas Club accounts
    as investments, 115–117, 124–125
    automatic transfers, 24
    balance computation, 110–111
    choosing accounts, 109–110
    establishing credit with, 67
    interest-bearing checking accounts, 27, 39–40, 114
    participatory savings plans for retirement, 156
    places for, 111–112
    regular savings accounts, 27
    returns on, 110
    security of savings, 109
    targeted savings, 108–109, 119, 134
    types of, 112–114

Savings and loan associations, 111
  checking accounts with, 23
Second mortgages, 64
Secured credit cards, 67
Security concerns, 215–223
  excessive concerns, 217–218
Self-help financial aid, 142
Seller-financing, 182–183
Selling a home. *See* Home-selling
Senior citizens
  checking accounts for, 38
  credit to, 65
SEP IRAs, 116–117
  retirement savings through,
    158
Series EE savings bonds, 116
Serious worries list, 98–106
Service charges on bank statement,
  55
Services summary on bank state-
  ment, 52
Set–aside accounting record, 16–19
  example of, 18
  for clothing, 19
Setoff, creditor's right of, 79
Share-draft accounts, 23
Shared-appreciation programs for
  home-buying, 170
Simple interest method, 110
Simplified Employee Pension IRAs.
  See SEP IRAs
Small credit accounts, opening of,
  66–67
Social Security payments, 152
Special aid programs for college,
  144–145
Special endorsements, 45
Special events, budgeting for, 12
Spending. *See* Expenses
Stability and credit, 65
Stafford student loans, 143–144
Stale-dated check, 41
Standard & Poor's, 126
State identification cards, 43
Status concerns and money,
  223–229
Stock-bonus plans, 156
Stockbrokers
  fees, 128–129
  mutual fund fees, 130–131
  working with, 203–204
Stocks, 127–129
  fees and commissions, 128–129
  individual company stocks,
    127–128

yield on, 123
Stolen checks, 47
Stop payments on checks, 48
Straight life insurance, 132
Subcontractors, liens by, 188
Success, money as proof of, 223–229
Super NOW accounts, 27
Superstitious behavior and money,
  219–220
Supplemental Educational Oppor-
  tunity Grants (SEOG), 142–143
Supplemental loans for students
  (SLS), 143–144
Surety bonds, contractors buying,
  190
Sweep accounts, 25
Symbolic functions of money,
  214–215

T
T & E cards, 28
Target benefit contribution plans,
  155
Targeted savings, 108–109, 119, 134
"Tax Information on Selling or
  Buying Your Home," 194
Tax Reform Act of 1986, 117
  limited partnerships, 131
Tax-sheltered annuities (TSAs), 156
Taxes
  college education savings plans
    and, 137–139
  credit and, 60–61
  home improvements and, 194
  home-buying and, 174
  investing to reduce taxes, 120
  property taxes, 174
  seller's perspective on, 184
T-Bills. *See* U.S. Treasury bills
Teacher training scholarship
  programs, 146
Temporary buy downs, 169–170
Thrift plans, 116
Thumbprints, for check cashing, 43
Tight budgets, 2–3
Total return, 123
Townhouses, 172–173
Tracking
  actual spending, 19–22
  cash flow tracking, 16–19
  cash withdrawals from bank
    accounts, 14–15
  credit costs, 74–75
Trade associations, scholarships
  from, 145

Traveler's checks, 34
Travel planning, 98
TSAs, 156
12b-1 plans, 130
Two-party checks, cashing of, 44

U
Uncollected funds (UCF) hold, 47
Unconditional lien release, 188
Unions, scholarships from, 146
Universal life insurance, 132
User accounts, 70
U.S. Savings Bonds, 115–116
U.S. Treasury bills, 125
    fees for, 128
Utility costs, 175–176

V
VA-guaranteed loans, 165
Vacation travel planning, 98
Variable annuities, 132
Variable life insurance, 132
Veterans, scholarships for, 146

W
Wages, garnishment of, 80
Wants and needs, 90–98

Warranties for home, 175
Whole life insurance, 132
Widowed persons, credit of, 69–70
Wills, 106
Women, credit identity of, 69–70
Worksheets
    balancing checkbook work sheet,
        56
    expenses worksheet, 8–10
    income worksheet, 5–6
Work-study programs, 142, 143
Worries list, 98–106
Worth, money as measure of,
        226–227
Writing checks, 40–43

Y
Yield
    on investments, 122–123
    on savings accounts, 110

Z
Zero coupon bonds, 126–127
Zoning considerations, 174
    variances, 185